THE RAZOR'S EDGE

THE SPORT RIDER STORIES

THE RAZOR'S EDGE

THE SPORT RIDER STORIES

JEFF HUGHES

For Mom, who hated that I rode, but pretended not to. And Pop, who rode back in the day, himself, and always understood.

A skittish motorbike with a touch of blood in it is better than all the riding animals on Earth.

- T. E. Lawrence

Contents

Preface

Descending eastward out of Tioga Pass, I expect it to be warmer. But, no. The track runs through high desert and I remain chilled. The cold, embarrassingly hurried run through Yosemite—there's all of one latent frame resting inside the film cassette in my Nikon F4—was a mistake. And now it's quickly getting dark, I'm tired, I'm hunched down inside the Aerostich, shivering, and I'm low on gas.

But then, even as the darkness unfolds, a few miles into the descent-that-wasn't, rt. 120 serves up something spectacular. The first one is a surprise, my 80mph pace bringing me out of my seat as I crest the rise. And then I'm into them. Mile after mile of whoop-de-do's, one after another, like a crazy-good curvy road turned on its side. I've never seen anything like it. Soon I'm laughing and warm and shaking my head at how amazing this world is.

Benton is a bust. When I had studied my map earlier I assumed I could get gas there. Nope. There's hardly anything to the little town. And so as I turn south it's with the wonder if I'll be spending the night on the side of the road. At least I've got my 100-watt, "off-road-only," halogen high-beam to help find a nice spot.

I drift into Bishop on fumes and with a sigh of relief.

Thirty minutes later I'm checked into the Thunderbird Motel and enjoying a lovely, fine meal at the Mexican restaurant down the street. And an hour later I'm at the bar, another couple blocks down, with a cold draft in front of me. It's all worked out splendidly. Like it always does.

My attention is divided between the several young people at

the pool table a few feet away, the heavy, frosted mug which I lift periodically, and the hardbound journal in front of me.

"Whatcha writing?" says the pretty barmaid, walking over.

I look up and smile at her. "Oh, just what happened today. So I won't forget."

She tilts her head sideways, a sudden quizzical look on her face. "You're not from around here."

"Nope," I shake my head. "From Virginia. I'm on a motorcycle trip."

It takes her a second to process. Then her eyes widen. "You've ridden a motorcycle all the way from Virginia?"

"Sure. Always wanted to see California."

"By yourself?"

My eyes crinkle into another smile. "Sometimes it's better that way."

She steps away, motioned by one of my fellow patrons a few stools down. But she returns a minute later with a fresh mug, dripping from the top. "This one's on the house."

I nod a smiling thanks. She'll get it back in her tip.

§

Sport Rider was my favorite from the moment Nick Ienatsch and company set sail with it in the early nineties. And so it was with something of a beatific happiness that I read Kent Kunitsugu's reply to my query, a handful of years after that cross-country trip.

In my early twenties I had sat down multiple times, pen in hand, trying to capture in words the feeling that came over me while on two wheels.

I couldn't. I found that describing the magic of a motorcycle—so intense that it nearly beggared belief—to be impossible. After awhile I stopped trying. I could, and did, write about everything else. Just not that.

A trio of decades and a half-million miles later, I was ready to try again. The words came slowly, haltingly. But finally, at long last, they were there.

And then, a while later, came the thing with *Sport Rider*. It was a cool gig while it lasted.

I'm proud of what I contributed. From the very beginning I sought to illuminate those motorcycling issues that I thought were important. To describe the lessons, the joys, the often subtle nuances, that slowly presented themselves to me across all those miles. To share the bag of talismans I had been given.

More than anything, I tried to convey the magic—what it was like to actually be in that seat... running fast through nice country on a good bike on a fine road. To wield well that incredible vehicle that so many of us love so passionately.

I'm grateful to Kent. First for seeing something in that original query of mine. Then for publishing the piece. But then also for being open-minded. Before I showed up the *Benchracing* column was reserved for guest authors—one hit wonders who would drop a story and then be gone. Kent didn't hesitate in letting me return again and again. With only a handful of exceptions, for eight years the *Benchracing* column became my space.

And, then, for giving me room. Most regular columns in most motorcycle magazines are on the order of ~900 words. One page. When I complained in a long letter that a writer could hardly get a story started in that amount of space, before he had to end it, Kent didn't blink. He let me wax loquacious with 1500 and 2000 and even a couple of 2500 word pieces. To those who know the magazine business, and how precious editorial content is, that was a rare gift.

I hope I returned the trust that Kent gave me. I always— save one I-somehow-forgot-the-date-and-was-a-day-late-miscue— made my deadlines. I figured Kent had enough headaches putting together each issue without worrying whether his contributors were going to get their stuff in on time. I always tried to act like the professional we're all supposed to be.

More than anything, I tried to craft good words. Words that were true to this, the finest sport I've ever known. Words that captured the magic of those amazing machines made of two wheels, bound together with a motor, and lit with a special grace.

The words that you now hold in your hand.

The Devil On My Shoulder

"Just a little faster. C'mon, just a little bit more—you know you can do it."

After a thousand miles in three days I'm tired, looking forward to getting home and seeing my family and relaxing for awhile. I split from John and Forrest a little while ago, back in Front Royal, and headed south down 340 while they continued on eastward. I'm almost home, after another fine trip into the mountains of West Virginia.

Like so many things, it starts with just a bit of happenstance. At Luray, as I turn onto 211, a large group of sportbikes—fifteen or so—have just turned onto the roadway in front of me. I trail them by a few hundred yards and watch with interest as we all roll towards the mountain. They're the usual mix—600 and 1000cc Japanese models, with a few standards and a couple of odd Ducatis thrown in. The assortment of gear is equally diverse, with about an equal split between the guys wearing one-piece leather suits, of all different colors, and the guys in street leathers. A few just wear jeans, but everyone has at least a jacket and gloves and boots. A reasonably serious group, it seems.

I hold my distance as we approach the Gap. The mountain rises up before us and, seeing it, even through my tiredness I can feel it begin. The strumming inside, the ratcheting of my heartbeat and the rushing in my ears. *C'mon, just let it be*, I tell myself. *Don't do this*. That is my every intention, to not do anything.

The first curve is delicious, like the first sip from a glass of fine wine, like the first drag on a cigarette after hours of abstinence. I don't need to reset my speed, only downshifting twice to get the revs up. The curving left-hand sweeper curls hard under my wheels, the suspension firming. The feeling is instantly mesmerizing, the lean angle and the pull of the g's and me meeting them with but a delicate grasp and the merest hint of a down-turned knee. My left hand extends a single finger towards the clutch lever, even though it'll be another two hundred yards before I'll need it again. No matter. My hands have gone all light on the grips and my boots have slipped back tight on the pegs and that sound has started in my head again, and in that moment I feel it all slipping away, all those good intentions.

The one turn has been enough to string out the pack of bikes in front of me, as some number of them slow for the turn. I've closed on the bikes in the rear and quickly swing into the left lane—there are two lanes heading up the mountain—and begin cutting past them. I figure the hot-shoes up front will flush out any radar-wielding LEO's lying in wait, and the last impediment in my mind melts away. Rolling into the first tight section I click another downshift, into third, and add a little more throttle. Bearing deeper into the rush, I feel the scurring of my peg feelers as they begin to reach down and kiss the tarmac. For the space of a handful of miles I'm in a place I can't escape from—grooved, in-the-zone—a place I wouldn't escape from if I could. Curve after curve, a rolling euphoria.

Through the narrowed slits my eyes have become the bikes still in front of me seem translucent, temporal. Ghost images, soft markers in the road as I continue rolling past. As I move towards the front of the strung-out pack I sense a growing umbrage. Maybe it's the saddlebags. For sure, this is not a race—there's no striving within me to get ahead; I'm not trying to beat anybody. The other riders out there just happen to be witness.

As something of a forlorn excuse, I can offer only that this is, after all, *my* mountain. Mine in the way that our heart lays claim to those places we especially love.

One of them accelerates out as I pass and pulls in behind me, riding my tail. A tag-team partner, he stays with me for the last mile, to the summit. There's not much left after that—the long right-hand sweeper that begins the descent, and we ride that hard—but then we come upon the brake lights of traffic in front of us. The one lane heading down the mountain will force a sedate pace.

The thing inside me disappears as quickly as it appeared and I sit back, relaxed, once again in cruise mode. At the bottom of the mountain the rider behind me beeps and pulls off at the store, pointing at me and turning a thumbs-up. I nod and wave back, continuing on alone.

§

"Hello. My name is Jeff and I'm a..." Well, I don't know exactly what I am, what the term would be. 'Speedaholic' maybe? Except that that doesn't begin to capture it.

It's always the same. Riding for miles, striving towards my wife's gentle admonishment before I leave to "be careful." And, now, "act like an adult." Sometimes she knows me better than I know myself. And I do, mostly, smiling inwardly at how mature I've become. But then we get to the curves.

For some people it's alcohol, or drugs. For others, gambling, or raising hell on the town. For me, it's speed. Not straight-line speed. Nor the simple speed which comes with acceleration—though those things hold their own allure. No, what gets me is speed on a motorcycle, running hard through the curves on a good piece of road. That's my manna, my heaven. But it's also where that devil on my shoulder emerges. The one that sits there with a crooked little smile on his face, the one that bends over and whispers in my ear, "just a little faster. C'mon, just a little bit more—you know you can do it."

Yeah, I'm a sucker for it. And it doesn't seem to matter much which bike I choose—the same nattering voice being as present on my K1200RS as on my GSX-R1000. It seems that a bit of sporting competence is all that is required. That and the addiction.

The track helps. Knowing I've got a number of track days sprinkled liberally throughout the riding season seems to keep the compulsions at bay. Not that the track doesn't have it's own little voice—it surely does. If anything, the voice there on my shoulder seems more animated and chatty than ever while out riding a closed circuit. But at least the track is a good environment in which to confront it. Or to let it somewhat have its way. But that's a subject for another day.

So does forcing myself to ride further back in the pack of whatever group of buddies I might be out with. I don't pass too often on such social rides, and so the pace of the guy in front of me becomes my pace—and please God let him have a quieter voice than the one that insists on nattering at me. Running with the hot-shoes up front is a sure recipe for having that voice turn all excited and happy.

And time. Trying to keep in mind that I'm in this for the long haul. I want to be like that 85-year-old guy I met this past summer at my local BMW dealer, the one who rolled in on a K1200RS, same blood-red color as mine, in the midst of a four-corners tour. All by himself.

You know that old saw, the one that says there are old riders and bold riders but no old, bold riders? Well I'm hoping someday to end up being that old rider, all the while being at least a *little* bold along the way. Doesn't quite seem fair, otherwise. Maybe we just need to ration that fun a bit, pick our moments with a bit of care. Not too much gas on the fire, too soon.

As usual when it comes to perplexing problems, I don't really have any answers. Only hopes. Looking around at other people, those with other addictions, I'm convinced I'll never be cured. Just doesn't seem to be in the cards. Not that I'd want to, even had I the choice. Sometimes addiction brings its own kind of reward. A bit of joy, tasted now and again, to go with the angst.

So I'll just continue the search, riding all those good roads and looking for answers—all while holding to a fervent determination to keep it more or less in check. And sometimes, between the babbling of that voice on my shoulder, finding grace while I'm out doing it.

August 2003, Sport Rider

Evening's Chance

The magic of a good motorcycle lies in its power to take you away, to a place better than all the other places.

The long days at work, seemingly ever more frequent, wrap themselves around me like a cloak, lending, after the long trip home, nothing but an aching tiredness. Sometimes, sitting on the train during that evening ride home, watching the cars stacked up on the interstate after the subway has emerged from below ground, a vision which just amplifies my sorrow at what my days have become, I'm struck with the thought of maybe doing an evening ride, like I used to. But it's inevitably another hour or more, after exiting the subway station and joining those very same throngs of drivers, before I turn my pickup into my driveway—long enough for the day's exhaustion to catch up with me. Maybe tomorrow.

And then, of course, tomorrow turns into all the other tomorrows—the day that never comes.

Which is all the more reason that I remain surprised about tonight. Because tonight the thought holds, even through the grim veil of my fatigue. "I think I'm going to go for a little ride," I tell Ginny after I've been home a few minutes. "I'll be back in a little while."

"A little while?" she laughs. "That's really funny. I'll leave a plate in the frig."

I know what I'm searching for, of course. A respite, however brief, from the melancholy which seems to have fallen over my days. It's strange how we never think of our lives turning out the way they do.

As a counterweight, sometimes there is magic. A spark where you believed there to be nothing but cold ashes.

Sometimes it's as simple as pulling the cover off of a motorcycle.

It emerges slowly, happiness, a nudge here and a poke there as I catch shy glances at the machine that will soon take me down the road. It always seems more than it is, that simple act. A start to the measured ceremony that precedes every ride: wiping down the tank and seat and fairing; throwing the little things I think I might need into the tail pack; retrieving the air tank from the shed and bending down to check the tires, first adding a couple pounds and then pressing my thumb over the release valve of the tire gauge, in little bursts, like a doctor taking a patient's blood pressure, until they're perfect. All the while willing myself to only look obliquely at the bike, seeing its lines and angles softly, out of my peripheral vision. Somewhere along the years all that preparation became more than just getting ready. It turned into ritual, a little ceremony.

Like that of a Samurai.

As is so often the case, I have no destination in mind. Just riding. I'll end up wherever I end up. But what is always the same is the instant relief. Once down my long gravel driveway, out onto the hard top, in the few moments it takes to throttle up through the gears, click-clicking up into fourth and 4000rpm—easy cruising while the oil and tires and suspension build some heat—and the detritus of my day falls away like so many loose scales. Then there's the first curve, another couple hundred feet down the road, and though I know it's just a whisper of what's to come, it nevertheless drops me straight into the heart of gladness. Even at this gentle pace it's like being spun up into a web of magic.

My path draws me inevitably westward, into the mountains. Like there was ever any other choice. There are maybe two hours of daylight left to this day. Not nearly enough. But then, you make do with what you're given. I'll spend those two hours as dearly as I can.

The Suzuki feels wonderful: a heady mix of airy lightness and explosive power, held to the road with a lithe suppleness. Beneath its thin veneer of civility lies a raw ferocity, ever a temptation. It feels like nothing so much as a magic carpet, gilded with a touch of lightning.

The landscape is bucolic, a mix of woods and pasture and corn fields, with cows and horses grazing—the odd one raising its head and watching me as I roll past. I suppose that's part of the charm, the rustic countryside ever a telling background to where the good roads are.

The first hour slides away like an unraveling, slowly abetting the hunger I feel, on roads I have long loved. By the time I get to the Mobil station and stop for gas I'm smiling inside. I nod at the sad-faced woman inside as I pay, seeing in her tired eyes a reflection of myself from just a little while earlier. I wish I could tell her about this magic I have found, but I know that she wouldn't understand. So I leave her with just a smiling "have a great evening," and head back outside to my bike.

Between me and where I'm going lies the chain of the Blue Ridge, the rolling hills of Virginia's Piedmont giving way to a sudden sharpening of the landscape. There's a quickening in my chest as well.

My riding on the street is normally marked by restraint, a catechism of don'ts, like carrying a very sharp sword, but kept in its sheath. Mostly. But every now and then, trusting to instinct, listening to a sixth sense that tells me everything will be alright, I loose the reins. The sword gets drawn.

That's how it is here. The road begins to twist, slowly at first, as it tracks over the starting-to-swell landscape at the bottom of the mountain, but then there's a quickening as its cadence accelerates into the swift-flowing song which is its character, like a rhyme gaining strength. Assuming the position, my boots slide back on the pegs and my stomach tenses slightly to hold my weight and my gloved hands reach down to lightly grasp the grips. Like a Centaur, the only tension in my body is held down low, my upper body purposefully relaxed. Soft hands, the better to wield that sword.

Mostly, it's in my head, this sense of where I am and what I'm about. A predator's eye fixed upon the landscape, leaking measured aggression. A willful attitude, tempered by a relaxed confidence. More than all the other things in the world, this is what I am. This is what I do.

The eastern face lies mostly in shadow and my eyes flash quick, burning looks into each of the darkened corners, searching intently for anything amiss—a twig or a leaf or a patch of gravel—anything which might interrupt the hunter's symphony in my head. I don't have to choose my lines. Having ridden this road hundreds of times, knowing each curve and bump and swell along its entire length, they come naturally, falling under my wheels without thought. And the Suzuki, having been under me for thousands of miles—joining with the ghosts of hundreds of thousands of miles of other motorcycles before it—has long-since moved into that realm where it ceases to exist. Like an oft-repeated musical score, riding it comes not from my head, but from a mysterious place inside which needs no conscious attention.

The road itself is like a flower unfolding, one dangerous and dark. In my heart is the desire to push the pace, faster and faster—right now—but I restrain that impulse, knowing that I must be patient. There's a natural rhythm to things which demands respect, a time to allow heat to build in the sides of my tires even as something inside me searches for and syncs to the cadence of the road.

Then it does and suddenly I'm there, in that place where it's all clean and effortless and where there's nothing left holding me to this earth but those tiny contact patches. Those are stretched and straining and, even through my flying rush across the road and the flooding stream of endorphins which accompanies it, there's a place of stillness inside me which allows me to feel them, exquisite and sensitive, in their elastic, grasping movement across the smooth-textured pavement.

I hold to that feeling carefully, all-too aware of how quickly the GSX-R1000 could sweep them away. My right forearm rests lightly against the flat tank of the Suzuki, my hand motioning the throttle with the gentlest of movements. I find that oddly beguiling—how in the midst of such a rush of speed and energy and power-unleashed, the one thing that holds it all in check is wielded with the delicacy of a kiss. Like a butterfly, softly alighting, in the eye of a hurricane.

Nearing the top of the mountain, the growing crescendo in my head finally breaks, a symphony's hurled denouement, as I spin through the last corner leading to the summit. Four miles. A glistening bit of artwork, now drying. I draw a grateful breath and allow myself a moment's pause, reflecting. Then I'm laughing under my helmet and the sword is back in its sheath and I'm over the top and beginning the descent, bathed in the last sunlight of a dying day.

Tomorrow will be okay.

June 2004, Sport Rider

Of Serious Intent

In every endeavor, amidst the multitudes, there are those who embrace it truly.

I call them the four horsemen. Not because of any ill will they bring, but because of their propensity for roaming the countryside with a swift, sure certainty.

They are an eclectic bunch, tending towards middle age, not especially notable when they're off their bikes. Just four friends who happen to share a love of riding. Typical sport riders, you might think, seeing them laughing and talking quietly to themselves there at the café. But you'd be wrong.

Their bikes are diverse and, some would say, uninspiring: a 929, a several-years-old GSX-R750, an RC51, and a first-generation R1. Not exactly cutting edge. But all four machines are well maintained. You never see any of them without good tires and chains and brakes and cables, the machines washed and clean. But they all also show the signs of much use—the little worn bits here and there, the dull rubbings on the wheels from countless tire changes, the not-quite-as-bright-as-it-once-was bodywork. These guys are definitely riders, not polishers. The first clue you get, even before you see them on the road, is written in their odometers.

A closer inspection of their bikes reveals a second clue: despite their age and miles and lack of flashy aftermarket accessories, each of the four bikes wears top-notch suspenders, fore and aft. The Ohlins and Penske units sit there in subtle contrast to the mundane plainness of the rest of the bikes. You see those expensive bits and you wonder a little bit, and then a dawning sense of these rider's priorities starts to emerge.

If you asked—you'd have to ask because they won't offer

it—you'd find that each of the four riders has been riding for quite a long time. One has a club racing background. All have done dozens of track days. And though they all obviously love the sport—you see them out most every weekend—you never hear the brashness and boasting that usually accompanies a group of riders getting together. Oh, they'll talk at length about good roads they've been on, or a particular corner that was fun or challenging or scary, and they'll regale each other with the technicalities of this tire or that suspension setting or who did well in the race last weekend. Just like the rest of us. But hearing it from them it somehow seems different. Somewhere along the line these four riders found a way to leave their egos behind.

They're friendly enough, freely talking to anyone who engages them. But with a smiling "thanks anyway" they'll politely decline the offers to join the large throngs of riders who get together on the weekends in the usual haunts. They tend to head towards roads of their own choosing, a little farther away than most, a little less well-known, a little less crowded. And, preferably, to ride those roads with just each other—a small circle of friends where trust and respect were long ago earned. Once the morning coffee is finished they'll be gone, four shadows flashing quickly across the landscape, not to be seen again for many hours.

Mostly, if you make the effort to get out there on those same distant roads yourself, you might see it where it matters most—in their riding. To trail behind them and watch is to see poetry in motion, a perfect, rolling form snaking across the landscape. Closely matched in terms of speed, temperament, and style, they'll swap off the lead occasionally, but otherwise you never see them pass each other. They just ride along in perfect sync, a half-dozen bike lengths separating one from the next, as if each were connected by an invisible wire.

Deceptively fast, their smoothness and lack of any abruptness lends a quiet sense of nonchalance to their cadence. You see them carving gracefully through the corners with lots of lean angle and lots of leaning *in*, but not a lot of leaning *off*. They make time, but without any sense of effort. After a while it comes to you what you're witnessing, what it reminds you of: the liquid flow of running water.

§

Like driving a car, the basic skills needed for piloting a motorcycle are pretty straightforward. The MSF manages to get rank neophytes up to a minimal level of ability in a brief, 20-hour curriculum, after all. Riding well, though, especially at speed— that's a whole different ball game. That requires a set of competencies and a collection of judgments which can be astonishingly intricate. Definitely not the kinds of things that can be taught quickly. Add to those complexities the considerable risk in not getting it right and riding a motorcycle suddenly seems to have a lot more in common with the aviation community than it does with our 4-wheel brethren on the ground.

Fortunately, motorcycling—and sport riding in particular— responds well to all those attributes that aviation has long found essential: consistent machine preparation, an openness to learning from others, an honest, thoughtful, deliberative outlook towards our own experiences, and an attitude that our ability is never quite good enough—training and improvement are a never-ending process.

Whether we adopt that attitude is up to us. Many don't. We've all known friends and acquaintances who shared this sport with us for a while, a year or two or three. But when you rode with them there was always that nagging feeling that they didn't quite get it, consistently riding over their heads or making too many mistakes or suffering too many close calls. And sure enough, eventually there would be the inevitable crash, or the close call that was a little *too* close. And then they quit, and for once you were glad, knowing that they were never really cut out for it in the first place.

Sport riders—and with that label I'm talking about the type of riding a rider prefers, not the kind of bike they own—are particularly suited to the aviation analogy. Our community sees both ends of the spectrum. On the one hand, perhaps because of the "cool" factor associated with sport bikes, we see a lot of very young riders, those with very little experience. Lacking the good fortune to hook up with an experienced mentor, a lot of these new riders unfortunately end up heading down the wrong path. We're all familiar with the typical squid image so I won't belabor it here, but suffice it to say that the vast majority of that squid population are very young and very inexperienced. Their riding choices reflect that.

On the other hand, the sport riding community also counts among its members many of those with the highest levels of experience, talent, and ability in all of motorcycling. These are the squinty-eyed veterans who long-since passed through—survived—those early years of riding innocence and came out on the other end with a set of hard-won skills and battle-tested experiences that can't be bought for any amount of money. Like hours in the air, the only way you get those is with seat time. These are the guys who consistently wear the right gear; they're the ones who study the dynamics of the sport, who think about why what works, does, and why that that doesn't, doesn't; who watch racing not just for the pleasure it evokes but also for the technical nuance it offers; and they are the riders who spend time on the track themselves, for fun, sure, but also because they know that's the best and fastest place to improve their skills. They've taken that dictum to heart that we, none of us, are ever quite good enough.

The upshot of all that being that these riders are often the ones exhibiting the highest levels of judgment, skill—and safety— seen in the entire sport. That experience, too, is reflected in their riding choices—which tend towards restraint and discipline. It's not that these guys never light it up—they do—but they do it in a way and in a manner of their own careful choosing. They know that some lessons shouldn't be learned twice.

Motorcycling—and sport riding, especially—is an activity that doesn't suffer fools lightly. It's too bad that we have to go through a process of Darwinian selection in order to arrive at the place we all want to be. But at least we have the satisfaction of knowing, having gone through that process, that what we're left with is a community of oftentimes exceptional individuals—riders of serious intent—who bring an extraordinary level of ability to the game. Something we can all aspire to.

Like the four horsemen.

September 2004, Sport Rider

The 80% Myth

*Every sport, every community,
has its beliefs. Conventions that are
accepted as distilled wisdom.
Sometimes those are wrong.*

The climb up the hill coming out of the area famously referred to as *The Shoe*, rising up along what would be the 'ankle,' is semi-blind. Visual cues are obscure, the horizon falling away towards bland nothingness. And because the climbing elevation itself serves to feel like a brake, you tend to ride up that climb pretty hard, throttle pinned to the stop. That perfectly describes my ascent.

Only thing, it's a mistake.

At the top, where the topography begins to flatten, turn nine comes in with a sudden, rushing abruptness. Having already run numerous laps this morning, I certainly know that. Not to mention that George McNabb, one of Reg Pridmore's CLASS instructors and a friend of mine, had warned me of that very thing two nights ago, pointing to the corner on the crudely drawn map on the back of the restaurant napkin. But in the exultation of the moment, reluctant to let go of my pace, I hold into the throttle for one more heartbeat, and then another, before I begin rolling out. By then I'm over the top and as my two fingers cover the brake lever, feeding load into the front tire, the whole corner suddenly snaps into focus.

The equation has changed.

With a jarring awareness I realize I'm in too hot, already way too deep into the corner. And although the rain stopped twenty minutes ago, the track is still very damp. I need to be off the brakes and turning hard left, right *now*. But what really has my attention is the splash of red in the center of my vision. As soon as

I see it, even before the synapses in my brain can make all the connections, I know instantly what it is.

The Ducati rider.

The hairball erupts with a mushrooming flood of adrenalin, the metallic tang sharp in my mouth. Even though I know I'm not supposed to—that I can't afford to—my eyes are nevertheless drawn inexorably to the obscene sight, just off the apex of the turn and a mere handful of feet off the track, of the motorcycle on its side and, right next to it, the rider in red leathers lying motionless up against the Armco.

I know all about target fixation—something, thankfully, that I'm not especially prone to. And I'm also aware that our vision is normally drawn to motion, to the movement of would-be prey, or danger. But in this case, perversely, it's the very stillness itself of the rider which strikes in me a fascinating dread, fixing my attention. That momentary freeze is the very last thing I need.

Floating in a sea of possibility—most of it bad—the calculus of traction flashes through my head as I try and come up with a new equation, some new combination of turning movement, body position, lean angle, and throttle setting that will get me out of this fix.

In the midst of all that my mind flashes back, for just an instant, to my arrival yesterday evening.

§

Watkins Glen. A mystical name, conjuring images of countless motorsports legends: Formula One, Alfa Romeo, Lotus, McLaren, Ferrari, Lauda, Stewart, Fittipaldi, Williams. All coming together in the crucible of this place called by the cognoscenti, simply, *The Glen.*

Having ridden the 500 miles from my home in Virginia, it's no wonder that I can't wait to see the place. And so instead of heading straight for the cabin that I've rented for the next two days, to the lodge where a cold beer and a hot meal await, I head first for that storied ground.

I can't get in, of course. The place is locked. But dismounting on the hard-packed grassy field of the spectator parking and walking over to the fence to peer inside gets me my first glimpse. Black tarmac snaking across the landscape. The big red Winston sign. Bleachers, devoid of fans, but I can imagine them full.

The sun setting softly behind me casts a warm glow along the fence, the last such light I'll see for several days. And, in my stomach, that edginess that always seems to accompany my arrival at a racetrack, the first fluttering butterflies, begins to take hold.

Scanning back and forth, my eyes take in the grandeur of the place. I see it alive in my imagination, the rolling landscape and the seductive sweep of the asphalt and the lovely light and the swift movement of wheeled vehicles in full song. But there's something else, something which adds a disquieting edge to the otherwise wonderful sights. No matter where I look my eyes are drawn to it: Armco. It's everywhere, just a few feet off the edge of the asphalt. Girding the place like a steel necklace.

The realization slowly dawns on me. Maybe tomorrow morning, with the benefit of some sighting laps, I'll find it's not too bad. Maybe this is just a bad section and the rest of the track has plenty of runoff space. Maybe. But I've always wondered why the AMA boys never run here. And as I turn away from the fence I have a sneaking suspicion I now know why.

As I walk back to my bike, thinking about tomorrow, a low breath escapes my pursed lips. "Eighty-percent, Hughes. Eighty-percent."

§

It's one of the most oft-repeated canards in all of motorcycling: The eighty-percent rule. The notion that a rider will ride at no more than 80% effort, leaving the other 20% as a reserve, a cushion to fall back on for when—not if—the inevitable aw-shit arises. It's the expectation that even when we're riding at a crisp, sporting pace, one that's fun and challenging, we've still got that piece-of-mind stash in our back pocket, ready to pull our ass out of trouble. It's our last line of defense against the litany of risks that otherwise imbue our sport. And if you talk to riders out in the hinterlands, to those sport riders carving through the canyons and dicing across the mountain passes, you'll almost always get a knowing nod. "Sure, I always keep it to 80%." And most of them believe it.

Only thing is, it's a myth.

Despite all those well-meaning assertions, in spite of the very real belief that they've left lots in reserve, most riders riding at pace in the hills couldn't ride 20% faster if their mother's life depended upon it. Not even close.

The fact is, those of us who push a sporting pace—even the most measured and controlled one—are a lot closer to the edge than we're generally aware.

How can that be? How is it possible that so many riders can truly, honestly believe that they're only doing eight-tenths, if in fact it's more than that? How can so many riders be wrong?

Because backing off just a few clicks from our pace is enough to make us feel totally at ease. It's enough to eliminate almost all of those butt-clinching "moments" that we all occasionally experience when really pushing things. It puts us in a place that's calm and relaxed and where we could ride forever. It seems like we're cruising.

It *feels* like 80%.

Think of any of the top racers, guys like Valentino Rossi or Colin Edwards. One of the things that separate them from us lesser mortals is their ability to consistently run close to maximum effort for long periods of time. Lap after lap they're able to, within the constraints of that particular race day's engine-suspension-tire package, put together lap times that are mere tenths of a second apart. They do that while routinely spinning their rear tires on throttle-up, aggressively braking right up to the point of washing out their front ends, and carrying what seem to be impossible lean angles, all while remaining constantly attuned to the declining amounts of traction left in their swiftly deteriorating tires. They ride, in other words, on the very edge of what is humanly possible.

To those same racers, a single, whole second is an enormous chunk of time. If they back off their pace that one second—around one percent at most major racetracks—they're instantly transported to a far less arduous place, one that's much easier to maintain without making a mistake. Back off three or four seconds—we're still only talking two or three percent— and they are positively in cruise mode. For someone like Valentino, the difference between a 1:44 and a 1:48 lap time at Mugello is like night and day.

It's pretty obvious that those of us who ride on the street, and maybe do the occasional track day, aren't anywhere close to being in the same league as Valentino or Colin. Certainly the maximum effort that we can bring to bear is worlds apart from theirs, as is our consistency—we're not anywhere close to being as attuned to what a motorcycle can do as they are.

But the principle of pace and effort still holds. Just as a top racer can go from full-bore to cruise mode by just backing off 2-3%, a street rider will see a similar drop in perceived effort by doing the same. Drop a few more clicks to account for the extra few challenges to be found on the street and we're right in the range of what most sport riders actually do.

So how much does that end up being?

I'm guessing that for the majority of experienced sport riders the total is no more than 6-8%. Maybe a little less for those with lots of saddle time. But it would rarely be any more except among true neophytes.

Which means that that 80% effort that we always talk about is, really, more like 92-94%.

Don't believe it? Then try it yourself. On your next track day have a buddy time a couple of your laps—one at what you think is 80% effort and one that is as absolutely fast as you are able. My bet is that those two times will be a lot closer than you expect.

Okay, so why is any of this important? Whether it's 80% or 94% or whatever the figure ends up being, we still need to keep something in reserve, don't we? So, big deal, as long as we do that—what's the difference?

The reason it's important—I'm not suggesting that riders change the pace at which they ride—is because that reserve we congratulate ourselves for carrying in our back pocket is a hell of a lot slimmer than we may have believed. It's important because a relatively small bump in our pace can quickly put us back at the edge, back to that place where things can go to hell in a hand basket in a great big hurry.

We just need to realize that, that's all. Having done so, we're then better prepared to make all those choices that we're inevitably called upon to make during a day's ride—and maybe we'll end up with a few less surprises.

As with most things, wisdom begins with understanding.

§

Back at Watkins Glen, still trying to sort out the mess I've made of turn nine, it's ultimately one of the other tenets of our sport—you go where you look—that ends up being my saving grace. The 80% rule may be a myth, but that one surely isn't.

At the very last moment I finally manage to dredge my eyes away from the sight of the Ducati rider and twist my eyes around hard to port, fixing them on a point far down the track. Holding fast to that spot like a beacon of hope, feeding in throttle as smoothly as I can, and leaning over on the damp pavement as far as I possibly dare, I manage to make it through the turn. Barely.

Back in the pits, I have plenty of time to think about what happened. That was way too close, a result of riding too hard on a track which inordinately punishes such indiscretions. Going back out after the red flag I once again remind myself to take it easy, to hold it to no more than 80%.

I mean… 94.

July 2005, Sport Rider

The Most Honest Place I Know

Truth is its own reward.

It's the first session of the day and it's still cool on this Autumn morning. I shiver in my leathers, not entirely because of the venting in the Dainese suit. The track still has patches of dampness from the fog which rolls in every night off the Dan River, but is drying quickly. We're helping it along with our laps. The last track day of the year. It's going to be a good day.

The South Course at Virginia International Raceway has a hell of a long front straight. More than half a mile. Coming out of Oak Tree, the hard right-hander leading onto it—where legend has it that years ago the car racers used to deliberately rev their motors trying to shake acorns loose onto the tarmac—I'm in third gear on the GSX-R1000. Deliberately overgearing it, trying to keep down wheelspin. Once onto the straight, speed builds in a rapid crescendo. Even short-shifting—trying to keep the front wheel on the ground—I'm soon on the far side of 160mph. God's country.

Some of life's experiences defy description. Braking hard from those speeds, in what your mind tells you is an impossibly short distance, is one of those. Those HH pads and six-pot calipers provide what seems to be perfectly fine braking—really powerful braking—everywhere else. Just not here. Past the braking marker, two fingers on the lever, squeezing like the trigger of a rifle, the pads of those fingers feeling for the load on the front tire. The rear end all light and softly shimmying, like the subtly-turning tail of one of those smallmouth holding station in the river over beyond the trees. There are damp patches here, too, and one can't help but wonder if we haven't overloaded that front tire as we roll through them. But, no, we're okay.

You never think you're going to make it. The end of the straight comes at you like the earth towards a crashing plane. It rises up like an unremitting wall, but with a rush like a cutting scimitar. Only at the very end, just when you've nearly given up all hope, does it seem like *"yes, I think maybe I can make that turn."* It always seems a surprise.

§

Look at a sportbike and you see studied, purposeful aggression. From the flowing bodywork to the race-inspired seating position to the short, stubby clipons, the message is unmistakable. There is power here, and speed. Wield it as you will.

Given that compelling message, we probably shouldn't be surprised that an entire culture has risen around it. That new converts are assembled every day. And that, as with most cultures, a hierarchy inevitably arises out of the multitude. Unfortunately, for a vocal minority, their place in that pecking-order is based on bluster and bravado and denial as much as on skill and talent. It's often the guy who exudes the most hot air, who's most in denial about the risks he takes, who lives the largest—at least in his own fantasies.

You see it every Sunday. Everywhere we sportbike types gather together. Along with the coffee and scrambled eggs and laughter you'll hear more exaggeration and embellishment and excuses than you can shake a stick at. Everything from how we saved that front-end tuck to why we ended up going wide in that one turn to how come we're not running up front today. We work hard to fashion that golden image of ourselves.

And then there's the track.

The track is many things. Obviously it's fun, like the very best stretch of curvy road imaginable, but without the trees and the traffic and the gravel and the cops, and run over and over again, as if by some miracle. So euphoric that it defies description. A magic place. A legal drug.

But the track is other, more-subtle things, as well. It is a teacher and a guide, not just on how to ride better but also serving up lessons in some of the more far-reaching qualities that affect our lives. Things like patience and persistence, humility and fortitude. The joy of rising above one's limits. The satisfaction of doing something better than we ever thought we could. Mostly, though, I love the track because of the truth to be found there.

Riding a modern sportbike on the street is kind of like leaving that supermodel at her door with naught but a goodnight kiss—satisfying certainly, but leaving much to be desired. Yet to hear many street riders talk about it, you'd think they hit the ball out of the park. Some of them actually try.

Sportbikes today are so remarkably good, their performance levels so astonishingly high, that one is able to extract only a small fraction of that performance on any public road. Fact is, riding really fast on the street is a whole lot less about skill and talent and a whole lot more about simply how big a bet one is willing to place on the table. The bet, the stakes, being you, of course.

Which leaves the track.

Only there can anything approaching the real truth about how good we really are be found. Only there does all the bluster and bravado and exaggeration fall away to a blunt reality, the certain truth, of the numbers on the stopwatch.

It's the most honest place I know.

June 2003, Sport Rider

Degrees of Control

Of all the stories I wrote for Sport Rider, this one probably touched the greatest nerve with readers. It certainly elicited the most commentary.

You slide in behind him—or maybe he glides smoothly on around in front of you—and within a handful of corners you know there's something special here. It's not his hardware, which might be most anything from an ancient BMW Airhead to a years-old Japanese Standard to the latest race-replica tackle. Nor is it his clothing which, if anything, probably carries a patina of age—the leather or nylon faded from long miles in the sun and spotted from uncounted bug-cleanings. Nor is it just that he's fast, though he probably carries a pretty crisp pace. No, what instantly gets your attention is the utter casualness—the sheer effortlessness—with which he rides along the road, dispatching the curves like they were so many pieces of candy. There's a relaxed assurance in his demeanor, a perfect confidence in his swift cadence, which gives rise to a certainty of what the next miles will bring. His speed is just—so. We watch for a while—assuming we're able to stay with him—and in our heart of hearts, where our desires stir and where our ego lives, we couch what we're seeing in the same way we always do. We know some guy, maybe we know lots of guys, buddies who are surely faster than Mr. Smooth and Effortless. Hell, maybe *we're* faster. But even as we think these things, salve for the ego, we can't escape the growing suspicion that this rider in front of us is just playing. Not with us, but with the road—with probably the merest touch of a smile tugging at his lips as he glides through the corners—even as our own heart hammers a staccato beat as we're carried along in the rush behind him. Maybe it dawns on us, in a moment of honesty, that he could just walk away if he wanted. One of those things you just know. So why doesn't he? Why is it that he seems content to just roll along, playing those curves in the road like they were so many riffs drifting easily from a well-worn guitar? We all talk about being good, about being smooth. Well, there he is, right in front of you. The poster child.

§

In a sport whose very appeal is built around the merits of speed—a sport where our greatest heroes are those that go the fastest, a sport where even the most mundane machinery comes dripping with performance, a sport where even the clothes we wear are based upon the need to attenuate the risk we perceive attendant to that speed—it's hard not to get caught up in the notion that speed is the *thing*. It's both the yardstick by which we measure ourselves and the mantle in which we wish to be draped. Hell, who doesn't want to be fast?

The corollary, an article of faith repeated so often that it seems to beggar any argument, is that speed—too much of it at least—is a *bad thing*. It's the bogey man waiting to catch us out any time we cross that imaginary line of *too much*. Most of us nod our heads when we hear that.

The thing is, that doesn't always jive with our experience. We see guys all the time who manage to crash at quite modest speeds. And we know some—admittedly a much smaller number—who ride really fast, and have for a long time, but who never seem to crash. Not as in they don't crash very often. As in they *never* crash.

We all undertake a modicum of risk every time we thumb the starter. We all know that—it's just inherent to the sport. But those of us who choose to adopt a faster pace deliberately assume more of that danger. We knowingly engage the laws of probability in a game of chicken. You play it long enough and you lose. That's what we've always been told, right?

Why is it, then, that that select group of riders manages to ride at an elevated pace over many miles, weekend after weekend, trip after trip, and year after year, with little in the way of mishap? Why are these riders seemingly held apart, aloof, from the carnage which too-often otherwise afflicts our sport? And how is it that so many other riders, riding at much lesser speeds, still manage to toss away their bikes with such depressing frequency?

Well, maybe we've been looking in the wrong place all along. Maybe, just maybe, it's not about the speed after all—at least not in the way we usually think of it. Maybe it's about something else, something as simple as the degree of control we exercise over a span of road.

§

It might happen on any ride, on any Sunday. We head out with some buddies, or maybe we hook up with that group of guys we were talking to down at the gas station, or maybe that devil on our shoulder is just simply a little more vigorous in his exhortations this day. However it happens, we soon get to *the road*. The good one. The one that brought us out here in the first place. And there, in that mix of camaraderie and good tarmac and adrenalin-laced delight, we find ourselves giving away that which we had sworn to hold tight to—our judgment. It doesn't happen all at once. We give it away a little click here, a little click there, like a ratcheting cord. Soon, rolling through the curves faster and faster and laughing under our helmets all the while, we enter a new realm.

We've all been there. We know instantly we're in a new place because suddenly it's different. Our lines are no longer quite so clean. We're on the brakes more, and we're making little mistakes in our timing. And instead of that Zen-like rush through the corners we were enjoying just moments ago—the state of grace which is the prize of this sport—we're now caught up, in the brief slivers of time between corners, in trying to fix those mistakes. They seem to be coming faster now—both the corners and the mistakes—and there doesn't seem to be quite enough time to do what we need to do, the mistakes piling up in an increasingly dissonant heap. Our normally smooth riding is suddenly ragged, with an edgy and anxious quality about it. Inside our helmet the laughter mutes, and then is gone altogether, replaced by a grim determination to stay on pace. We start to mutter little self-reproaches with each newborn error.

Soon enough we'll blow it. We'll get into one particular corner too hot—realization and regret crystallizing in a single hot moment—and from that instant until whatever's going to happen, does, we're just along for the ride. It will be what it will be. With a touch of luck we'll come away with nothing more than a nervous laugh and a promise to ourselves not to do *that* again. That and maybe one more little debt to pay. You know, the one we just made to God—if he would please just get us out of this mess we'd gotten ourselves into. Just this one last time, promise.

Just one of those moments, huh?

§

It has to do with choices. When we ride a challenging road—at whatever speed—there is an observable, knowable, degree of control which we exhibit. Not just over one corner. Not even over just one section. But over the entire road. On some days our mastery is complete—we've chosen to stay well within our own personal skill envelope. On other days—well, on other days maybe we choose to push towards the edge of that envelope. To a place where our mastery begins to diminish. To a place where the degree of control we exhibit becomes less and less.

Ultimately, to the tipping point—where all our skills seem to go to hell and gone in one big hurry.

There's a predictability to it. A good rider, riding within his proper envelope, will have none of those "moments." There will be no spikes in his heart rate. No sudden bursts of adrenaline. Nothing but a smooth, flowing movement across the road. He is this side of the tipping point—the tipping point for him. It'll be different for each of us. And it'll vary from day to day, maybe even hour to hour, depending upon how we feel. Sometimes we're in the groove, and sometimes we're not. But I think the key is that as long as that rider stays this side of that tipping point he can probably ride a surprisingly long time without ill effect.

And that's the message. The predictor of bad stuff, the closest thing we have to a crystal ball, are those "moments." They are part of the landscape, part of the sport. And they happen to all of us. But for any given rider they need to be very rare. If they are happening with any frequency at all, I'd say the tipping point is at hand. And if that's a place you choose to hang around much there's probably something very ugly waiting for you somewhere not far down the road.

Think about all those riders who've ever impressed us, like our rider at the beginning of this story. They all seem to have a smooth, fluid, easy quality about them, an assurance which belies any stress or fear. They're always balanced, always in control. I suspect somewhere along the line they've acquired a germ of wisdom, hard-won over many miles, which has given them an appreciation of their own limits. They know where that tipping point is—where their mastery of their bike and the road and the environment begins to slip away—and they long ago made the decision to stay this side of it.

When you do find them testing their limits—surely there's an argument to be made for exploring the edges of one's ability—it's likely to be at a time and place of very careful choosing. And probably involves a racetrack. Much of wisdom involves simply knowing when and where to loose those impulses which we all carry.

And so maybe it's never been about speed after all. Maybe that's why that small, select group of riders are able to ride year after year without crashing—the fact that they ride fast is secondary to the fact that they're always in control. They know their own limits.

And that's the lesson for the rest of us—at least for those of us who wish to enjoy this sport for a long, long time. There's a choice to be made, every time we thumb that starter.

Not that it's easy. If it were we wouldn't see the carnage among our ranks that we do every weekend. But for those who manage it, for those who bring restraint and discipline to mix with their skill and daring, there's an upside, even beyond the gladness of bringing one's bike and body back unscathed after an afternoon's ride. There's something to be said for gathering up one's powers, like the magician that motorcycle makes us feel like, and wielding them well along a good road. There's art to be found there.

Art and magic.

October 2003, Sport Rider

The Razor's Edge

Yes. The story from which the whole collection takes its name. There's a reason.

The mountain rises up before me, a cut jewel, and a tingle of anticipation hums in my chest. The mid-morning sunlight is perfect—diffused by a soft overcast which throws even illumination into all those curves that, even before starting my ascent, I can see in my mind. In front of me the road tracks straight ahead, upward, for three hundred feet, lifting us—this fast motorcycle and I—from this beautiful valley. Then it jinks hard left, following the contours of the rugged landscape. That's where it begins.

Approaching, seeing the road twist away out of sight up there ahead, there's a single, baited moment, a coy little tease, like when gazing with desire upon a girl about to be courted. Then that passes, replaced by an outright willfulness. My boots slide back on the pegs and my knee swings out and then back in a stretch and I roll my shoulders in an exaggerated arc. My own little habit—the quick little routine which prompts me to gather myself mentally and get loose physically for what is to come. A motorcyclist's version of a batter taking a few false swings as he readies himself for the pitch. As the first curve approaches I'm exactly where I want to be, body compact and low and relaxed, hands soft on the grips. There's a growing excitement in my chest and a buzzing in my head. The next handful of miles are among the best in Virginia, across one of my favorite mountain passes, and I haven't been here in awhile.

Clicking a downshift and now, quickly, another. Back in the throttle, the bike steadies, its demeanor suddenly changed, hard now into its powerband. It knows I have charged it with the task it was built for and it sings its own song of delight. There's a subtle tension, an aura, around us now—me and this machine I love—a purposeful edge.

Pushing the motorcycle hard into the first turn I feel the elastic firming of the tires and suspension as they compress, the frame and engine and everything all suddenly alive. The diving pull of the turn is electric, and a flush of exultation washes over me. There's a smooth texture to the sensation, like running one's fingertip along a piece of silk, and I can't restrain the laugh which breaks out under my helmet. God, I love it!

With the first corner having set the stage—this will be an aggressive run—I'm now in attack mode. The corners come quickly, like stabbing punches from a boxer, and I work the motorcycle like the musical instrument it has become. The engine has that "packed" feeling like it has when it's singing high in the sweet spot of its rev range. I revel in the delicacy required by the throttle, how the merest movement changes the motorcycle's whole demeanor. Two fingers are extended to the brake lever— not that there's any hard braking here. Only an occasional gentle caress, trail-braking easily into the corners, like lightly brushing the face of that girl.

After a dozen curves I sense a danger, a need for caution in my growing delight. *Easy,* I tell myself, *stay loose.* It's with conscious effort that I keep my hands and arms and shoulders relaxed even as my lower body is tight with the physical effort of shifting my weight back and forth. But even with that tiresome effort below, the lifting movement from my calves and thighs feels good, a sprung feeling, like I'm part of the bike's suspension.

Halfway up the mountain the curves tighten even more, like the ever-shorter coils of a rope piled upon itself. The exit of one feeds almost instantly into the entrance of the next and there's no time for contemplation. Seeking to maintain my pace, I shift my lines slightly, placing my track so as to capture as much of the road's wrinkled camber as possible. Pushing. Pushing. My eyes in a flashing glance grasp the story of what the road is telling me. Like a game of instant chess, the constant stream of input demands an instantaneous response, a judgment edged as much in instinct as anything in the here and now, and then I'm exiting that corner and am into the next. There's a verge here, something deep and dark. I'm on the cusp of where it all gets deadly serious, and I know it.

It's been there all along. The knowing. But it's one of those things that I—like many of us—when faced with the choice of experiencing this euphoria, this transcendent delight of the rush along a good road, sometimes turn away from. As if simply ignoring it might make it go away.

Alas, it never does.

It breaks back into my consciousness on one of the hard right-handers near the top. In one of those corners where, for just an instant, I see myself in my mind's eye, in the whole context of what I'm doing. A flashing glance away from the road—from the entrance and exit points and the road camber and the texture of the tarmac and the is-there-gravel question, all the things my attention is normally focused upon—and my peripheral vision captures the picture of my fairing and its angle to the road and I realize I'm carrying an awful lot of lean angle. Having stopped a few times over the years to take pictures, I know what the landscape from this mountain holds. A dozen feet beyond the track of my tires, across the single oncoming lane and eighteen inches of guard rail, lies nothing but a sheer drop off. If you blow it here you'll probably die. And that's been my bet: every one of my corners will be nigh perfect. There will be no mistakes.

§

Among the activities that are reasonably accessible to most of us, motorcycling is nearly unique in the dual promise it holds. Imagine a rheostat, one of those round dials with a raised lip in the middle to be grasped between thumb and forefinger. Inscribed on the right side of the dial's flat face, in bold lettering, is FUN. Inscribed on the left side of the dial, in a rather more subdued font, is DANGER. As we twist that dial, turning up more and more of the fun that brought us here in the first place, the degree of danger advances too, right in lockstep. They are inextricably tied together.

Therein lies the dilemma of every sport rider, from the very first moment we swing our leg across that seat when heading out for a day's ride. "How much fun shall we have today?"

Our cruiser and touring brethren have long since answered that question quite neatly for themselves: just twist the dial a little bit, right to where it says "mild" in easy script right above the switch, and leave it there. But for those of us who lean more towards the sporting end of the spectrum, there are choices to be made. For us, a day's ride is likely to encompass a whole range of experiences. Everything from a gentle, one-hand-on-the-bar easy cruise; to that bread-and-butter, crisp sporting pace which always makes us smile; to—maybe—a WFO sprint across a favored road which has our pulse pounding and heads shaken later in disbelief at what we've just done.

I liken it to having two lines, drawn in parallel, each representing a side of that risk/reward duality. The gap, the space between them, is the place where we spend our time. It's where we live, as riders. It's in that imaginary space that we make all our decisions, where we make all the adjustments to our lines and braking and pace, where we tend to all the technical nuances of our sport. It's the place that each of us has chosen as an acceptable balance between fun and danger.

It's our comfort zone.

If that's all there was to it—just find that reasonable balance, that spot where we can each nod to ourselves that, "yeah, I'm okay right here," then go out and have at it—we'd all be golden. Unfortunately, for us sport riders it rather quickly gets more complicated—'cause we still have that dial.

What happens is that when we start wicking it up, looking for more and more of that exhilaration, those two lines start to converge on one another. That space wherein we operate, the gap that represents that degree of separation between fun and danger, swiftly gets narrower and narrower. Until, ultimately, there's hardly any discernible space between them at all—we've reached that rarified place where the two lines have merged into one, a single blood-thin line. A place where no margins are left, no mistakes are possible. A place where it's all on the table in a single, bet-the-house wager. The razor's edge.

Not that we ever mean for it to happen, of course. We always leave home in the morning intending to be reasonable and smart and have some fun but—surely not—we won't be crazy. No siree, not us. But then we get out there, where the roads are perfect; where the laughter and the camaraderie lull us into believing that it's all okay; and where, sometimes, it seems we are blessed with a special grace. And it all starts to go away. Sometimes the difference between just right, one more afternoon's delight to add to that box of memories, and too much, a disaster etched in stark relief, is but the breadth of an angel's hair.

That challenge, somehow hewing to that balance, is the burden we carry in return for all the extraordinary pleasures this sport brings us. One thing's for sure—no one can live very long at the razor's edge. Eventually those house odds surely catch up with us, trumping all our skills and all our intentions. The place is a slippery slope, with a comeuppance as inevitable as the sun. So for those of us who intend to stay in the game for a long time, those of us who can't possibly fathom not doing this, we have to figure it out.

On this particular morning, recognizing what I'm doing and the place I've gotten to, I decide—reluctantly—to back it off. Not a lot—just a click or two. But enough so that the humming urgency to get it all perfectly right—every second, every corner—

mostly goes away. There's still a rush along the road, still a delight in the doing of this thing, but now there's some space here. A crack of daylight between Mr. Fun and Mr. Danger.

That extra little bit of space lets me see other things. Coming up the mountain I saw nothing but the road. The world outside the narrow boundaries of that ribbon of asphalt was little more than a blur of color, unnoticed and uncared for. Hooking the hard right-hander that marks the summit, my now slightly-lesser pace affords me an occasional sneaking glance sideways, as I begin my descent. And what I see is the world. Something that even those of us who aren't smell-the-roses types maybe ought to take a look at every now and again.

On this day I'm lucky on many levels, and I know it. I'm lucky to have had that wonderful, flying lap up the mountain—I can't deny the joy in that. I'm lucky that that same flying lap didn't end in disaster. And I'm lucky now, slicing my way down the mountain, seeing it all for what it is.

It's never easy. Those of us who find our delight in tip-toeing through a landscape which just also happens to be littered with dark horrors, like Dorothy on her yellow-brick road, need all the help we can get. Like moths drawn to a flame, our challenge is, in that nexus where joy and disaster intersect, to find the light without falling into the fire.

It reminds me that an awful lot of the people attracted to our sport aren't very long for it. Think of all the buddies you used to ride with five or ten years ago. Chances are that a lot of them are still there, out with us on the roads. But I'd bet that for every rider that still suits up every Sunday, there's another that has long-since traded in his helmet for something else. And while a lot of that has to do with motorcycling in general—things like getting married and having kids and changing jobs have always taken a toll on our ranks—there's another factor that causes riders to disproportionately leave our sportriding fraternity.

Fear.

The fear that comes from the sudden, inescapable understanding that yes—damn straight—it can happen to us. Most of us don't willingly walk up to that understanding. Most of us come to accept it only after something has happened. Usually after the big *it* happened; or because it very nearly did; or because it did to one of our buddies. Then comes the ringing uncertainty around every corner and over every rise, and all of a sudden riding doesn't seem nearly so lighthearted and carefree. A few wooden rides later, just to prove "hell yeah, I got back on that horse," but they're not fun anymore and it's hard to imagine that they'll ever be fun. And there you go—we've lost another one.

Which is a shame. And why I think this is all so important. Because, although I may be a little over the top in my passion for this sport—I have been accused of such—I honestly believe that out of all the fun and inspirational activities we might aspire to, riding a fast motorcycle over a good road is as good as it gets. And that's why it's such a pity every time we see another rider walk away.

Which is why we need to figure it out. Why we need to find that balance that allows us to keep on riding, forever.

In the end, it's a pretty basic question. We're all torn with wanting to go faster and faster, yet knowing that we shouldn't. The choice we make—a choice we'll be presented many times on every single ride—is probably the single most important one we make.

How much fun shall we have today?

December 2003, Sport Rider

Motorcycling's Dirty Little Secret

This was the very first piece of mine that Kent published. It elicited quite a response. A lot of people nodded their head in agreement. Quite a few took umbrage. I was happy, simply, that it made people think.

We were railing at a pretty decent clip across the Cherohala when we spotted the helicopter. "Police chopper," was our first thought, as we checked our speed. But a little further along, when we came around the corner to the blue lights and the flares and the double-handful of bikes parked along the side, we realized the real reason. Medivac.

That one was sobering in its clarity—there was lots of blood on the road. We would find out later that the guy survived. Barely. The Armco had taken off one of his legs, just above the knee. The police estimated his entry speed into the corner at nearly 100mph. Of course he'd been with a group of other riders. Naturally.

Riding with a group of like-minded friends can be one of the best parts about our little sport. Being able to talk about and laugh and share the experiences on the road can be a real kick. But it also has an ugly side. Group riding is nothing less than our dirty little secret. Why? Because that is where an extraordinarily-high percentage of single-vehicle motorcycle accidents happen.

The simple fact is that most of us—and especially us guys— have an investment of ego and pride and desire for self-inclusion and, yes, even competitiveness, which too-often drives us to do things in a group setting which we generally wouldn't do when by ourselves. Including piloting a sportbike at too-fast speeds. It takes a *really* mature individual to defy those instincts to "stay with the pack." To not stay on the tail of that rider in front of us even though the pace has elevated far beyond what we feel comfortable. Frankly, most of us simply don't have the discipline to *not* do those things.

The blunt reality is, mile for mile, our chances of being involved in a motorcycle accident are sharply higher when riding with a group than when riding alone. I don't know of any formal statistical study which proves that. The Hurt Report didn't elaborate on that particular dynamic. Yet the empirical evidence is overwhelming. It happens wherever motorcyclists and good roads meet—the Sunday Morning ride in Northern California, the Angeles Crest, Deals Gap, route 211 in Virginia, or any of the countless other lesser-known places favored by local sportbike-riding cognoscenti. Just turn your gaze towards any of those places and contemplate the crashes that happen there virtually every weekend—the vast majority of those involving riders in a group. Funny how the solo riders running those same mountains manage to mostly stay on two wheels.

So what's the answer? Not to ride with friends? Refuse that invitation from one of our buddies to go on that overnighter just because we don't know the rest of the riders? Never dare to ride with that group of strangers we hooked up with at the gas station?

One thing is for sure—there aren't any simple answers. There's certainly no panacea. But it can work. There *are* groups of sport riders who routinely ride together without incident.

We have to start by acknowledging that group riding does indeed carry extra risk. Always has and probably always will. The ego thing is very real. And if you're a guy, figure you're doubly-susceptible. More than one woman, on observing a bunch of male riders together, has remarked that "the testosterone is running mighty thick." We need to beware the consequences of that.

More experienced riders, usually the ones who set up and lead these rides, also have an obligation to assert some manner of leadership. Simply pretending that everyone will "ride their own ride" clearly doesn't work much of the time. Smaller groups are better. So is more spacing between riders. So is a willingness—too often absent—to point out to riders that something about their riding is unsafe, or that it's clear they are pushing too hard. So is insisting on proper riding gear. So is making it emphatically clear that the ride route may include sections that are more challenging and that will likely cause some of the slower riders to fall back and perhaps lose sight of everyone else—and, oh, by the way, not to worry because everyone will wait and re-group at whatever checkpoint. So is appointing one of the more experienced riders to run sweep, tagging along with and keeping an eye on the slower riders.

And, of course, there's always the track.

Those are some of the *things* we can do. But they alone won't fix the problem. Even more important is the *attitude* that everyone brings. An insistence by each of us that we will not be involved in an incident on this day. One day at a time. Just like those guys in recovery—a notion not too far from the truth for some of us.

The problem isn't going to go away on its own. If we don't do something, if we don't—via self discipline and peer pressure and self-policing—begin to insist on better behavior and less carnage within our own riding community—it'll be done for us. We'll see ever-more draconian enforcement of traffic laws, more police stings, and more road closures. That's not the kind of environment any of us want to contemplate riding our next sportbike in.

February 2003, Sport Rider

Day of Broken Dreams

This was the first of two of my stories that dealt with real people who died. To this day, when I ride past the place where it happened, I quietly whisper "Hey, John." I'm pretty sure he hears me.

It's one of those rare days of summer when the air is so crystal clear and the sky is such a deep shade of blue and the sun is so sharply bright that everything has that etched-in-stone look. As I descend the Massanutten on my way home I catch a glance through the trees of the south fork of the Shenandoah, somnolent and timeless as it wends its way down the Page Valley. The sight makes me catch my breath in wonder. Even having been stopped earlier—and thus having to make do with the slight reduction in pace that I had promised—it's an extraordinary gift, this day.

A day on which it seems impossible to believe we might die.

§

"Zero tolerance." I'm stopped at the Mobil station on my way out. The half-dozen riders clustered along the side of the building are talking about an article in the local Rappahannock paper. "That's what it said. They're not cutting anyone any more slack. Yesterday they were even running radar out on 647."

They're talking, of course, about the police response, itself a reaction to community outrage, to us—sport riders. Because we keep crashing, there up on the mountain. It seems to be the one thing we've gotten down pat.

Even the news of the crackdown doesn't dampen many spirits, though. It's just too nice a day. The cool front—rare for August—was forecast several days ago. Enough in advance so that everyone could line up their chores and adjust their schedules so this day would be free. And now everyone is determined to enjoy it.

As I finish my doughnut and orange juice the group of riding buddies mount back up. In seconds the air is rent with a joyous cacophony—raspy inline-fours and bass rumbling v-twins and the rattle of dry clutches. It's the sound of what we do, music to my ears. You can't hear it and not feel the ratcheting in your chest, promise implicit in those edgy notes. Hearing it, I have to fight the urge to hurry and mount up myself. I have all of this day in front of me and I want to savor it.

It's less than ten minutes to the mountain. Only mid-morning, still a few hours before the crowds of two-wheelers will be here. That's intentional. The law enforcement crackdown isn't a surprise to me, of course—this is, after all, *my* mountain. I'll get a run in now, while it's still relatively quiet, then continue on and hit the good roads west of the Gap.

Beyond the twisted nature of the road itself, the great benefit of the mountain are the two lanes heading up in each direction—no double-yellow passes necessary—with one lane for each of the descents. It's the finest motorcycle road in a long way.

The westbound ascent starts slowly, like broad strokes of a painter's brush. A couple of fast sweepers, flashing across tarmac dappled in sunlight and shadow. Then the hard right, a prelude of what is to come, clicking one downshift to get the revs up. That's the first one with a hard apex, the spot where you first feel the suspension compress. Then there's the long, lazy left-hander, winding up your heart along with your speed, round past the gravel turnout there on the left to where it begins. The serious stuff. There's a floating sensation, an aftermath of the delight from that first good curve, and a last moment's appreciation that nearly the whole mountain lies in front of you. Then you're not thinking about the mountain anymore—just riding. One more downshift, the engine now wound up into the meat of its powerband, just in time for the hard left-hander, pushing now—but not too hard. You're thinking about your tires, and the need to get some heat in them. The next turn is the decreasing radius right-hander—the one that has caught out so many riders. It sucks you in, the visual cues promising. But I've been here before. I know of the deception and exactly how much the corner will give. Backing out of the throttle for a heartbeat or two right when one would normally be winding it on, that restraint rewards me with a line which scribes a path just out to the dotted line dividing the two upward-climbing lanes. Then the dance begins. From the deep shadows you emerge into the sunlight, a short, deft little swirl with that painter's brush as you go throttling up through the next left. The strokes become delicate after that, fine strokes drawn in swift, tight arcs, again and again, blood thin.

I love this place.

§

I know immediately that I'm busted. Over the top and beginning the descent, I've accelerated in a quick little burst to move around the lone vehicle up in front of me before the two lanes squeeze down into one. As I draw abreast of the car I see the cruiser come around the corner two hundred feet in front of me. Even as I chop the throttle, my pass aborted, I know that it's not enough. Sure enough, there they are, blue lights flashing.

Damn it.

After the usual pleasantries—and noting what a nice bike it is—the young officer matter-of-factly states "I'm going to have to write you a summons. Do you have your registration?" With the conversation back at the gas station just a few minutes before still echoing in my head, I smile wryly. "Sure," I reply, popping the seat to retrieve the paperwork.

Maybe it's my resignation, the certainty that at this point that it's all a given. Or my apology, genuine, disgusted at what has become of this once-wonderful stretch of road. Whatever, the officer offers me an unexpected gift. "I'm going to let you go with a warning."

The weather is not the only thing fine about this day.

It's a mixed blessing, of course. With the officer's stern admonition that my reprieve is good for one time only—my get-out-of-jail-free card has now been punched—I know I'll be on the hook for anything else that happens today. That, and the fact that I feel an obligation to keep the promise I made. A promise which gets additional emphasis from the officer's parting comment— "I've never given a warning to a motorcyclist before." All of a sudden I feel like I've become a representative for our entire sorry lot. And I'm determined that nothing must happen which later might make that officer regret his moment of clemency. I want the story to end with the notion that maybe cutting a motorcyclist a break now and again isn't entirely unwarranted.

It's suddenly become a day to chill. But that's okay. Even with the edge off my pace it remains a gorgeous day, the next few hours an almost mesmerizing mix of sunlight and shadow and movement along crooked little roads, across a landscape beguiling and wondrous. A day to remind us of why we bother in the first place.

§

John Kosztolnik and his brother Peter are a couple hours behind me. Their ascent of the mountain begins near midday, with the sun high in the sky. Like mine earlier—like most all the riders out on this golden day—theirs is a perfect run up the mountain, spiraling up the corkscrewing esses in a smooth, flowing ballet. How could it be otherwise? This road seems touched with something special, a magic which seems to gladden the heart with the curl of every curve and every foot of elevation gained. And they've come here on this day—a perfect day to match with a perfect road—for the same reason we all have: to be touched by that magic.

John is in front on his 929, with Peter running a few bike lengths behind. Skilled, experienced riders, the brothers tag-team their way into the last mile of the ascent. It's been a good run and if they feel any disappointment at all it's only in the knowledge that it's almost over. There are only a handful of curves remaining until the summit.

At the same time, above them, an R1 rider is making his descent. His track brings him past the long, sweeping right-hander which marks the first serious turn in the downhill slalom, then through the two-hundred-foot-long straightaway leading into the following left-hander. That little straightaway is the last place to gather one's thoughts—and to get set up properly for the turns which follow. The left-hander is a sweeper—easy to negotiate— but not as open as the fast right-hander which preceded it. It requires a modicum of restraint. Overcooked, it can lead to a busted entrance into the right-hander which follows—a turn which is hard and abrupt and which has none of the friendly forgiveness of a sweeper.

John and Peter, heading up, approach the turn at the same time. Just one of those countless confluences of time and space which pass through all our lives without thought or acknowledgement. For the brothers the turn—a left-hander from their perspective—is fairly open, the extra radius from being on the outside and the extra space afforded by the double-lanes heading up serving to moderate the turn's abruptness. But to both the Kosztolnik brothers heading up and the R1 rider heading down, the turn is blind. John's first glimpse of the R1 is in an already-blooming moment of crisis, after the Yamaha has come across the double-yellow line and has swept across the oncoming lanes, right in front of him. There's no time for him to react.

§

I'm still lost in my reverie, enjoying the day. After descending the Massanutten I head back east towards the mountain, retracing my route from a couple hours before. It's only a few minutes away.

Heading up the western face, a track I've ridden a thousand times, I'm in casual mode, happily thinking about which routes I might choose once I'm east of the Blue Ridge. With the spectacular weather there's no need to head home just yet.

Past the summit, I lean hard into the long right-hand sweeper, the same one that R1 rider would have negotiated just a little while before. Around the turn, one last, long graceful sweep of that painter's brush, until the exit, where I can see into that two-hundred foot straightaway. Off to the side at the end, right at the entrance of the left-hand sweeper, sits a Park Ranger with his light bar flashing. His window is down and as I approach under trailing throttle he motions me to slow down. The first intimation that something has gone terribly wrong here today. Moments later, winding slowly through the carnage of twisted metal and leaking fluids and flashing lights and grim-faced officers—and blood and tears—the day has suddenly turned. At the bottom of the mountain riders are everywhere, sudden-seriousness in their faces, talking about what happened. The sense in the air is that something long-cherished has irrevocably changed. The time of innocence has passed.

John Kosztolnik died this day, in his brother's arms. As that news circulates among the riders down below, I suddenly want to be away from here. This is no longer my place—not today.

As I ride slowly home, wondering about things and why they happen the way they do, I pass other riders heading towards the mountain. Riders still unaware that a tragedy has unfolded. Riders who see nothing but a stunningly beautiful day and the chance to ride a great road. And I'm struck by the contrast between that promise—held by every single one of us who ride, when we awakened on this day—and what has become of it.

When will we ever learn?

February 2004, Sport Rider

Crisis of Confidence

The after, *after it all goes* wrong.

"I worry more about damage to my bike than I do about hurting myself." Paul looks at me with a quizzical expression.

"Really?" he asks. "Why would that be?"

I shrug. "I don't know. I guess I just figure that riding with the right gear will mostly protect me. But modern bikes, with their plastic fairings and such, always seem to take a pretty rough hit when they go down. And having my bike out of commission while parts are ordered and repairs get made really sucks, you know?"

Paul nods, without saying anything, a thoughtful look in his eyes.

It's a week before the Daytona 200—the real start of spring, if you ask me—and I'm in Maryland getting new tires shod on my bike. Hanging around the shop while the service guys in back do their work. Shooting the breeze with Paul Milhalka, sales manager, friend, and supremely accomplished rider. With experience counted in decades, over half a million street miles under his belt, and thousands of track miles, Paul is as good as they come. There isn't much in the motorcycling pantheon that he hasn't seen or heard. Even in his mid-sixties, Paul can still give most anyone a run for his money. He's forgotten more about motorcycling than most of us will ever know.

I'm not sure he buys my argument about the wisdom of worrying more about one's bike than one's body.

§

A couple hours later, having traversed the 70-odd miles from the dealership, I'm only a few miles from home. Still only mid-afternoon, I decide that a little detour is in order—a couple of the local country roads are calling. I'm slightly chilled from the long ride back on the freeway, but I'm not thinking about that. I'm thinking about how glad I am that March is finally here. It's been a long, cold winter.

Wending my way out along Georgetown and then down Blantyre, roads now thankfully clear of the salt smears which were here just a few weeks ago, I'm daydreaming, thinking about the race in eight days and wishing I could be in Florida to see it. But no matter. It's hard not to be happy at the start of a new riding season. Those intermittent rides during the winter months are never nearly enough.

Past the last couple of horse farms, approaching the little cluster of houses at Bethel, I'm in that mindless zone you sometimes get lulled into. After riding nearly 200 miles today, I'm only a mile from home. I haven't seen another vehicle on the road in the last ten minutes.

It appears like an apparition, out of nowhere. A sudden looming shape rising in front of me, almost as if by magic. I'm surprised, astonished at the sudden appearance, jerked out of my reverie. Then I'm back focused again, hard on the brakes, swiftly calculating lines and time and distance; flashing through my list of options. It only takes the space of a heartbeat to realize there aren't any. My last thought, in the final ticking microseconds, is the irony of my words to Paul, just a couple hours earlier.

Son of a bitch.

§

I live near a rolling dervish of a road. It's only six miles from end to end but those six miles snake across the landscape in a turning, twisting roller coaster of a ride. It's long been one of my favorites. And as I turn down this little jewel on this cloudy morning in May I'm relieved to finally be out riding again.

The last couple of months have been hard. The crash back in March, which totaled my bike and left me with a broken wrist, suddenly changed the whole complexion of my riding season. I'm still waiting for the slow-turning wheels of the insurance bureaucracy to cut me a check so I can replace my bike. In the meantime, I'm fortunate to have this ancient old Yamaha to ride.

Except… except that this doesn't feel fun at all. The first turn is blind—hell, they're all blind on this road—and approaching it I suddenly have the feeling that there's another SUV, a twin to that one back in March, just around the corner, waiting to get me. I try and dismiss the notion, telling myself how ridiculous it is. But the feeling sits there in my chest, leaden and unmoving.

There's something on this road trying to kill me.

§

Crashing. Sometime, somewhere, it happens to all of us. If it hasn't yet happened to you, it will. And if you've already gone down—well, you will again if you stay in the game long enough. That's just the way it is. Which is a big part of the reason why so many of us work so hard at getting good, at improving our skills and refining our judgment so that those little escapades are as far apart as possible. It's also why we wear the gear that we do, to hopefully moderate the effects when that unfortunate day arrives. Eventually, though, despite all our best efforts, that day *does* arrive. Then there's only the afterward.

The after effects of a crash may be subtle—to the point that we may not even be aware that they exist—but they're almost always there. They oftentimes have a profound effect on our psyche and on our future enjoyment of the sport, introducing fear and caution where once there was nothing but joy and abandon. They oftentimes make fast riders slow. They take what once was a delight and turn it into an exercise in overcoming fear. And they are one of the biggest reasons people leave the sport.

It starts, in the beginning, with denial. Like coming down with cancer, or being one of the unfortunate passengers on an airliner falling from the sky, the thought that we might actually crash on today's ride is an abstraction that we refuse to accept. Sure, we recognize intellectually that it *could* happen—that's why we wear the gear, after all—but in our heart of hearts we don't really believe it. Crashing is one of those things that always happens to someone else.

Up to a point, that sense of denial is healthy. It's what allows us to climb aboard our bike and go charging off with our buddies on Sunday, to go flying into that corner on our favorite road, and to load up the trailer as we head off for yet another track day. We'd have a tough time doing those things if, in doing so, we truly believed we were going to crash.

But it also sets us up for a fall—a big-time reality check when it does happen. We're then suddenly faced with some serious head games. That road which once brought us such pleasure now seems filled with demons out to get us. And instead of the joy that we once experienced on every ride we now have an edgy fear pressing on our nerves, a scalloped, uncertain path through all those corners instead of the smooth lines we used to scribe, an involuntary hitch on the bars every time a car comes around the bend. What do we do then?

The good news is that there is an answer. The bad news is that, as with most things involving our psyche, it's not necessarily simple or quick. There's no magic bullet to instantly make things better. How long or difficult the recovery process might be depends a lot on the particular circumstances of a given crash.

There's something of a continuum to where we end up emotionally—the starting point for our recovery—following a get-off. That point seems to vary, according to several factors.

The first of those is physical injury. Which makes sense.

The more severely we're hurt, the more likely we are to come away with serious reservations about this thing we've chosen to do. The worst extreme, of course, being a truly close call with death or very-serious injury. Those can be tough to come back from. Conversely, being injured very lightly, or not at all, will typically leave us with far fewer demons to slay.

The involvement with another vehicle is another negative factor. Maybe because out of all the things we have to deal with out there on the street, we intuitively know that other vehicles pose the single greatest threat to us. Most serious motorcycle crashes involve a 4-wheel vehicle. So having them involved in your incident can bring lots of mental baggage to the party. Single-vehicle crashes, as bad as they might be, at least don't have that issue to contend with.

A long layoff can also make things worse. Whether caused by a bike needing repairs, an injury which prevents one from riding—like my broken wrist—or simply because a rider chooses not to ride for a while, the longer one goes without getting back out there seems to make it harder when you eventually do. It's as if every day of the layoff allows one's subconscious to conjure ever more ghosts, to add ever more excuses.

The environment also makes a difference. Two of my three racetrack crashes were high-speed, violent affairs—enough so that they totaled my motorcycles. Yet in both cases I walked away with no physical ailments that a few Ibuprofen tablets wouldn't fix—and little in the way of mental baggage to work through. Conversely, and not a little ironically, both of my street crashes happened at far lower speeds—yet left me with lots of emotional issues to overcome. Just one more reason to save the really extreme stuff for the track. It's a safer environment in more ways than one. Ever notice those racers who crash hard in practice on Saturday, then go out and win their race on Sunday? Chances are that wouldn't happen if it involved the street.

And ambiguity. We all tend to dislike uncertainty.

Especially with a risk-laden activity like motorcycling, we want to feel that that those risk factors are known and controllable. So understanding the cause of a crash—especially if it was a mistake that we can correct—goes a long way towards assuaging how we feel about it. Having that left as an open question leads to the inevitable feeling that it's out of our control and could happen again.

Okay, so understanding that these are some of the factors affecting how we react to a crash, what's the answer? How do we get past those ghosts and demons? How do we make it fun again?

You have to ride. Simple as that. You have to ride as soon as you possibly can, and as often as you can. If you commute, keep on commuting. If you were planning on going on an overnighter, keep those plans. If you've made a habit of getting out on Sunday mornings, well then, get out *this* Sunday morning. If in your riding you usually run a spirited sporting pace you might want to back your speed down a couple clicks, that's fine—but whatever else you do, get out there and spin some miles. They may not seem like a lot of fun at first. They may, in fact, seem haunted and anything *but* fun. But they'll get better sooner than you think. The one constant I've observed in all of this is that perseverance will always bring one back. Riders who are determined not to let this thing beat them inevitably gain back their confidence and skill and smoothness. It all does, indeed, become fun again. Those who walk away—well, they just gave up too soon.

Which leads me to my last thought. Those who have been riding a long time are far more likely to bounce back from a bad crash than those who are relatively new to the sport. I think that's because by the time we have to start using multiple hands to count our years on the road, motorcycling has become too important to us, has become part of how we actually define ourselves as human beings, and most of us would do most anything to get that back. Some of us cannot imagine not doing this.

Keep on riding, forever. Not a bad prescription for what ails us.

April 2004, Sport Rider

Different Strokes

This year's crop of sportbikes emphasize—with an exclamation point—the extraordinary capabilities available to today's sport rider. When you step back and think about the performance that we have available—at stunningly affordable prices—it just makes you shake your head in wonder. If anyone tries to tell you about how great things were back in some distant past, tell 'em they're full of it. Today, right now, is the golden age of motorcycling.

Most things in life aren't free, though, and neither is this brilliance we've been given. Much of the superlative capability displayed by today's bikes comes standing on the shoulders of a new design paradigm—increased specialization.

Years ago bikes were far less focused. A road bike—save the rare chopper or full-dress tourer—was expected to do pretty much everything: get you to work during the week, be suitably cool-looking while cruising the local hangouts on soft summer evenings, provide a capable touring platform to get you out to the beach on your vacation, and, of course, pull yeoman sportbike duty on the weekends. Some of them even got tagged with number plates come race weekends, since that was about the only way to get out on a racetrack—track days having yet to become widely available.

In contrast, look at the universe of motorcycles available today and you'll see a very different landscape. Most bikes are purpose-built and can be dropped neatly into one of several classes: cruiser, full-dress tourer, sport-tourer, or sportbike. Sure, there are some niche models out there—adventure-tourers and standards which attempt to straddle multiple categories—but for the most part the bikes available today have become quite specific in their design.

In most respects this has been a benefit, allowing engineers to design models tailored to a specific market segment without the compromises that inevitably resulted back when they were required to build do-everything bikes. Nowhere is this more evident than in today's sportbikes—which often have capabilities which are a mere whisper from the top-flight race machinery of just a few years back.

The downside is that those very same attributes that make a bike so focused and capable in one area also often detract from others. Most modern motorcycles aren't terribly versatile. Which isn't to say that you can't take your R1 on that cross-country tour you've been planning; or choose your Gold Wing for your next track day. Only that those might not be the best choices.

The answer—one usually far more obvious to us than to our significant others—is to own more than one bike.

Owning different kinds of motorcycles cuts instantly across the problems posed by the lack of versatility in today's specialized machinery. Want something to carve up the canyons on the weekends? No problem. One of today's superlative sportbikes is just what you need. Feel like criss-crossing the country on the interstate? No worries. There's a touring rig out there built just for that. Want something with some sporting character, but that also affords a bit of comfort and carrying capacity? No sweat. A sport-tourer or one of the new standards is just your ticket. Whatever category of riding you prefer, there's something out there to meet the need.

Doing that, though—owning more than one kind of bike—brings yet another issue to the fore: the need to constantly re-acclimate when you switch from one to another. First there are the differences in ergonomics to adapt to, often vastly different between classes of bikes. Second are the differences in weight and suspension compliance, again often very different. And lastly there are the differences in handling and general response. Given all those differences, stepping off of one motorcycle and onto one of a different kind can feel as strange as going from two wheels to four.

My current rides are a K1200RS and a GSX-R1000. Both are reasonable examples of what pass as current state-of-the-art in the sport-touring and sportbike worlds. Both do a great job in their respective roles. Like children, they each have their own personalities; their own individual strengths and weaknesses. But owning both, and swapping back and forth on successive rides, what I find interesting and challenging is the experience of constantly switching between bikes of widely differing character. And both of mine, at least, are tilted towards the sporting end of the spectrum. Toss in a full-boat touring rig or a heavyweight cruiser into the mix and there'd really be some changes going on.

When I go riding there usually isn't a whole lot of rhyme or reason as to why I choose the BMW versus the Suzuki. Sometimes I clearly want the deadly-serious sportbike capabilities that the Gixxer provides. And sometimes I want the longer legs and greater comfort of the BMW—and it'll obviously get the nod for an overnight trip or when weather issues intrude, just like the Gixxer is the obvious choice for track days. But most times, there's no difference. A typical weekend will have me riding one on Saturday and the other on Sunday. I ride both on the very same roads, with exactly the same entrance and exit speeds, using the same lines, and at precisely the same pace. On the street the limiting factors are not to be found in either bike, in other words. What *is* different is how the two bikes feel—and the need to accommodate to that difference every time I switch between them.

Stepping off the KRS and onto the Gixxer, the first thing you notice is the position—the far more severe ergonomics. And as soon as it's rolling you quickly notice the suspension—firm to the point of feeling harsh. Your first thought is that this is an uncomfortable bike to ride. But you also notice how light and airy it all feels. And after only a handful of miles the overriding character of the bike begins to emerge—a feeling of power and aggression and quick responsiveness. There's a directness to this bike, a feeling of focus and of everything happening the instant you command it. There's a sense of everything being part of a unified package. Soon, that suspension that at first seemed harsh all of a sudden has a compliant, lithesome feel. You realize how well it tracks over the road and there's a delight in the feedback you get from the tires and suspension. You suddenly realize that the overall sensory input seems more intense. The Gixxer is nothing if not about vibrant communication.

The next day, climbing on the KRS, the first thing you notice—just like on the Gixxer—is the position. Like most sporting motorcycles the BMW has a forward-leaning crouch, but far less than on the Suzuki. So much less of it, in fact, that, in comparison, you feel like you're sitting almost upright. There's an immediate feeling of spaciousness compared to the Suzuki. And that roominess gets reinforced as soon as you start rolling—the softer suspension combining with the much more relaxed ergos to impart a sense of luxurious accommodation. Your first thought is a happy one—you could ride this bike forever.

As you bend into the first corner, however, that smile fades. The suspension suddenly feels not just soft, but has wandering, roly-poly character to it. The precise, joyful, tracking of the Suzuki has been replaced by a feeling of being disconnected and distant. And as the twisty stuff gets tighter and tighter you realize how big and heavy this motorcycle really is. It feels large and unwieldy and only barely competent. Had you never ridden the KRS before you surely would instantly dismiss it as having any sporting character at all. "Get me off of this thing" would be the likely sentiment.

But you have been on it before—and you know better. You know what this bike can do. And sure enough, like a dull blade whetted on a stone, growing sharper and more impertinent with every draw, until what once was dull and slow-witted has transformed itself once again into a weapon one might confidently wield in anger, so does the KRS slowly begin to reassert its character with each passing mile. Soon enough, you're smiling once again—and the BMW is kicking ass.

It just takes patience.

The next ride, back on the Gixxer, and the process starts all over again. Just like putting down a Bowie knife and picking up a straight razor.

And that's how it is for those of us blessed with more than one bike. Constantly having to readjust to the day's ride. It's not a big deal. The re-acclimatization period is usually pretty brief, especially when going from anything else to a sportbike—whose sharp focus typically prompts a very rapid adjustment—but it's nevertheless something that must be dealt with.

The crux of the matter lies mainly in the differences in speed at which different bikes respond. Starting at the sportbike end of the spectrum, things happen instantly. There's a direct, laser-like feeling of connectedness between you and the bike: you think it, and it's done. As you move to other kinds of bikes, though, those with more weight and softer suspension and longer wheelbases, that feeling of responsiveness diminishes. It simply takes more time between initiating a movement and having it take effect. As one of my riding buddies recently quipped, "you have to dial ahead…"

That's the piece we need to adjust to. We have to re-map our own nervous system responses to those of the bike we're on. The more widely divergent our choices of ride are, or if we spend lengthy periods of time on one before swapping to another, the longer it'll take. But once that's done, once those neural pathways are again in sync with our chosen platform, we're good to go. That's when a bike comes alive again. That's when you can rail.

§

As you might expect, that's not the end of the story. For

many riders, for those who only own one bike, none of this is an issue.

Ever hear the old western adage "beware the man with one gun"? The inference there, the second part, is "because he probably knows how to use it."

Whether we're talking about a century-old single-action Colt Peacemaker or the just-introduced Kawasaki ZX-10R, our ability to get the most out of a tool is largely dependent upon our dedication to it. Having only one of anything—something that gets used all the time with no distractions from other, similar, tools—allows us to gain a familiarity with it which is sometimes almost spooky. Riders who own only one bike often gain a nuanced, uncanny understanding of their machine which sets them apart from their buddies who have multiple platforms. They come to know, at an intimate, unconscious level, exactly what their bike will do. There's no need for any kind of acclimatization—these guys are attuned to their bike's specific characteristics the moment they swing their leg over the seat.

Which is to say, at the end of the day, that you're in good shape regardless of which side of the fence you're on—whether you own one bike or many. For sure, there's a distinct pleasure in having a multi-bike stable, in being able to choose exactly the right kind of platform for a given ride. But there's also an equal delight in knowing the one bike you do own like an old glove.

And what I said at the beginning—that thing about not wanting to take your R1 on a cross-country tour? To hell with it. Take it anyway. You'll have a great time.

Enjoy today. It's the golden age.

October 2004, Sport Rider

Hubris

*We're rarely quite as good as
we imagine.*

Turn two is supposed to be the hard one. Every lap, flying hard up the hill off the long front straight, the wide pavement and that very same climbing elevation serving to soften the edge off of turn one, you're cooking. Carrying lots of corner speed and winding on lots of throttle and your heart hammering with the rush. Rising into the sky, your mind is already fixed somewhere beyond your vision. There over the hump of the hill, after the landscape has flattened, lies turn two, soft and beckoning. You know, having done it countless times before, that you've got to check your speed more than you want, more than feels right. Because the exit of two tightens, almost imperceptibly at first, but then with a flash of urgency. Like most decreasing-radius turns, the curling pavement of the hard right-hander disappears sooner than feels natural. If you're carrying too much speed into two, you'll blow the entrance into three.

So it's only natural that after getting through that sequence you relax a bit. The downhill esses which follow aren't terribly technical. You just follow your line as you wind up more speed on the descent. Your head is already wrapped around turn five, another few hundred feet in the distance, with maybe even a thought or two already intruding about the quick six-seven combo at the end of the finger beyond, and the long, scary-fast backstretch which follows.

§

As the third session starts on this July day the Georgia sun is already high in the sky and the early-morning comfort is quickly giving way to serious heat and humidity. Road Atlanta can be a hot place in the summertime. As I zip up, with trickles of sweat already running down my arms and back, my hands clammy under the Held gloves, I'm thinking the track might get greasy this afternoon, with tires quickly going off in the heat. I've got to watch that, especially since I've got yet another track day scheduled here tomorrow. And tomorrow—the advanced-only session—is the day I really expect to push the pace. Today is just a warm-up, a day to have some fun and get reacquainted with one of my favorite racetracks.

The first lap of the session is easy, of course, just getting heat back into the tires. As I hook turn seven and head back down the long back straight I marvel again at the changes along that section. The old Gravity Cavity—that suspension-draining, stomach-churning black hole of American racetracks—is gone, replaced with a double set of ninety-degree turns. I miss the old roller-coaster feel of Gravity Cavity, but the new turns are certainly more demanding, more technical. As it is with most things, you get back something with everything you give away. The new layout is still way cool.

Turn twelve, my favorite, remains the way it always has. You go firing hard up the hill, blind to what's on the other side, running on hope and belief. Then there's that flashing transition when you're flung over the crest and suddenly the pavement is falling away from you and your suspension has extended and the bike has gone all light and the pavement is curling hard to the right and you're pressing, pressing. And in that moment the hot, floating exultation wrapping around you is like nothing else and you suddenly remember why you're here and why you do this.

Starting my second lap, I begin to push some speed. Not a full-on press, but probably not more than a click or two down. My pace still feels relaxed, but now there's a bit of an edge to it.

Up the hill out of turn one I'm mindful of that turn two-three trap and I work my way carefully through there. It's actually pretty easy right now, with my speed still building in a slow crescendo, still a few ticks down. It'll be harder in a lap or two, when the prelude is over and the tires are warm and there are nothing but hot laps, done as quickly as one can. You hate to give up speed then.

Into the esses, first a left, easy, then pulling the bike back upright and hard over onto its right side. Ahead, down the hill, through the tunnel of vision clamped around me by the vortex of speed, I can see the black top of the pavement tinged in orange, runoff from the red Georgia clay. I'm thinking I need to adjust my line ever so slightly because of it, the fine red dust a mild impediment to the exemplary traction this track offers. There's plenty of space, and shifting over a few inches won't affect my entrance into five.

There in that downhill right-hander I'm half aware that my toe-slider, even with my boots tucked in hard and tight, is pressing on the ground, trailing invisibly-tiny fibers of ground-off plastic behind me. At the between-sessions break I had already begun worrying about that, having started with a fresh set of sliders—but having no more and knowing they would have to last two full days.

Mostly, I'm thinking about turn five and that line I'm aiming to change. And maybe, just maybe, a little bit about why this morning, on the subtlest of levels, doesn't feel quite as connected and grooved as it usually does.

Then, with as little drama as it takes to say it, I'm down. Just like that, without any warning, just that quick. I've got an instant headache from where my helmet has smacked down and my right ankle hurts from the weight of something hitting it and my vision is a blur of color and motion as I tumble along the ground. It takes a fraction of a second for all these things to coalesce into the realization—one of the most surreal, disbelieving moments I've ever felt—that I've crashed.

This is not happening…

§

I could have guessed it, of course. I should have seen it coming. But I didn't, mostly because I didn't want to. Crashing was, well, beyond the pale. Something that happened to other people—poor bastards. Never to me.

In retrospect, looking back at the warnings I had received along the way, there was one particular shot across the bow, an especially stern rebuke, if I only I had had the wisdom to see it. At Mid-Ohio, eleven months earlier, on another double-set of track days, I had ridden the hardest and fastest I ever had. It was one of those times when everything seemed to come together with amazing alacrity, a time when it seemed I could do no wrong. A couple of days to feed the ego.

It never occurred to me that, quite apart from the polished display of riding skill I thought I was exhibiting during those two days, I was in fact dancing around the edges of conceit and vanity. It never occurred to me that I had gotten to a place of illusion, that I was peering into an abyss I didn't even recognize, that I had ventured to a place of implacable, remorseless odds. It didn't occur to me in that moment when my gear shift lever touched down in 13 and snicked up into a false neutral, or when the rear end broke loose on the long, sweeping turn one—that maybe, just maybe, I was pushing a little too hard.

It never occurred to me that I was a crash waiting to happen.

§

When we look at this sport of ours we tend to think of new and inexperienced riders as the ones most at risk and the ones most likely to be involved in an incident. And, indeed, statistically that's true. But sometimes things happen even to riders of long experience. Sometimes that's just the long odds of the sport finally catching up with us. But sometimes it's because a rider keeps pushing beyond what is prudent—first just a little bit, but then more and more—believing himself infallible, until the inevitable harsh reminder that we're all subject to the same laws of physics and the same vicissitudes of chance. None of us are exceptions.

It's a progression a lot of us end up going through. Somewhere after our long apprenticeship in the sport something changes. We come back from a ride one day to the realization that that fast rider we've long admired is no longer some abstraction— we *are* that fast rider. And so we start adding on track days like they're pieces of candy, tokens to our growing addiction. We go hard-charging with our buddies on the street, getting faster and faster all the time. And all the while we revel in that sense of invincibility that comes from doing something long and well.

And then the worm turns, like it always does.

Most of us aren't quite as good as our fantasies would sometimes have us believe. These days, I try and remember that.

August 2004, Sport Rider

To Thine Own Self Be True

This might be the only motorcycle story ever entered into official court records. Page County, Virginia. The copy of Sport Rider passed from the bailiff to the judge, who thumbed through the issue until he came to the article. Evidence of my attitude as an upstanding, responsible motorcyclist. The charge subsequently reduced from reckless driving to simple speeding. The court kept the magazine.

In the beginning it was simply the road that drew me. Black asphalt, a serpentine layer of coils laid down across the mountain, like God himself had maybe once decided to play with a cowboy lariat and, having tired of the game, let it fall in twisted folds to the ground.

Later, with time and miles, the other things would get added.

The road rises, as inevitably it must in order to track over the mountain. But the rising is more than just physical. It rises in other ways too. Those, too, I would find.

In the end, it would become my catharsis, an oasis, the place I would ever return to whenever things seemed amiss. A place of refuge.

Fortune plays a part, of course. I am blessed to live where I do, with a good road at the end of my driveway, with that leading to other good roads, and those to still more. A patchwork quilt of possibility in the routes I might take. But however else I might put together the pieces of my ride, whatever variations I might toss in on a weekend morning, the mountain has always been a part of it. The part that, even in the hour or more of riding beforehand, has always been there in the back of my mind, whispering its promise.

§

This particular morning, with summer edging into fall, seems no different from the countless many which have come before. Simply a beautiful time to be out, enjoying the world on two wheels. The coolness in the air—different, sharper, than the textured, sultry feel of a summer morning—hints at the changes soon to come. There's a bittersweet feeling to that, the delight in moving through the low-humidity air with its achingly-bright sunlight tempered by the knowledge that the riding season—the good one, at least, the one not requiring layers and layers of clothing—will all too soon draw to a close.

But we'll not worry about that. Today is a time to rejoice in the gift of this day we've been given.

Out of town along Old Waterloo, past the school where my kids used to go. They're grown now, gone on to other things. But the road is still there, for me, just like always. That, too, is a gift.

A half-mile past the school leaves the last small cluster of homes behind. Then there's that first, long, left-hand sweeper, the first really nice corner. That's like a doorway. You step through it into another world. After that it's just country, a rural landscape I have long loved.

The opening miles are special, like they always are. There's an intensity to them—the feeling of the road sliding past my tires; the controls, still fresh to the touch, not yet dulled by time and miles; the air sneaking through the crack in my visor, cool against my chin; the visual cacophony flowing past me on both sides, like I'm in the middle of some sort of high-speed motion picture show; and the feeling of the motorcycle itself, working, moving, alive. It wraps around me, all those things, and I'm swiftly captured by that old magic of being lost in the moment. All the worries and stresses that too-often hang around, whispering in my ear—no different from the things that afflict us all—for a little while are cast aside.

The most special gift of all.

In a studied twist on our usual there's-too-much-to-do-and-I'm-already-late world, the next hour is a contrived effort to *not* make time. My route, casually mapped out in my head as I ride along, has but a single commandment: make it as circuitous and remote as possible. It's a wonderful world where being late getting somewhere is considered a virtue.

That route takes me across Virginia's western Piedmont, a cornucopia of narrow roads and woods and fields and horses and cows and creeks and sunlight and shade. Out Old Pine, downhill through the esses that I long-ago nicknamed "the slalom," where a few times I've seen deer along the side and you know you have to be careful. Then there's the slow, curling right-hander leading up onto the single-lane bridge, past that and down through the canopy of trees, where it's always cool, even on the hottest days of summer. Then up the hill and it opens up, the woods giving way to farms on either side. Over in the field an old man on a tractor is baling hay. I raise my hand and he waves back.

Good roads. Good people.

There's something else out here, though, something drawing me. However much I love these roads, however I might choose to piece together the parts of my ride today, I'm edging ever westward, towards my beloved Blue Ridge. Towards the mountain. I've never had a choice in that.

And soon enough I'm there, the north-south ridgeline of rugged, age-old peaks, mountains which have gazed down across epochs, rising across my view. Even knowing where I'm going, there's a mystery here.

The first turns at the bottom are just like they've always been, creamy smooth and tinged with expectation. I've got eight miles of this in front of me.

But, climbing, now heading into the entrance to one of the deeper corners, my reverie is suddenly interrupted by a bumpy, jarring chatter coming from my tires: rumble strips. Lifting my eyes I see the sign with the new—lower—speed limit, and suddenly, sadly, it all comes back to me.

This place is not what it used to be.

§

Having a great bike is only half the equation necessary for enjoying this sport of ours. If the wonderful machines available today are to mean anything other than simply being interesting engineering exercises, they must be married to equally-wonderful roads.

In that, too, we've been blessed—there are a great many roads across this land which are suited to taking the measure of our machines.

We have them today. It's not at all certain that we'll have them tomorrow.

If they do go away, if, in the end, we end up losing the privilege to wake up early on a weekend morning, heart charged with the anticipation of the day's ride, we won't have far to look for the reason. We'll need only look in the mirror.

We'll rationalize it six ways to Sunday, just like we do today. But if we're ever honest with ourselves, we'll have to admit exactly where it lies. It's not our cruiser-riding friends on their Harleys. Nor is it our touring buddies on their Goldwings. It's not the folks riding through on four wheels. And it's not those people who live along the roads we ride. And much as we might grouse about their part in it, it's not the cops or the prosecutors or the judges charged with enforcing the law, either.

Go talk to the paramedics, if you still don't know.

Mea Culpa. The blame is mine.

Some people think it can't happen. They insist on living in a make believe world where no amount of excess, no degree of egregious behavior on their part, no number of crashes, ever gets a response.

They're wrong. We're already seeing lowered speed limits and sharply stepped-up enforcement on many of our best roads: Deals Gap, the Angeles Crest, and the Blue Ridge Parkway, just to name a few. And they're serious. Come to Virginia and ignore the limit on that long-time favorite road of mine and you *will* get busted—trust me on this.

And who can blame them? To say that the carnage on the road has gotten out of hand is a study in understatement. When things get to the point that we *expect* to encounter a crash on the day's ride—when we come back home in the evening and log onto the local internet forum just so we can see who went down that day—something is terribly amiss.

The irony is that all of this is happening at the very same time that public access to racetracks—where a rider can ratchet things up to just about any level he desires—is at an all-time high. Track days, unheard of when I started riding, are now ubiquitous, cheap, and easy for just about anyone to attend. Any excuses you hear anymore about why someone can't are just that—excuses.

We can continue to simply ignore the problem, of course, to act all surprised when our favorite road suddenly gets targeted. But if you've ever ridden a once-great road that is now suddenly receiving that sort of attention, where the speed limit has been dropped and the cops are out in force and you know they're there looking at *you*—because you're riding a sportbike—and you know that if you so much as sneeze wrong they're going to be on you, you know what I mean.

The blunt, simple bottom line is this: we've got to start doing a lot better job of keeping it on two wheels. The people charged with enforcing the law are remarkably tolerant, I've found—up to the point that we start crashing and making a nuisance of ourselves. That gets their attention. And when people then start dying they'll step in and do whatever they need to to stop it. Not much of a surprise, huh?

That road of mine, the mountain? The place that for two decades has been my own special place? I don't go there much anymore. It's not a lot of fun when you can't throttle up even a few mph coming out of the corners—the new speed limit doesn't afford much head room. And it certainly takes away from the pleasure of a ride when you feel like you're under a microscope all the time. So now I just go there for an occasional cruise-through, just to remember what it used to be like.

§

Life is funny. Most of what we can expect from tomorrow is hidden from us, a mystery yet to unfold. Occasionally, though, we're blessed with a glimpse into that future, given a vision that shows us what the world will look like a little bit down the road.

That's the last gift we've been given. We can clearly see the dual futures that sport riding holds. One is of continued advancement of our machines and ourselves; of enjoying many more years of waking up with that humming excitement in our chest. The other is barren; one of road closures and machine restrictions and draconian traffic enforcement and sharply-curtailed riding opportunities; one where the carefree freedom long associated with our sport is long gone.

Which will we choose?

February 2005, Sport Rider

Katie

Death is a part of life. We all know that. But when it happens unexpectedly, and especially when it happens to a young person, we struggle to understand it. As if the orderly universe we like to imagine suddenly twisted itself into an errant wrinkle. Surely there must be a mistake?

At the last minute I decide not to go to the funeral. I don't really know the family, after all, or even her other friends, and so there is no one there to try and console, no one to whom I might feel obligated to try and explain the unexplainable. Instead, I go for a ride. That seems like the right thing to do. She would have understood that.

So it is that the early morning's slanting sun finds me chasing my shadow westward, into the mountains, seeking respite in the wind and the road and the glories to be found in a fast motorcycle. Lord, how many times have I done that?

The Suzuki feels vibrant and alive, a mixture of things that normally make me laugh inside my helmet. Today is imbued with a quiet seriousness, though, and my thoughts are locked into wonder at the mystery of why things are; why they happen the way they do. As I bend the Gixxer into the turns, the sensory input from the road feeding its ever-soothing effect, like a mainline hit straight into my psyche, the bike soon disappears beneath me. I'm cruising today. Instead of the taut focus I normally bring to my rides, constantly evaluating the lines and angles of the road, the shadows from which it's sometimes hard to tell what the upcoming traction is likely to be, and the feel from the tires and suspension whispering their story—all the endless variables that riding a sportbike brings to bear—I move into autopilot. Riding on instinct, with all the technical minutiae moved away into some murky region of my brain, a place of which my conscience is only dimly aware, I'm left alone with my thoughts.

Into the mountains, traversing all those roads which she and I both loved, the only place where our separate worlds intersected, I'm reminded of how she looked the last time I saw her. Like me, riding made her happy, in a much deeper way than the mere passing of a pleasantry might. It showed in her eyes, in her laughter, in the exuberance she brought to Sunday mornings.

Realizing where I am, I roll out of the throttle, engine braking slowing me down, and then pull off onto the gravel pullout. Switching off the ignition, I dismount, pulling off my helmet and slowly shrugging out of my jacket.

This is where I took the picture, carefree ponytail streaming out behind her, smile hidden beneath her helmet, but her happiness nevertheless lit just as brightly by the joyful arc she scribed through the corner. A single moment in time; a single moment of grace.

Today, as on that day, I have my Nikon SLR in my tail pack. But for once I feel no compulsion to take it out. There's nothing here now but a memory.

§

It's a tragedy when anyone gets killed. But it's especially disheartening when it's a young woman with nearly her whole life in front of her. Then the tragedy is amplified by the painful wonder of what might have been.

Katie Ashton was killed commuting to work on her motorcycle. The details don't matter. Suffice it to say that it happened in D.C.'s dense suburban traffic, one more lousy statistic in a concrete jungle already littered with a long list of such sad stories.

What does matter is what she was like as a person, and as a rider.

She brought her own special brand of adventure with her, an enthusiastic partner in exploring this life we lead. She was compassionate and kind. And she touched many people with her spirit and her generosity.

She was also a single mother, leaving behind a young daughter. For that she has been criticized. Some cannot understand how a person with her responsibilities could so willingly embrace the risks of a sport like motorcycling.

I think something different. I think Katie left her daughter the greatest gift she possibly could: a lesson in what living life really means. The wisdom that being alive is much more than just the accumulation of years.

She was no poseur. Sportriding cast the same spell on her that it has on many of us. And she responded to that enchantment by approaching it with the same dedication as those rest of us similarly afflicted. For her the sport quickly became much more than something in which to pass a few happy hours. It became part of who she was.

She was one of us.

So much so that in the hours immediately after the news of her accident began to circulate, there also began a series of self-appraisals by a lot of local riders. Riders who were suddenly voicing questions about whether they ought to continue riding, whether the risks were worth it.

No one could know what Katie would have counseled, of course. But I think I know. I think, after all the crying and remembrances, after the cards and the flowers were finished, after all the trying-to-help-all-those-she-could who had been touched by the tragedy was done, she would have said "let's go for a ride."

Because she got it.

She knew that riding carries risk, of course. Just like life itself. But she also knew that riding carries an enormous capacity to heal, a power to make things right when nothing else seemingly can.

§

Mounting back up, I point the Suzuki down the mountain. Accelerating up to speed, then holding a constant pace through the sweepers on the descent, I'm left with the pull and tug of the esses, swept up in that rising note of excitement as something mysterious changes, as the bike cleaves to the road, becomes a part of it. The old magic. She would have ridden here before. Would have felt that.

A few miles on, having bottomed out down in the valley, I turn down a small, little-used road, one that climbs up along the ridgeline of the next mountain in the chain. It's one of my favorite places, a sun-dappled route running for much of its length along an ancient trout stream. A road which is at turns both beguiling and technical. A dozen twisting miles up is a pond and a church and a tiny, old cemetery. There are only twenty or thirty graves there, but some date from the early 18th century. Time enough to give one some perspective.

It's been awhile. I determine to stop there.

Those esses on the run down the first mountain have left in me a tinge of something. No longer content just to cruise, my throttle hand wields just a little bit longer throw, a slightly sharper edge. The Suzuki harkens to my touch, heartened as it always is by the promise of a spirited run.

In my mind's eye I look back one last time, remembering that ponytail dancing behind her like the tail of an ebullient kite, the girlish smile, and the courage to step outside the stereotypes of her gender. Then I wind up the Gixxer and, for a few miles, for her, ride like the wind.

Godspeed.

March 2005, Sport Rider

The Sport Tour

The early morning air is cool as we head down the mountain, leaving behind the rented condo which has been our base of operations for the last few days. John Holt is in the lead, as usual, followed by Kevin Hawkins and Dave Sulser, three of my long-time riding buddies. Behind them comes new-guy Scott, who I warned last night about the tighter, technical roads we'd be hitting further south—and counseled that as the pace sharpened on those to not try and stay with the guys in front—unless he wanted to crash. I bring up the rear, and so have the advantage of being able to watch this conga line as it snakes across the serpentine road.

Down in the relative flat of the valley—rolling terrain is actually more apt, since there aren't any really straight roads here in the Potomac Highlands of West Virginia—and we turn south, towards breakfast at the state park an hour a way. I'm hungry for more than just the promise of eggs and sausage.

The first hour of the day, with the sun hardly over the horizon, is always a gift. Everything is fresh and clean—most especially your senses. Today will be hot, and we might even get some thunderstorms this afternoon, but right now the air has that sultry, smooth-like-velvet coolness which feels so seductively good. It puts you in mind of perfection: of perfect roads, ridden with perfect companions. That's how you end up with perfect days.

Snaking south at an even 70mph has an effortless quality. It feels like we're floating as we crest the hills and bend through the turns. Wisps of vapor tack off the hillsides like slow-moving ghosts, last vestiges of the fog which would have enshrouded this valley last night.

The sharply-slanting sun casts deep, bluish-dark shadows

into the roadside along our left flank. That adds a bit of an edge to the ride as we pass through, watching for deer. More than once over the years we've had one bound across the road in front of us. Coming back in the afternoon we might add ten to our pace.

Then we're there at the foot of the mountain. The first one of the day and one of my favorites. Rolling into that first hard right-hander and suddenly feeling the suspension and tires firm up, that feeling of gravity suspending itself, is the elixir. My focus instantly sharpens and I become absorbed in the task at hand— another gift, this concentration, maybe the only thing I ever do where I'm totally lost in the moment.

The road here has small bits of positive camber, smooth, subtle undulations in the pavement which give a rider advantage, and I deliberately place my lines so as to catch those. And there's that rising: My heart beating faster to match the ascent, exultation growing with every curve.

Then we're over the top and flying down the other side, the descent dropping us onto the eastern flank of the mountain. As we round the first cork-screwing right-hander the panorama of the valley below opens up to us. Lifting my eyes from the road for a moment, I'm jolted by the sight: A broken tapestry of cottony clouds lies below us, at turns flashing yellow where it is lit by the sun or blue where it lies in shadow, interspersed by the odd tiny farmhouse or barn far below. The vision is arresting enough—it's not every day that you get to ride above the clouds—that I roll out of the throttle so I can continue to gaze at it.

You can't look at something like that and not be put in mind of larger things. You're reminded of how some things are timeless, that some things are forever a mystery.

Reluctantly turning my eyes back toward the road, I smile slowly to myself.

§

Most of us get our sport riding fix in measured doses—the several hours on Saturday or Sunday that we're able to get away, with maybe the occasional track day during the week thrown in for good measure. If you're like me, that's not nearly enough. No matter how great a ride I might have on those days I almost always come back wanting more. Even after having ridden half a dozen or more hours, sitting there on my deck on a summer's evening, cold beer in hand and a couple of yet-to-be read motorcycle magazines in front of me, the distant sound of motorcycles down on the road still tugs at me. That feeling of never ever quite being sated is probably healthy in terms of sustaining interest in the sport for many long years. But, still, it leaves an ever-present ache; a desire that never seems to be completely fulfilled.

So it's nice, now and again, to give rein to those impulses. To cut a big, fat slice out of the sport-riding pie. To, just occasionally, get to know what it's like to truly have our fill of riding. How?

The sport tour.

As its name suggests, the sport tour combines attributes of both sport riding and touring. For most of us it means mapping out a route across the curviest countryside we can find, seeking escape in both the road and the landscape. And the very breadth of that opportunity, the multitude of adventures it promises, gives rise to dimensions of the sport that simply don't exist in our regular I've-got-a-few-hours-and-then-I-need-to-be-home rides.

Think of it as sport riding on steroids.

The first difference is one of the most important: The very roads that are open to us. Since sport touring by its very nature is a multi-day event, it affords us the opportunity to reach out and ride roads that are otherwise too far to get to. For some guys—like my buddy, Jay, in Florida—who live in areas bereft of good riding roads, a longer trip is the only opportunity they have to ride the good stuff. But even for those of us blessed to live in places rich with good roads, a sport tour gives us a chance to extend those choices. And there are few things as delightful as discovering a terrific new road, or re-discovering an old friend of one that we haven't seen in awhile.

Of course, traveling long distance means having to pack a lot more stuff. Extra clothes, foul weather gear, tools, maybe even camping gear if that is the chosen end-of-day venue. And those choices need to be made judiciously, as nothing messes up the handling of a motorcycle quicker than adding too much weight. But even going through the process of selecting and packing gear is exciting. There's something immensely satisfying about pulling together the stuff you need to be self sufficient, even if it's only for a few days. It harkens back to those nomadic impulses of our long-ago ancestors.

Through all of it—the planning and preparation and the talking of the trip with our buddies—runs a thread of anticipation. It lends an air of excitement which subtly colors your world in the days and weeks ahead. During the work week I always look forward to the weekend, to all those day rides which are so important to me. But on those periodic occasions when I have a sport tour coming up, there's a tinge of something else, a bit of extra magic in the air. Kind of like a kid waiting for Christmas.

Eventually the day of departure arrives. The leaving always has a crisp sort of feeling to it, a delight in finally getting to what seems to be a great adventure. And then you're in it, riding, moving across the landscape, and suddenly awash in the multitude of things which attend to life on the road: The taste of hot coffee in the early morning light, the best coffee you'll ever drink; mounting up while the air is still cool, still laced with the morning's mist; burning off a quick half-tank before breakfast; having the road, a really good one, almost to yourself for a few precious hours; being on your game, because finding that groove, that rhythm, is a lot easier when you're rolling miles everyday; seeing everything with fresh eyes, because you don't live here and haven't been dulled to what's around; the exultation of a road run well, knowing there are many more to come; the surprise when that little line on the map that you didn't expect much out of turns into a delight, one more little secret to tuck away; the laughter and the camaraderie, regaling each other with our own unique versions of this shared experience.

And then, of course, there's that thing of just being out in the world. I mean really being in it. Motorcycles, being exposed to the elements, have long been touted as giving one a far more intense experience than our automobile-bound brethren ever see. Which is true, of course—up to a point. But I'll be the first to admit that I might bag a regular Sunday ride if the weather turns nasty the night before. And in any case the 4-8 hours I might be out on those day rides sharply limits what I'm likely to be exposed to. When you're out for several days at a time, though, and especially considering the micro climates which often seem to exist in mountainous areas—the range of weather possibilities that you're going to be exposed to suddenly gets a lot broader. There'll be heat, there'll be cold, and there'll be rain.

Which is fine with me. Because that's the way the world is. I figure we ought to experience that stuff now and then. Besides, there's nothing that will make you appreciate clean, dry pavement like having run for some hours—or days—in the rain. That wet stuff will give you a nuanced understanding of traction like nothing else will.

And, finally, there's that wonderful downtime at the end of each day, relaxing with whatever your favorite beverage is as the aches and pains of a long day of riding slowly melt away; rewinding the hours just-passed in your mind, a few more memories for the archive; and wondering what the morrow might bring. You're tired, but it's the very best tiredness I know.

In the end, I think that heading out on the road for a few days is the very epitome of motorcycling, the highest form of our sport. It'll put you in a place—physically, mentally, and emotionally— that few people in this modern world of ours ever really get to experience anymore. And it provides that rare opportunity to, finally… get enough miles.

So pull your maps out, talk to your buddies, and—as they say in that commercial—just do it. You won't be sorry.

August 2005, Sport Rider

A Calmness Inside

There's one thing that good pilots, good gunfighters, and good motorcyclists all have in common.

Two hours and 125 miles from home, with the midmorning sun hanging brightly aft of my left shoulder, and I'm in my favorite place—deep in the mountains. It's been a glorious start to what I can already tell will be a special day. Terrific weather—slightly cool when I left at daybreak, but now warming nicely. Mostly, it's the roads. Fine, curvy roads. I have them nearly to myself.

I mark where I am by the cut in the trees and the small rockslide on the mountain opposite, across the western side of the divide. Passing it, I glance down at my odometer, noting its number. Two more miles. At elevated speeds the turnoff comes swiftly. I've blown past it more than once.

I'm on cue this time, though, backing out of the throttle as the tenths on my odometer click down. Mark. And there it is, the gray shape of the tarmac appearing suddenly on my left.

Wheeling down it, second gear, and the bike pulls smoothly around the first right-hander. Then there's a little slalom, a tease, and there's the stop sign.

Visibility is poor in both directions. The T-intersection sits square atop the very crest of the mountain, with a quick drop-off in both directions. I've always liked it here. The airy peculiarity of the intersection prompts the feeling of being suspended in space. That, and knowing it's the start of a really good run.

Turning east, I accelerate quickly into second, just enough to obviate the risk attendant to the blind crest. But then I relax, enjoying the anticipation of what is coming. The road meanders slowly down the flank of the mountain for the first half mile. A lazy, lolling, prelude. Then it sharpens suddenly, curling hard right, as it breaks into a series of high-speed sweepers that sluice down the mountain. That first right-hander has good camber and its g-forces trigger in me the heightened sensory acuity that always accompanies an aggressive run. It puts me into that edgy place— the nexus of joy and chance and consequence—that I've always been drawn to.

Eight miles later, down on the valley floor, and we're done. The ebullient feeling that defined my run down the mountain quickly abates, leaving behind the quiet satisfaction of a road run well. Turning now north, the local road is interesting and fun, but lacks that sense of expectation that a truly serious stretch of road possesses. I'm actually glad of it. It gives me a chance to relax for a few minutes, like a boxer between rounds, and think about the road a few miles ahead.

The pause also gives me a chance to reflect on how our riding tends to vary a bit over the course of a long day. Usually not a lot. But over many hours our sharpness will fluctuate enough to be noticeable.

I've been happy so far today. I've felt good, with lines crisp and certain. An in-the-zone day.

Fifteen miles further on I come to the stop sign. I haven't been here in over a year but the lightning-blasted pine tree still stands awkwardly askew across the road. It's funny, the little things we notice.

I hold at the intersection for a moment, enjoying the odd mix of emotions I'm feeling—a calm confidence, yet tempered with the realization that the next nine miles will challenge me well beyond anything I normally experience. This is a road that, at speed, is forbiddingly technical. And its rock faces and sharp drop-offs pose a sobering consequence to getting it wrong. My heart hammers an anxious beat in anticipation. I could back it down to cruise mode, of course—that would be the prudent thing to do.

But that's never been in the plan.

Finally, nudging the shift lever down into first, I turn left down the road, westward. Back into the mountains.

Within a hundred feet the butterflies, and all those extraneous thoughts, are gone. My mind moves into that place where everything is gone save an intense focus on the road itself.

Since this is an ascent, I have the benefit of climbing elevation. I use that to advantage, leveraging gravity to help in modulating my entrance speeds. Tugging on the bar here, pushing on the tank there, I'm only distantly aware of the bike beneath me.

A mile rolls by. Then another. I'm lost in that exuberance, that special magic, that comes with piloting a motorcycle at speed.

Halfway up there's a kink that leads into a blind right-hander. Downshifting into second, the motor settles as I roll hard into the turn. Because of my inability to see through the corner—and the risk of what might be coming the other way—I've adjusted my line well to the right. Right where the 12-inch chunk of granite lies, having fallen from the cliff above, as it turns out.

No problem. A quick nudge on the bar shifts my line towards the center, enough to miss it. But even as I do the world on the other side of the turn is opening up to me. I see the fractured rubble of the rest of the rock slide only an instant before I'm in its midst. The rear-end breaks hard left. And that's when I see the car.

The wry thought that flashes through my mind in response to the unexpected flood of sensory inputs, is that my day has suddenly gotten very interesting.

§

Wyatt Earp, the famous western lawman and gunfighter, once was asked how he managed to survive so many deadly confrontations. Earp replied that "Fast is fine, but accuracy is everything. Shooting at a man who is returning the compliment means going into action with the greatest speed at which a man's muscles are capable, but mentally unflustered by an urge to hurry."

It's hard to imagine a more stressful situation than having a man a few feet away raising a gun and blazing away at you. The urge to fire one's own weapon as fast as possible must be overwhelming. That first-to-clear-leather scenario is certainly the one played out in countless western stories, songs, and movies. And yet Earp's point was that speed is only as good as one's ability to use it in a controlled fashion. Earp insisted that the very best gunfighters were fast only up to a point. The key quality which most distinguished them from those that fell before them was a studied deliberateness. They were far less concerned with getting off the first shot, than with getting off the first shot that counted.

Unflustered, indeed.

Motorcycling, like other risk activities, carries with it the need to occasionally respond to extreme stress levels. Unfortunately, our natural responses to those occasions are often exactly counter to what we would wish. Keith Code pointed out years ago in his "Twist of the Wrist" books how, when confronted with an unexpected situation, our native, instinctive motorcycling responses typically make things worse, not better. We grab the brakes when that's the very last thing we should do. We punch inputs into the bars which unsettle the chassis or which steer us in exactly the wrong direction. And sometimes we simply freeze, riding quietly into oblivion. The unfortunate reality is that we tend to respond to panic with scripted, wired-in reactions which are rarely helpful on a motorcycle.

And so the key is to never allow panic to emerge in the first place. We must work to engender that inner calm that those gunfighters of old had. To foster the equanimity that gives us the chance to work through whatever mess it is that we've gotten ourselves into.

That calm comes from one place... confidence. From

having experienced—and survived—a multitude of could-have-been-bad situations. The first time a new street rider feels his bike break traction is terrifying. By about the tenth time it happens to him he begins to realize that that kind of situation is not the inevitable prelude to a crash that he once imagined it must be. And by the time it happens to him the hundredth time he recognizes that, though certainly not desirable, a loose bike is in most cases a very manageable event.

And so time and miles—simple seat time—will eventually give us most of what we need to get to that place of inner calm. If you're a new rider—have patience. It will come. If you want to accelerate the process, get to a racetrack and do a bunch of track days, or do a little club racing.

After that, it's just a matter of believing in yourself, having faith that no matter what situation the world throws at you, you can handle it.

My little escapade back up on the mountain? It turned out okay. I stayed on the throttle, my rear-end hooked back up, and I was able to steer to the right of the oncoming car, missing it by half a foot.

Just like I knew would happen.

June 2008, Sport Rider

A Most Amazing Thing

Charlottesville, Virginia is a pleasant little town. It's the old stomping ground of Thomas Jefferson, he of founding father fame. And the university which he begat still colors the surrounding community with the youth and vigor and openness to new things which are common to college towns.

Alas, its roads suck. It bestrides rt. 29—the primary north-south artery through central Virginia—like a sick colossus, determined to make the errant traveler pay.

Which is why we are avoiding the place altogether.

Hidden among the faint swirls written into old maps, there exists an alternative. A tiny little secondary road which hooks far westward, and then south, looping around the urban metropolis and avoiding all that mess of traffic. My riding buddies and I optimistically refer to it as *The Charlottesville Bypass*, though it's a strange bypass that takes twice as long to get somewhere. Only a motorcyclist, more interested in the quality of time than its quantity, would appreciate it.

Since I'm the lone Virginian in the group—the rest of my buddies are from Pennsylvania and other points north—I'm in the lead. Our destination, on the first day of this 5-day adventure, is a bucolic little bed and breakfast a ways down the Blue Ridge Parkway. Supposedly, I know where I'm going.

Or maybe not.

The "bypass" is not well marked. And to stay on the route you have to be careful to make several turns. I know I've made a mistake when I go flying around a corner only to find the pavement has suddenly turned to gravel. Nope, this ain't it.

Jim, the rider behind me, and I do a quick U-turn and start heading back. A mile up the road, at the intersection where I should have turned left, the rest of our party is patiently waiting. Earle, who had been running third, had correctly divined the correct route. He knew we'd be back.

"Have a nice ride?" he laughingly quips.

"Yeah, what a terrific road!" I laugh in return.

Earle is the normal road captain of our little group. He takes off, once again assuming his accustomed place at the front. But not before I glance down at the cockpit of his K1200S and note the GPS affixed there and the colored line on its screen clearly pointing out the correct route.

It's a bit of an epiphany.

Several days later, after having run south most of the length of the Blue Ridge Parkway and enjoying many of the great roads in western North Carolina, I'm heading back north again. Alone this time—I've left a day early—it's late morning and I need gas.

The Blue Ridge Parkway is a wonderful motorcycle road for lots of reasons. But access to gas—or even just knowing where it can be found—isn't one of them. You pretty much just end up turning off on one of the occasional side roads which intersect with it, ride down the mountain, and figure sooner or later you'll come to a little town. I've drifted into town riding on fumes on more than one occasion.

I'm in no danger of that this morning, but what I do find— after finding the town, gassing up, and cooling myself down with a liter of bottled water—is that I've come far out of my way. Studying the paper map, I see that had I continued just a few miles further north on the BRP, a different road would have gotten me to this same town in half the distance. Not a big deal. But with a 600-mile day in front of me I'd just as soon spend it doing quality miles, not the 20 miles of hot, mostly-straight road I'd just run, stuck behind a slow-moving pickup truck. As I tuck the map back into my tank bag and mount back up, my mind goes back to Earle and his GPS.

§

The box containing the Garmin Zumo 550 arrived a week later. Ironically, before I even had a chance to mount it on my bike, my wife Ginny and I had the opportunity to try it in the car, using the included windshield mount. We had a funeral to go to.

Like most guys who've lived in a particular area for a while, I've always felt I have a pretty good handle on the local roads. As motorcyclists, we're especially attuned to them, after all. In this case I was quite smug about the time and distance involved in getting to the funeral home. I knew exactly how the Zumo would route us.

I was more than a little taken aback then, when, halfway there, the friendly little woman's voice coming out of the GPS unit said to turn right.

"That can't be," I said. But she was quite emphatic. Ginny laughed. "You better do what she says," she said.

So I did. A few miles later she had me turn left, down a scraggly-assed road I had never heard of or been on. And within a hundred feet I had two thoughts. The first was that I have to bring my bike back here. The second was that this GPS thing might have more going for it than I had thought.

§

I'm not at all a Luddite. Look at what technology has brought to our sport—everything from sophisticated engine and suspension technologies to amazing braking systems to user-selectable engine mappings to truly exceptional tire designs—and one is hard-pressed not to see the enormous advantages inherent in those things.

But I also tend to be very focused when I'm out riding. I'm not at all into gadgets. Radios and music players and intercom systems and cell phones and CB's and the host of similar devices that riders sometimes attach to their bikes have always struck me as not-so-benign distractions. I'd prefer to keep my attention directed towards the road, thank you very much.

And so when the first motorcycle GPS units began appearing some years ago, I mentally pegged them in the same category. Just another distraction to avoid.

I've now been convinced otherwise.

My overarching philosophy of riding—that one's attention must remain unequivocally on the road—hasn't changed. That remains as true as ever—especially as our pace increases. But I've found that a GPS can confer two very important advantages.

First, it can find new roads for us. After having used my Zumo for a couple of months, I've disabused myself of the notion that I know the roads around where I live as well as I once thought I did. It's almost uncanny how the routing on a GPS unit will find roads you've never been on. Some of those roads will be entirely forgettable, of course. But some of them are true gems—out-of-the-way routes that almost no one knows about. I've always enjoyed "exploring"—turning down a road I've never been on and seeing where it goes. Unfortunately, a lot of those roads turn to dirt or gravel some ways further along; and a lot them simply dead-end. A GPS allows you to do that kind of exploration without, mostly, worrying about those things.

The second thing a GPS unit can do is actually free up some of the attention that we otherwise spend in navigation. We've all had occasions where we're headed some place in particular and we end up looking around for landmarks, street addresses, and other such cues. We end up spending part of our attention—and sometimes a lot of it—on navigating rather than paying attention to the road and to traffic. A GPS will tell you at a glance how far until the turn is, allowing you to quickly return your focus to that SUV piloted by the soccer mom with the cell phone in her ear.

A dozen years ago, on one of our first trips to Deals Gap, some pals and I were stopped, hours after darkness had fallen. We were tired, cold, and hungry after a long, wet, and foggy 500-mile day in Appalachia. We still had a couple hours in front of us—we thought. The road that we had been on had turned to gravel a few miles back; and then even that had petered out into but a rough dirt trail. We were clearly lost.

The maps and Delorme atlases came out, illuminated with a couple of flashlights, and much discussion ensued. We eventually got it all sorted, of course. We finally made it to the hotel that night, got some food, and eventually enjoyed that end-of-the-day brew. And it's also true that that was a memorable evening—in a twisted sort of way.

But I think I'll take a GPS next time. And find other ways to make the ride exciting.

January 2008, Sport Rider

Good Roads, Bad Days

Sometimes, we're our own worst enemy.

Once again, just like they have the last couple of years, the weather gods have served up a late summer respite from the usual dog day doldrums: low humidity, crystal clear air, and an azure blue sky. A Sunday filed with promise. You can't not ride on a day like this.

So I'm out midmorning, intending to enjoy every minute of it. I usually get out on both Saturday and Sunday, most weekends, but I spent most of yesterday doing household chores and didn't get a chance to get out. All the more reason to treasure the few hours I've got today.

The K1200RS is running really well and I take a meandering route out towards the western roads that I love so much. I pass a sheriff's cruiser when heading out of Salem, him coming into town as I'm heading out, and so I'm kind of chilling. Can't afford another ticket like last year's, you know?

Out on Hill Crest, and I'm thinking about that sheriff's deputy and that the day is so nice and that there will be lots of squids out. If I were a trooper with a quota to meet, it wouldn't be a bad day to bag a few. So I keep on chilling.

Sure enough, heading down the hill towards the little one-lane bridge about a mile shy of Stone Hill I see a car stopped and a guy lighting a flare. Before I even get around the corner I know what I'll find.

One of the guys working the crash scene says I need to turn around. I ignore him and pick my way slowly through the short line of stopped cars, the half dozen bikes, and the two police cruisers. It's a slow-speed corner and I know it's not too serious.

Serious enough to catch the attention of the local constabulary, though. Just like the scene I came upon *in* Stone Hill last weekend, where the motorcycle, lying on its side, was mostly up under the pickup truck. Cripes, how the hell do you do that? The road is straight and the speed limit is 25, for chrissakes.

So as I motor away I just shake my head in wonder at the countless ways we manage to bring all this attention upon ourselves.

I'm thinking the same thing ten minutes later as I'm rolling down Stackhall Road. I'm guessing maybe the word has been passed along the radio and the heat will be on today. So I keep chilling.

Out past Jefferson to the 4-lane. At the stop sign there are two sportbike guys, full race gear, stopped on the shoulder and looking down at their bikes. I pause for half a second, debating whether to stop and see if they need a hand. But I'm not in the best of moods, what with all this chilling and all, and quickly decide to hell with them. Four minutes later they confirm my suspicions, blasting past my being-careful-to-keep-it-to-62-ass at about 100mph. Assholes.

Two minutes later I'm playing my day out in my head. I usually eat a few hours later into my ride, on the way back. But I haven't had any breakfast and so decide to stop now. As I pull into the little carry-out burger joint there are the two sportbike champs. Small world sometimes.

The pretty girl takes my order and I hang outside the door for ten minutes waiting for my sandwich. When it comes I wander over to the picnic tables there at the end, under the trees. As I walk past their bikes I glance down at the clues written in their tires. Just old habit, you know?

After eating I climb back aboard the KRS and continue on west to the Gap. I point to the two sportbike riders as I pull out. They wave back.

Before it got screwed up by guys who thought they were a

lot better than they really were, the Gap at Beahm was hands-down the best motorcycle road within a hundred miles. Living as close to it as I do made all those 4-hour-a-day commutes worthwhile.

Like most good roads you could find a rhythm on that mountain, like it was a living thing. Not anymore. Now, with the 45mph speed limit and the draconian enforcement, you just kind of glide along, remembering how it used to be. Your suspension only just begins to firm up at those speeds. Not enough to get you into that special place.

I'm thinking of that as the one lane heading up breaks into two. That's the place where my heart used to lift a few beats, a promise in the making. Now it's just a weird kind of marker, my reminder that they're after my ass and there's zero tolerance here and all the rest of it. So I glance down and make sure that the needle on my speedo doesn't slide more than a whisker past the 50 mark.

There's that first good right-hander, the place where, back in the day, you'd tip it in under throttle at 75 and feel for the rhythm, what the road would give you that day. It was, maybe, the first point of surprise for the squids who would sometimes hook onto your tail and who kept waiting for you to brake and got caught out when you didn't.

Then the long sweeping left-hander, coming around past the pull-off on the left and the prelude done and the serious stuff beginning. Click down into third—and that's the only thing I do today that is the same as it was back then. Just another old habit, I suppose.

Like awhile back, at the first crash scene an hour ago, there's a car stopped in the right lane. And just like then, wired into the ether somehow, I know what I'll find. Just like I knew that that one wasn't bad, I know that this one is.

Slowly around the corner, my eyes sweep past the half-dozen parked bikes. Two guys on the other side of the Armco are bent over the prostate rider, one with the forlorn stiff-armed please-don't-let-it-end-like-this posture of CPR, the other doing mouth-to-mouth. My eyes rest for a moment on the silent scene, then I motor slowly up and around the corner. I know it's futile. They don't, yet.

I guess they must have a special code for the really serious calls. As I descend the mountain on its western flank there must be twenty different emergency vehicles, of every description you can think of, heading up.

Calculating, I figure it'll take them an hour, maybe an hour and a half, to clear the road. So I take my time heading up Indian Valley. And on the Barbieville-Georgetown loop I stop for a good long while at the little country store and sit out on the bench eating an ice cream cone and drinking a bottle of cold water. I always like sitting out on that bench. It kind of reminds me of how things were when I was a kid. Back when things were simpler. I glance over at the KRS and think what a great bike it is and how nice it looks—even after all these miles—and all the special places it's taken me to over the years and how lucky I am to have it.

And then I mount up and head on back. It's been just over two hours and I was right. Nothing but a few marks in the road.

Just like always.

March 2007, Sport Rider

Heart of the Hunter

*Motorcycling   sometimes
touches our most primal instincts.*

An off-camber, downhill, 5mph horseshoe-shaped hairpin marks the beginning of the descent. The road up to this point has been pleasant, a mix of gentle sweepers slowly rising in elevation across a softly undulating landscape. A section to enjoy for its rustic beauty and mellow charm. A couple of miles back the road began to sharpen as it began its ascent, but the gradient on that side of the mountain is fairly even and so are the turns. This side is where it gets serious.

Dragging a touch of rear brake through the horseshoe settles the chassis. Then there's the rising of the exhaust note as the engine spools, a perfect complement to the falling away of the road itself.

My boots slide back on the pegs and my hands go soft as I point the GSX-R1000 towards the first of the long series of curves snaking down the mountain. My eyes flash through the deeply-shadowed corner—rain wash-off frequently leaves gravel on this upper section—and a smile pulls at my lips as the Suzuki carves its first razor-thin slice from the mountain.

Feeling for the feedback the bike provides, my head is wrapped around the contact patch of the front wheel. A downhill slalom is characterized more than anything by the need to manage load on the front-end. Rolling in and out of the throttle allows me to minimize use of the front brake. But even so the sprint downwards leads to a slowly rising pace. If the first corners heading down are akin to drawing a slightly dull blade across a whetstone, with their ever-so-tiny feeling of resistance, the last ones are like that of the final strokes of metal upon stone, when any sense of drag has disappeared into infinitesimal smallness and the blade has reached that magical quality of absolute rightness.

That special place.

The descent doesn't put me into a valley. After dropping a thousand feet, the road simply jinks northward, along the crest of a smaller series of peaks in this mountain range. The road opens up slightly, with alternating sections of tight corners interspersed by sections where the road is more or less open for anything from a few hundred feet to a quarter mile. Holding the same pace across the roadway's entire length, the little straight sections give me a chance to relax and to enjoy the beauty of this place. To glance down at the flat topside of the Gixxer's tank and marvel at what a remarkable machine it is. To enjoy the mellowness that comes with feeling like you're in sync with the world.

And then I see the riders.

There are three of them, specks in the distance as I exit a clump of curves and enter a straight section they are just leaving. My first thought, since I'm obviously gaining on them, is that they must be cruisers. But when they reappear on the next straight section a mile or so further along, this time a little closer, their more compact profiles tell me something different.

"Well, hello boys," I murmur to myself. My narrowed eyes take in their presence with a studied interest. Part of that is simply my avid passion for anything to do with motorcycles. But by the time they disappear back into the trees, then reappear in my vision half a mile further along, I realize that my pace has bumped slightly and my chest is imbued with that old, slightly breathless feeling. The one where the air itself seems to hum with a mix of anticipation and excitement and possibility. The one I feel every November when, alone, still hunting deep in the steep forest mountains of southwestern Virginia, I cut fresh spoor and shift my rifle to the other hand as my eyes squint upwards at the ridge above me.

§

My wife Ginny knows, even though we never ever really talked about it. Years ago, upon returning home from some errand or other, she would often joke "they're out there." She'd balance those smiling teases with frequent admonishments to "be careful" and "act your age" as the thought settled and I couldn't stand it anymore and began pulling my gear together. But the underlying message was always clear, even if I was reluctant to admit to it.

The thing is this: at its heart, sportbikes and sport riding are built upon a foundation of purposeful aggression. We may couch that in euphemisms, crafting a whole dialogue that pretends otherwise. We may outright deny it. But at whatever point we're honest with ourselves, what we're left with is that truism.

So what does that mean?

It means that an awful lot of those things that we do and that we espouse are counter to our basic impulses. All of those exhortations to exhibit restraint and take it to the racetrack and "ride your own ride" are counterintuitive. Much as they make sense logically, they don't always resonate with us emotionally. They simply don't come naturally to a lot of us.

A sportbike is, by its very nature, an instrument of sharply extralegal speed potential. Combine that with a testosterone-induced desire to at least occasionally experience that performance potential, along with the sport's cultural affinity for competition— what other activity can you name which is so associated with racing—and it's no wonder we have what we do.

At a personal level, it's a little embarrassing. You'd think someone entering their fourth decade of riding, someone who has had plenty of opportunity to experience first hand the deleterious consequences of bad decisions, would be a bit more mindful of what can happen when one amps up the throttle to run down another rider—or run away from one if we happen to be in the lead.

I do know this: that go-for-it response is, for many of us, an unconscious reflex. Were it not for that suddenly-charged-with-electricity feeling, we might not even be aware of it. I also know something else: when I go on rides with my buddies I purposely ensconce myself somewhere back from the lead rider—and then resolutely stay in the position I've chosen. I know myself at least that well. As Ginny has often reminded me, "you're weak."

It's not all bad. Our too often politically correct world would have us believe otherwise, but a hint of aggression is inherent to many of the activities we see as constructive—success in business, success in politics, success in art, success even, sometimes, in affairs of the heart. You're probably not the only guy with an eye on that pretty girl out on the dance floor. And as for sport riders, I don't know that I've ever met a really good one who didn't exhibit a degree of aggression in his riding style. It's not always immediately apparent, because those are the same guys who also consistently demonstrate the most smoothness and precision in their riding, but look beneath those qualities and you'll see it.

Those who have read my columns here over the last few years will recognize that I have long been a proponent of reasonable behavior on the street. Many of my stories have revolved, in one way or another, around the question of speed, of *pace*. How much is okay? How much can I get away with? What happens if I exceed whatever that measure is? The reason for that emphasis, on what some might think is an incredibly simple question, is because... it's not simple. It's anything but. In fact, I'd argue that it is the singularly most difficult riding question any of us ever have to answer. Some of us have wrestled with it for endless years and countless miles—and still don't have all the answers.

What we can do, though, is to take an honest look at

ourselves and try and understand what prompts us to do the things we do. And from that humble beginning, maybe, we can start to craft a riding strategy which gets us to that ultimate goal—being able to enjoy this, the finest of all sports, for as long as we ever would wish.

§

In 17th century Japan their lived a fellow by the name of Miyamoto Musashi. Probably the greatest swordsman who ever lived, Musashi spent years roaming the countryside, engaging in duels—usually to the death—with other martial arts adepts. It says something about Musashi that he was confident enough in his abilities that he purposely chose to use a bokken, a wooden training sword, in many of those duels. It's safe to say he knew a little bit about aggression and the instinctive compulsion to prevail over one's fellow warriors.

Legend has it that once, having approached a famous lord regarding a position, Musashi sat in the lord's parlor while awaiting his interview. While waiting, he pulled out his pens and paper and drew a picture of a flower.

During the interview, the lord acknowledged Musashi's great martial prowess, but wondered if he had the other kinds of qualities he was looking for. Musashi bowed respectfully and took his leave. It was only later, upon discovering the picture left behind in the parlor, that the lord realized his great mistake.

§

Within a few more miles I've run down the three riders. But having done so, something suddenly reminds me of that little vignette from Musashi's life and its message that the sword need not always be drawn. That restraint can sometimes be its own reward. Feeling suddenly guilty, I dial it back and hang back a ways. That gives me an opportunity to just watch them for awhile, enjoying the spectacle of sportbikes carving across a landscape, that beautiful ballet that never grows old. Some miles further along they turn off on another road, waving back to me as they do.

Back alone, I'm reminded of what a wonderful day it is, of how clear everything seems, and of how extraordinarily lucky I am to have such a fine motorcycle as this.

And that it still has much to teach me.

October 2006, Sport Rider

Kitchen Points

Of wives and rides… and going or not.

I'd never been to a motorcycle rally before. I'm not really into crowds of people. Good, curvy roads are invariably what I'm looking for when I head out on a motorcycle trip. Not burning precious daylight hanging around a campground somewhere.

But Earle convinced me that a rally need not be just a social gathering. He said a lot of riders use them simply as a home base for riding the good roads in the area. A place to stow one's gear and come back to in the evenings—much like we do at the condo or cabins we rent during our periodic multi-day trips into the Blue Ridge Mountains. The camaraderie and entertainment at the rally site is just a bonus. Kind of like an extended family to enjoy that end-of-day brew with.

And so when he pushed out our usual May run down the Blue Ridge Parkway to coincide with the BMWRA rally in June, I decided I'd give it a go. I figure most things are worth trying at least once.

I had already scheduled a couple of shorter, 3-day motorcycle trips—our annual Memorial Day weekend "Chicken Run" into West Virginia; and another long-weekend trip into southern Virginia. As I happily recounted in an email to some of my motorcycling buddies in late May—"I'll be on the road three of the next four weekends, eleven days in total. How great is that?!"

And it was. If there is something better in this world than being on the road with a good motorcycle, I haven't found it.

Alas, that's not the way it is for a lot of guys. The notion that they might be able to get away for days at a time to enjoy their motorcycle is... extraordinary. It's not that they don't want to. It's not that they can't afford it. And it's not that they can't imagine how much fun a trip like that would be.

It's that... they can't get permission. Hell, a lot of guys can hardly get away for a good, full day-ride.

I'm far luckier than most guys, and I know it. I'm away from home on at least four or five multi-day bike trips every year, along with a week away for hunting. And I've been doing that for years.

I'll grant that my long-suffering wife, Ginny, has the patience of a saint. And notwithstanding her understanding that motorcycles are an enormously passionate thing for me, I'm sure if you asked her you'd probably get a very different perspective on my repeated wanderings! But the point is that some of us are lucky that way. We're able to get away and enjoy our bikes the way they were intended, with long miles and adventure in the making. Others aren't so lucky.

So why is it that some of us can, while others can't?

John, one of my older riding buddies, one with much experience at this, long ago coined the phrase *kitchen points* to describe that currency of exchange between husband and wife. John reasoned that our marital relationships are inevitably a series of puts and takes, and that doing something like heading off at dawn's light for several days on the road, sans wife, requires a commensurate payback in kind. That might be anything from an outright gift, to the completion of a chore that one's betrothed especially wanted to have done, to embracing the thought of her having her own free time to indulge her own passions.

We all laughed the first time we heard John's depiction of marital wisdom. But as with most things humorous, we recognized the grain of truth inherent in what he said. It's funny how, over the years, our small gang of riders has repeatedly evoked his *kitchen points* characterization to describe the value proposition of something. We'll be back at the condo, sitting around with beers in hand after a long day of riding, kicking around ideas for future rides and new places to visit. Inevitably, at some point someone will shake their head and wryly disclaim "nah, would cost too many kitchen points."

That's only part of the picture, though. Without delving too far into the area of gender psychology, I'll offer the observation that women, generally, seem to be wired to not want us to leave. With all due respect to the fairer sex—and they are, indeed—but most of 'em would rather have us at home, puttering around the house. To a guy who has never been on a trip away without his wife, all the gifts and chores—and concomitant wealth in kitchen points—won't seem to matter. He's got a different sort of problem, as in how does he establish the precedent for doing that kind of thing in the first place? And then, if he achieves that, how can he continue to take such trips on any kind of regular basis?

The answer is—it can't be a choice. It can't be asked as a question. And it certainly can't put out there—like so many guys do—as a quest for permission.

I wish I had a nickel for every rider we've ever spoken with over the years, who upon hearing about one of our upcoming trips, enthusiastically expressed an interest in going along. They'd be there through all the talk and planning—"damn right I'll be there!" Right up until the end, at which point they'd quietly bail. There would be all sorts of excuses quietly offered for the sudden change in heart. But we always knew the real reason.

They couldn't get permission.

To all the guys in that boat, here's a suggestion: Be mindful of your better half's feelings. Truly try and understand her fears and concerns. Honestly ask yourself what seems to be an appropriate—and fair—mix of being at home and being away. And give her lots of notice, lots of time to get used to the idea of your being away at a particular time, on a particular trip. But at the end of the day, don't pose it as a question. Don't ask "would you mind if I went on a motorcycle trip with Jack and Dave in a couple of weeks?" You'll probably get a less-than-direct response, but you already know what the answer will be.

Far better is "Jack and Dave are heading down to Deals Gap on their bikes next July, and I think I'll go along."

You're still going to get some push-back. But the whole tenor of the conversation has changed, from why you *should* go, to why you *shouldn't*. And if a truly good reason can be articulated for why you shouldn't go—well, then you probably shouldn't.

Don't expect a panacea. I honestly don't know a single guy, even those like myself who are blessed with wives of remarkable tolerance, who don't still occasionally run into a bit of unhappiness when we leave. After thirty years with Ginny—long-conditioned to my wanderings—there are still sometimes a few tears as I head down the driveway. But at least she understands that my leaving has nothing to do with her... and everything to do with this two-wheeled passion that she married into. And she knows that I'll be back in a few days, or a week, or whatever the case might be.

She also knows—and this is the other side of the coin—that when she wants to do something herself, without me, that I'll fully support her in that. She often spends a week away at the beach with one her sisters, or a few days away at some race with a few of her running pals, and she knows that I'll do everything I can to make sure she's able to do those things, including burning vacation time if necessary so the domestic chores at home will be covered while she's away.

In the end, it all comes down to respect. She's got to respect you, and the things that are part of your nature. And you've got to respect her, and the things she does that are part of hers.

That and making sure there are enough kitchen points in the kitty.

April 2008, Sport Rider

Old Roads

Sometimes you can go home again.

The last vestiges of daylight are but a narrow smudge of pink on the western horizon. And as I roll down the county parkway even that disappears, leaving everything in darkness save the points of light from the headlights from the cars in the oncoming lanes. The four lanes constitute what I consider a big road—a marked change from the lolling country route which used to run through here—and I struggle to maintain an orientation as to where I am. It's been a long time since I've been back.

Rolling past the new shopping centers and housing developments, I shake my head. It's amazing how you can live in a place for so many years, to the point where you think you know it as well as you'll ever know anything—and then the bulldozers come in and in the space of a handful of years they transform everything so utterly that it might as well be on a different planet. Nothing here keys even the remotest recollection and I'm left trying to figure where the turnoff is by dredging a distant calculus of time and distance from the recesses of my memory.

I almost miss it. There's a traffic light and a church where before there was nothing but a stop sign, but the green road sign catches my eye at the last minute. *Hampton Road.* Seeing it stirs a moment of cognitive dissonance—in fifteen miles of changed landscape it's the first thing that has struck a familiar chord.

Quickly downshifting the Suzuki, I turn down the road. Once past the church the blacktop still wends it way through dense woods—another remembered puzzle piece—and within a couple hundred feet the speckled lights and urban sounds of the parkway have disappeared, leaving me in blackness. The halogen light of the motorcycle plays out in front of me, bright white where the road tracks straight, but in another hundred feet the road begins its twisting dance and the headlight beam turns discordant, absorbed by the trees.

At first tentative, a smile slowly breaks out on my face as the first few miles unfold and I realize that this is all pretty much the same. They haven't changed this yet. Still, I ride with restraint. It's hard to see in the darkness and the wired certainty of what this road holds, the script that I carried in my head for so many years, is now muted and uncertain. Has it really been that long?

The Gixxer, ever wanting to run, seems disappointed. I can hear the slightly raucous exhaust note even through my ear plugs and the inline-four emits its flow of power with an almost rheostat-like smoothness. I barely touch that well of power, the 1000cc mill needing the merest turn of throttle to accelerate through the corners.

But then there's the long downhill to the causeway, mostly straight, and I give the bike its head. I must have done that here a thousand times—the goal always the same: get to triple digits before arriving at the water. The GSX-R1000 makes short work of that, crushing its way past the ton in a few quick ticks. By the time I get to the reservoir and roll off I'm a third of the way into the second ton. It makes me start laughing.

The landscape isn't the only thing that has changed.

From there the road contorts its way for another dozen miles, lending both a remembrance and a lesson. This isn't in the mountains—there aren't any in this county—but you'd never know it by the character of the road, the way it twists and turns in a drunken symphony.

By the time I start down the hill into the tiny, little village twenty minutes later I'm struck by how lucky I was. Though I never realized it at the time, the small network of roads around here—probably no more than a hundred miles, all told—were the very best teachers I could have ever asked for.

The village itself seems little changed. As I slow to a stop across the street from the old general store, I have the same feeling that I remember from back then: that I have this all to myself. There are a few lights in the windows of the several houses along the street, but no one other than me is outside. Turning off the key to the Suzuki, it's suddenly quiet.

The horse railing is gone. The one I used to lean against as I smoked a cigarette and listened to the ticking sound of my cooling engine. But looking around, everything else seems pretty much the same as it was. I find that somehow gratifying.

I haven't smoked in years, so I don't have that to occupy me, but the introspective reflection of what this all means remains. Spending a few minutes contemplating what an enchanting thing a fast motorcycle is. And how it is that so few of us are given the gift to understand that.

Mostly, I'm thinking about the roads. How special they were in giving that fast motorcycle a place to live. A place to run. A place to allow us to be free of everything else, if only for a little while.

Even as these roads were my teachers then—all the lessons of our sport you'd ever need written in their infinite variety—they remain still. The young men who challenge them today, if they simply listen, will learn all they need. They can be as lucky as I was.

That strikes me as a comforting thought, a bit of continuity in a world which sometimes seems overly given to improving things, only to find that what was lost was greater than what was gained.

May there always be at least a few such roads as these.

Tossing away my imaginary cigarette, I shrug back into my jacket and mount back up. Thumbing the starter, the bike starts instantly and the sound prompts in me, once again, the feeling that all is well with the world. Slowly over the railroad tracks, then gently spooling the engine as I lean into the right-hander which leads out of town—and with speed the world comes alive.

The night has taken on that velvety smoothness that often comes after a hot summer day and the wind rushing past my face and arms and torso, my half-zipped jacket billowing full, is mesmerizing in its feel.

The preceding miles have given me a touch more confidence in my memory of how the road tracks, so my pace quickens. A mile rolls by across the darkened, rural landscape. Then another.

Almost missed, a quickly-looming shadow on my right marks the intersection with another small road. My mind reaches down it a half-mile, to a double-tap set of 10mph curves, and a long-ago crash. There were lessons aplenty that day.

I think to turn down it, but quickly decide against it. I'll come back another time for that. I've another thought in mind tonight.

Two more miles and the Y-intersection is there, just as I remember it. Taking the left-hand leg, the road curls around in a counterclockwise direction, almost like it was trying to turn back time. The Suzuki feels lithe, alive, wired to the road; its suspension uncannily sorted.

The salutary feeling prompts me to feed in more speed, slowly over the next mile, until finally I'm edging into that place where everything tightens up, where it all becomes taut and focused and purposeful. The good place.

With speed, the darkness that blankets the landscape imparts a floating sensation, as if hurtling through time and space, unhindered by natural laws. As if we—this bike and I—are some kind of meteor of light and energy, anchored to the ground by magic.

And suddenly it's there, in that nexus of blackness and motion and power, the world wheeling beneath me, that I find the answer I've been searching for.

That the world changes, inevitably. Especially those things

that we can see and smell and touch—the buildings and the roads and the landscape. All those things that we think about all the time, that seem to be the map of our world. But that there are other things, things that live deeper, that are untouchable. They exist within us, eternal.

As long as we live, they remain.

September 2007, Sport Rider

Racer Road

Though it happened many years ago, I remember it like it was yesterday. A cloudy autumn evening, comfortable from the Indian Summer temperatures we had been enjoying, but tinged with that knowing-it-will-soon-all-be-over feeling. There was that sense that the season's riding days—the good ones, at least—were numbered. I had toasted a set of tires the previous week in a trip down into the Smokies with some buddies and had since replaced them with a fresh set. I was enjoying that wow-the-handling-is-so-much-better feeling that fresh rubber imparts and was trying to squeeze in every last mile of good riding I could while the nice weather lasted. Leaving a couple hours early on this Friday afternoon seemed like exactly the right thing to do.

Weekday rides are always cool because most of the good roads—those most likely to attract attention over a weekend—are usually devoid of traffic. And so it was for me this day. I had the road virtually to myself.

Spooling up the engine at the bottom of the mountain, it didn't take more than a couple of corners to get synced, to find that rhythm. Then, snick, it was done. After that it was just riding, effortless, flowing through the corners without really thinking about it. The bike and I were wired, in the zone. Other than the engine—the sound of which seemed to be coming from somewhere deep inside me—the rhythmic scurring of footpegs on asphalt was the only thing to be faintly heard.

Halfway up, the tortured coils of tarmac perceptively tightened. No matter. I was in that rare place where everything seemed possible, where every nuance of the road and all the complexities of the moment were distilled into a singular clarity. I maintained the same road speed, simply carrying a bit more corner speed through the turns.

Ahead, a blind right-hander. Even though I couldn't see it, I knew what it presented: a conventional sweeper going in, but then tightening ever so slightly as it ran towards the apex—a bit of subtlety all but lost at less serious speeds. I knew the pavement was good—there was a single ever-so-rough patch of asphalt but it was a good foot to the left of one's normal line. The only complication was a faintly visible 6-inch-wide diesel smear which some vehicle had laid down in the lane heading up the mountain several weeks prior. Time and weather were slowly scrubbing that nuisance away. But I had modified my line a few inches to the left to avoid it ever since it had appeared, and was still playing to that caution.

It was at the moment of tightening, while dialing in a little more lean angle, when the rear end broke. It wasn't that flexing sort of shimmy we've all felt, when the tire breaks traction a little, the back end suddenly loose. It broke hard, like the sear of a rifle, with an abject this-is-no-drill certainty.

I should have been scared. Any rider who has ridden for more than a few months has experienced those chilling moments of surprise when, for a few puckering microseconds, our reality has become both tenuous and palpable. Those gotcha moments when we get that adrenaline dump and the explosive spike in our heart rate and that howl of disbelief in our heads. I've certainly had my share.

Only, not this time.

It was almost like I was a disinterested observer, casually watching the show. With the rear end stepped out something approaching a foot, I knew I was in danger of high-siding. But I also knew—with a dead certainty that even today I have a hard time describing—that the tire would hook back up in a controllable way. I knew, as much as anything I've ever known, that this was all going to be okay. And so I just stayed on the throttle and kept on riding.

A dozen years later, at Virginia International Raceway, I'd be confronted with almost exactly the same scenario—a badly loose rear end and a spun-up tire. There was no quiet certitude that day and I ended up getting pitched on my ear. But on that day long before, back home on that mountain, I found something strange and wonderful.

§

We've all got one: Our own little racer road. That piece of tarmac that we return to time and again, the place where we're most likely to loose the reins and let that bike of ours run. It's probably the best motorcycle road within a reasonable distance of wherever it is that we live. And for most of us, being "best" is defined by having a bunch of quality curves—the number of those and their temperament being dependent upon the local topography we happen to inhabit. If you're fortunate enough to live in an area rich with good roads, you may end up factoring in other things when selecting your marquee route—traffic density, scenery, along-the-route complications like houses or driveways, how well-known the road is to other riders, or how the road can be connected to other good roads to make a longer riding loop. For you riders who aren't so fortunate to live in an area of grand, broken geology, your favorite road may be as obvious as taking a map, scribing a hundred-mile-radius circle around your house, and pointing to the one good road within that space.

However we arrive at it, that favorite road of ours is unique. Regardless of whatever other characteristics it might hold, there is one thing that makes it immeasurably different from all the other roads that we ride: Our intimacy with it. That changes everything.

Riding a motorcycle at speed is an enormously complex activity, one that floods a rider with a multitude of sensory inputs and requires a constant stream of split-second decisions. It's a pursuit which insists upon near-perfection in execution and which rewards mistakes with an immediate and undue harshness. It's probably no surprise that only a small percentage of the population is drawn to it.

For those of us who are, the rewards of mastering that complexity are immense. There's something sublime about doing it well, riding at speed along a good road. And at its zenith are those rare moments, every now and again, when we somehow manage it all perfectly across a span of miles and are rewarded with that state of grace that no amount of money can buy.

Riding well can happen anywhere. There's no reason you can't climb on your bike, ride across six states, and end up on a strange road which you immediately make a connection with. It happens. But it's undeniable that most of us will ride better on roads with which we have some familiarity. And that's why that old favorite road of ours is so special. Having ridden it countless times, we end up with a nuanced understanding of its qualities. Not just the obvious things like the best line with which to connect its corners or how much traction in general that the pavement affords, but also much more subtle things. Things like knowing where the camber rises or falls, for instance, or those places where the pavement has some irregularity or other; understanding those places where our suspension comes in or goes out, or recognizing those points where you transition from throttle to brake and vice versa. And since it's in the mastering those inflection points, those points of change, that we raise our riding to a new level, that favorite road of ours holds a unique promise.

For years, that road of mine across that mountain was my home away from home. It was where I went for fun, whenever I just wanted some quality miles. It was where I went for solace, whenever other things in my life seemed crappy and I needed a lift. And it was where I went for education, whenever there was a new riding technique I wanted to try. On more than one long, tortured day at work, I'd find my mind creeping back to the shadowed hollows of that mountain, a momentary reprieve.

The downside of any racer road, of course, is the racer part. A lot of guys never learn the difference between riding a road well at speed—and simply riding fast. They end up crashing, of course, and if your particular racer road happens to be popular enough with such riders it'll draw the inevitable attention of local law enforcement. And when that happens, you're done. It's been a long time since I last rode that that old mountain road of mine, the one I so loved for all those years, at speed.

So when you do find that special road, the one that you find yourself returning to again and again, don't tell anyone save for your closest riding buddies. Like so many other things in life, the best racer roads are the secret ones.

June 2006, Sport Rider

Rain

I awaken to a dry heat. As I step out of the bedroom door it feels like I've stepped into an oven. Jeez. Someone left the heat up and we're all going to get sick.

Downstairs, the first one up, I open the balcony door to let some cool air inside. It's still pitch black outside but I can hear the patter of rain. It's both cold and wet.

I put the coffee on and step into the shower. In a surprise, by the time I come back out most everyone is up. It's mighty early for most of them.

We might as well have gone ahead and slept in. It's a miserable day for riding. Cold, foggy, and wet. After a while we walk up the hill to The Junction for breakfast. Even with a leisurely meal, the weather hasn't improved any by the time we're done. No one wants to go out. There are a bunch of movie videos on the shelf and Neil selects *The Pelican Brief.* That keeps us entertained for a couple of hours.

By late morning, everyone is getting antsy. Finally Andy announces he's going out for a ride. John and Neil and Eric tell him to wait up, they'll go with him. Left behind are Kevin and Forrest and myself. We watch more TV, I read a book I've brought along, and after awhile Kevin puts on the left-over chili for lunch.

I keep looking outside. Though wet and foggy, the sky is bright. I'm reminded of that one day on a trip years before when we stayed at the Inn down at the bottom of the mountain. The weather that day was similar to today. John and Dave and I had been out riding all morning and had circled back around. When we stopped at the store at the bottom, who should we run into, but Suzanne and Melanie. They had come up with Mac and Tom, and—like us this trip—were staying in a condo on top of the mountain. Observing the ugly weather outside their window, the two men had decided to hang out inside their condo, while Suzanne and Melanie chose to go out for a ride. I remember looking up at the fog-enshrouded mountain that day and realizing that Mac and Tom had no way of knowing that down below things were, if not great, nonetheless much better. They could have been out riding.

I wonder if today we are similarly being deluded by remaining on top of the mountain, up amongst the clouds. Especially as the hours tick slowly by and our friends continue to remain absent.

The sky remains a tantalizing puzzle, a tease. At 3pm, knowing there are only a few hours of daylight left, I finally decide to go. To see what's below.

My bike is a wet mess and it takes a few minutes to wipe it down. It quickly gets wet again, of course, but at least the pools of water on the seat are gone. More time is spent climbing into my electric fleece liner, my Aerostich Roadcrafter riding suit, Gore-Tex gloves, and Arai helmet. And since I don't know what down below holds or how long I might be gone, I take my tank bag with all its camera gear and the rain cover to protect it all.

Descending the coiled loops of asphalt heading down the mountain, I'm first struck with pessimism. Whatever promise I might have seen up top in the bright sky certainly isn't apparent here. Instead, I'm wrapped in a dark, gloomy fog and the rain, though light, is steady. Finally though, nearing the bottom, I break out into relatively clear air. It's such a welcome relief that I almost don't mind the rain.

South on 219, I really don't have a plan. Whatever else, it's clear that I wasn't missing a whole lot. My hope-against-hope that it might be mostly dry down off the mountain, maybe even with patches of dry pavement here and there, is quickly dashed. The sky is solid gray, with a light, steady rain. But the effort to get packed and dressed was more than trivial, so I continue on.

I'm glad I did.

The K1200RS feels wonderfully compliant, tracking steadily over the wet roads. My touch on the bars is gentle, easing into and out of the throttle and the brakes. I'm holding near 70mph, not all that much under my usual dry-road pace along here. But it feels good. Amazingly good.

In no time at all I've arrived at the mountain north of Marlinton, one of my favorites. Even today, in the wet, I flow around its turns at a good clip. Like scribing arcs with the tip of a narrow sword. Easy, gentle. With just a hint of aggression.

And as I roll out of the last curve, towards the summit, I laugh at myself, suddenly realizing that this is a lesson I somehow have to keep re-learning. That beautiful, warm, sunny days aren't the only nice times to be out riding. Sometimes it's actually fun to be out when things are wet and ugly. There's something special about being warm and dry and comfortable in spite of the miserable weather you're riding through.

§

One of the advantages of riding that we motorcyclists often point to is being out in the weather, interacting with the environment in a far more intimate way than do our friends in their 4-wheel boxes. And it's certainly true that most of us find that close interaction—the tactile feeling of immersion—to be one of the pleasurable aspects of the sport. It's a little ironic, then, that so many of us studiously avoid that same interaction as soon as it turns a little wet. Some riders outright fear it.

None of which makes sense when you think about it. Rain is an inevitable part of the environment for most of us. Stretch the miles on those weekend day-rides, out a ways from home, and sooner or later you're going to be caught in rain. Go on a few multi-day trips and you're bound to spend some of your time riding in it. And if you commute regularly on your bike it's a cinch that you'll get plenty of wet weather miles.

So we might as well accept the notion that riding in the rain is a normal part of our experience.

The key, of course, is good gear. Most riders grudgingly spend forty or fifty bucks on a waterproof-but-doesn't-breathe rain suit and call it a day. It's no surprise, then, that their wet weather experience pretty much sucks.

Make Gore-Tex your friend. Invest in quality, waterproof, breathable riding gear—including boots and gloves—and you'll soon experience that oddly satisfying feeling of being warm and dry even in a torrential downpour.

Having done that, it's just a matter of being smooth with your control inputs. Modern tires are amazing and there is far more traction available in the wet than many riders realize. Just watch a rainy day MotoGP or Superbike race and that is readily apparent. But that traction is brittle—when its limit *is* reached it goes away suddenly, with far less of the progressive feedback that dry tarmac provides. So soft on the throttle, soft on the brakes, overlapping transitions, and avoiding abrupt direction changes are the watchwords for the day.

There is a final benefit to wet weather riding: the sense of utter mastery that comes when the roads finally dry. I remember a track day years ago at Road Atlanta where the morning sessions were run in horrendous conditions, with a steady, cold rain. The asphalt surface at Road Atlanta provides excellent wet weather grip, but even still it was a chilly and stressful few hours. As we neared the noon lunch break, though, the rain began to slow and the sky to brighten. And by the time the first afternoon session got underway, the sun was out and the track was rapidly drying.

That afternoon was one of finest slices of riding I have ever experienced. The feeling of control, of being able to rail with absolute confidence, was dramatic.

And so it has been on countless other track days and street rides over the years. Rides that started in the wet, but then dried up after awhile. These rides are wondrous, sprung from the confidence that emerges from the extraordinarily nuanced feeling for traction that develops after long hours in the wet.

I'm not for a moment going to pretend that riding in the rain is as much fun as riding on a beautiful, sunny, 70-degree day. But given their inevitability, rainy day rides certainly have a place in our library of motorcycling experiences. So we might as well embrace them, understanding that not only are they not nearly as bad as we often make them out to be, but they actually have positive things to offer.

As I turn my bike back towards the condo, still enjoying that feeling of being cozy and dry while the BMW cuts through the wet landscape, I remind myself I need to remember that.

July 2008, Sport Rider

Rhythms of the Road

Leaving before dawn always seems special. The breaking sun meets you out on the road, light spilling into the crevices of the world just as your anticipation of what the day will bring gladdens your heart. So as I turn out of my driveway and point the bike westward, my back towards the smudge of light tingeing the horizon, I can't help but smile.

A five hundred mile day awaits.

I eschew the secondary roads that normally comprise my weekend riding diet—those delightfully convoluted rural routes which take forever to get anywhere. The first couple hours today are for making time. And so the first thirty minutes passes in thoughtful deliberation, the mostly-straight road I'm on demanding little attention. It's actually a pleasure to just sit back and ponder what the day will bring. My mind wraps around a particular fascination—how it is that this thing, riding, can remain so deliciously enticing ride after ride, year after year. It never becomes tiresome.

I'm gently pulled from my reverie when I reach the foothills of the Blue Ridge Mountains. The hardening landscape and the swiftly tightening kinks in the road put an end to any daydreaming. It's a delight to have the road suddenly imposing demands upon me, knowing that there is a none-too-subtle consequence in not getting it right.

With the sun just now breaking over the horizon behind me I remind myself of the deer. The forest I ride through is a national park and they are ever present this time of day. With that caution in mind I'm just a touch restrained, the tarmac rolling under my wheels with a modest degree of aggression. Like flexing your muscles a bit, but knowing there's more to be had.

Descending into the Shenandoah Valley, I turn southward,

enjoying the gently rolling road which flows through this storied place. It's the final bit of prologue to the day and the last chance for introspection. Like the first road I traveled this morning, this one requires but a modicum of effort.

Ninety miles from home, I stop for gas. A quick splash-and-go for both me and the bike. Then I'm back aboard and climbing the ascent, sudden impatience welling up inside me. The sun is an hour in the sky.

Perfect.

The Blue Ridge Parkway is one of the finest motorcycle roads in the world. Purpose-built as a scenic highway, stretching nearly five hundred miles across a hardened mountain landscape, it has no traffic lights, no stop signs, no intersecting traffic, no trucks, no cell service, no soccer moms, and no gravel. It's a roadway which runs through a landscape of stark beauty. But within a half mile of having turned onto it I'm reminded of the real reason I have always found it so special—its amazing rhythm. Curve after curve rolls in upon you like gently breaking waves. There is a symmetry to the road. Even at seriously extralegal speeds its even cadence imparts a smooth mellowness, not unlike the whiskeys that once came from the stills in the hollows down below. Of all the roads I've ever been on, this one is probably the most cathartic.

The reason, of course, is the vague similarity in all the curves and the deliberately-engineered turn radii which remove any abruptness. This is not a road with discrete turn-in points and braking markers. This is a road to be ridden with the deft swirling touch of a surgeon's scalpel.

Two hours later I turn off on one of the occasional side roads which lead down off the Parkway, the next leg in the grand loop I have planned for today. And within a hundred yards I know that this one has an entirely different character. If the BRP is even and consistent—this is anything but. The turns here come at you in staccato, abrupt bursts, like jabs from a boxer. Far more technical, the road has a ragged and edgy quality. And whereas a road like the BRP can be enjoyed—even at speed—with a relatively modest amount of attention, this one demands a far more intense focus. It puts me as close to a racetrack mindset as I ever get on the street.

Eight miles later, down in the valley, with the road having unkinked itself and my frenetic focus having abated, my mind mulls over the contrasts in the roads I've ridden so far this morning. Everything from that mostly-straight, get-there-quick road I started with, to the moderately technical road over the first mountain pass, to the road meandering in a gentle lope down the valley, to the Blue Ridge Parkway and its constant but easy curves, to this latest highly-technical road so laced with challenge and danger that it was emblazoned across its length with numerous public warnings.

And it occurs to me that each of those roads has its own unique character. Each must be ridden differently. What works on one might not work at all on another. A riding style that gets you down the Blue Ridge Parkway perfectly well might just get you killed on that last road I was on.

At a superficial level that distinction between roads is fairly obvious. But at a deeper level it's full of nuances. There's more to it than simply paying greater attention to a road which is somehow "harder."

Riding well involves, among other things, establishing a rhythm. Finding a cadenced set of responses to the demands imposed by a particular road. It's not unlike the metered time signature which sets the backdrop to a piece of music. In our case it sets the baseline for the pace, effort, riding style, and focus we'll bring to bear.

We can choose to ignore that baseline, of course. The easiest example of that is pushing the pace beyond what our skill level or the road conditions suggest. Doing so, we'll find that our riding quickly deteriorates. It turns ragged. Without a rhythm we're left simply riding corner to corner—rarely the smoothest or fastest way to get down a road. It's a truism on the racetrack that one oftentimes must deliberately take a particular corner more slowly in order to be better set up for a subsequent turn. A racer looks at a racetrack in a holistic fashion. He will gladly cede corner speed in one place in return for a faster overall lap time.

The same thing applies on the street. A good rider doesn't simply bull his way down the road, trying to impose his will upon every corner he comes to. He doesn't take each turn as a single entity wholly unto itself, but rather recognizes it to be part of a larger tapestry. He seeks to understand what the road demands, and what it will give him. He searches for the rhythm inherent in the road itself.

And then, finding it, he syncs his pace and riding style to match it.

How does he know when he has found it? Because it will feel right. Riding to the rhythm of a road will feel smooth and effortless, even if the pace is very intense.

If you sharpen a knife upon a whetstone, there is a proper angle at which to hold the blade. Held at that correct angle, drawing the blade's edge across the stone feels uncannily smooth. It has an almost perfect "rightness" to it. Drop the angle a little bit, or increase it a little too much, and the blade instantly tells you that something is amiss. The difference between a man who knows his way around blades and the vast majority who don't is that nuanced feel—the ability to quickly and consistently find that proper angle.

The same holds true in riding. Many riders treat the road they are on as simply a surface to ride along, something separate from themselves and their bike. They don't see it as an environment with which they should actively interact. And they are unable to read the nuanced cues that the road communicates.

The rhythm of a particular road will be essentially the same for all riders. But that doesn't mean that all riders will ride that road in exactly the same way, or that their individual paces will necessarily be similar. Rider skill level, the type and condition of motorcycle one is on, and familiarity with that motorcycle are all factors in that equation. But the rhythm buried in the heart of a road sets the same stage for everyone.

A few miles further along I turn left, on a road I've never been on before, prompted by one of those yellow caution signs which warns of a curvy road ahead. Throttling up gently, my senses are on high alert as I roll through the first handful of turns. Wondering what is here. What is being offered.

And listening for whispers.

May 2008, Sport Rider

Saturday Service

As I head down my long gravel driveway in the pre-dawn darkness, with the headlamp lighting my way and the orange glow from the instrument panel of the GS reflecting back into my face shield, it occurs to me that I don't get out for many nighttime rides anymore. I used to, back in the day. But anymore it seems that most of my miles seem to happen when the world is well lit. I wonder if maybe I've gotten a bit lazy.

This morning is different, for a reason: I'm heading to Bob's BMW for some minor service work. Saturday service is first-come, first-served at Bob's and I want to get there early enough so that I don't end up waiting all day. I've learned from hard experience that the longer one hangs around a good motorcycle dealership, the more damaging to your wallet it becomes.

The ride there from my home in Warrenton is 70-odd miles of interstate slog. I66, the Capital Beltway, and I95 are hateful routes during the work week, consuming far too many hours of my life. But as I roll through Gainesville and pick up I66 eastbound, with the first edges of dawn light tinting the horizon, I'm actually glad to be here. There's no traffic to speak of, the air has a dusky sort of feel to it, and I'm rolling at pace on a fine motorcycle. Not a lot not to like.

Across the American Legion Bridge, a few miles inside the Maryland beltway, there's a secret: a few miles of twisting slalom. You'd never notice it in a car. And even on a bike it's only during those rare moments when the road is devoid of traffic and you can push the speed a bit that the character of the road is revealed. But it's there. Playing to my imagination as I roll the GS through the kinda-sorta-sweepers, I pretend that I'm on some kind of Isle of Man adventure, smiling to myself inside my helmet.

The old magic.

The morning hours at the dealership pass softly. There's the easy banter with the other riders who likewise are there having stuff done. There's a lot of walking around and looking at each other's bikes and talking about this thing or that accessory; of roads and trips and weather; of tires and speed and racetracks—all the minutiae that concern serious riders.

I'm lucky to be one of the first ones in line. While waiting the couple hours for the service technicians to do their thing I wander around, idly talking to the folks who work there, many who have been there for years. It's funny how the business/customer relationship at a good motorcycle shop is different from almost any other kind of business. Money changes hands, sure, but that seems like just a niggling little detail. Mostly, it seems like we're co-conspirators in the grandest of schemes, members of some sort of secret society. You can't help but feel like you're part of something special.

By late morning they've finished working on my bike. Whether it's just a routine service—like mine today—or whether it's getting something fixed or having new tires shod or whatever, it's always a good feeling when you get your bike back. That nagging, worrisome feeling that comes creeping when a mechanical issue emerges is suddenly gone and everything again seems right with the world. Having a motorcycle in good shape—ever ready to run long miles—is important to many of us.

If the trip in this morning was special because of the early hour, the one going home is special because it's… free. I have a freshly-tuned bike, a half a day in front of me, and the freedom to spend it however I wish. It doesn't take me long to dismiss the thought of heading back on the interstate—it'll be the insane mess it normally is. No, I believe I'll take the long way. Mapping possibilities in my head, I point the GS east and south, down a tortured route that only a motorcyclist would ever conjure.

Three hours later I'm back across the Potomac in Virginia.

Having decided to detour down Virginia's Northern Neck—my route home becoming ever more convoluted—on a sudden impulse I turn down the road towards Colonial Beach. My parents used to take us there when we were little kids, a long, long time ago. I haven't been back since and now, riding slowly through the little town, I look at things carefully, searching for a connection, a bit of memory, to something I can barely remember. Turning down one of the side streets leading to the water, I park the GS and walk down to the sandy beach. Gazing out across the water, I wonder if the kid I was back then ever imagined that the man he would become would be back here one day checking up on him.

Continuing down the peninsula towards Montross, the afternoon turns slowly. Having decided that today is not a bad day for impulses, I've turned down a lonely, unmarked road and ridden it the few miles back to where it dead-ends at the water's edge. Standing there gazing back across to the Maryland side far in the distance, listening to the sound of the water and watching the birds wheel in the air and feeling the breeze on my face, I'm struck by how rich this day has been. And I'm reminded, as I so frequently am, of how strangely important a motorcycle can be in taking us to those special places, in imbuing even our most mundane activities with meaning and fun.

As I climb back aboard the BMW, this time to finally point it towards home, it occurs to me that it will be well into evening by the time I get back. Almost dark. Thinking back to when I left home this morning, a thought begins to form.

Maybe I'll ride for a bit longer, yet.

August 2006, Sport Rider

Sleeper

Glancing down at the cylinder heads hanging out and then back up at the rather cheesy windscreen reminds me of a conclusion I reached many years ago: the BMW GS may be the ugliest motorcycle on the planet. This latest 1200cc incarnation dropped quite a few pounds on its recent predecessors and acquired a rather more svelte physique in the process. But even so that's kind of like putting lipstick on a pig. It still begs the question of why.

Which is one reason when I fall in behind the small group of sportbikes beginning their ascent of the mountain I have little in the way of expectations. Were I on my GSX-R1000 or K1200RS I'd expect to hang with them for awhile. But a tall, lumbering dual-sport doesn't exactly come dripping with sporting promise. And even though I've been mightily impressed with the road-holding skills of the BMW in the few weeks since I added it to my stable, that's been tempered by many years of focusing almost exclusively on sport and sport-touring bikes. I long ago bought into the conventional notions of what fast is.

Life can be full of surprises.

Simply brisk at first, a subtle change of body language in the rider in front of me cues me to the change in tempo. They'll be intent on getting knee pucks on the ground, something I in my Aerostich can't do. Not that I'd be inclined to anyhow—not to mention how ludicrous such a thing would look on this bike. But even as the sweepers at the bottom give way to the tighter, more technical sections of this road; even as I feed in enough throttle to stay with these guys, I have to marvel at how effortlessly this bike turns, how fast it transitions, and how steadily it tracks. By the time I break off a handful of miles later I've come to a startling conclusion: up to the last few percentiles of what could be considered reasonable on the street, this is the easiest-to-ride-fast bike I've ever been on. My Gixxer would catch it in the end—and would flat smoke it on a racetrack, of course—but at the cost of a hell of a lot more effort. My KRS would never even be in the hunt.

§

It starts, I think, because most of us aren't just riders—we're also gearheads. We have become so attuned to the advances in motorcycle technology over recent years—technology which is most apparent in the sportbike category—that we've lost sight of the fact that motorcycles of all stripes have shared in those advances, and have for a very long time. Motorcycles today aren't simply good. They are extraordinary. By almost any measure you can think of they exceed the capabilities of all but a tiny percentage of riders.

Which means that—on the street—our notions of what is fast are becoming increasingly irrelevant.

I should have known that. When Suzuki introduced its SV650 some years back it was originally positioned as an economical beginners bike. But its outstanding frame, responsive geometry, and jewel-like motor quickly found a cult-like following among many much more advanced riders. It may not have looked like a sportbike, but it sure hammered a curvy road like one!

The same can be said for a lot of bikes. Bikes that because of style or age are too-soon dismissed as having any serious sporting competency. And that's a mistake.

Up until a couple years ago, one of my buddies, Kevin Hawkins, used to trailer two bikes to track days: an 85 FZ750 and an 00 ZRX1100. Neither one exactly cutting edge. The FZ failed to arouse much interest because of its age. The ZRX because it didn't have the sculpted bodywork and bend-over-and-grab-your-ankles posture of a proper sportbike. Yet when the early morning benchracing ended and the real sessions began Kevin was always one of fastest and smoothest riders out there. There was always a lot more interest in those two bikes at the end of the day than there was at the beginning.

Which kind of says it all. It reminds us that in a world where all the hardware is pretty damn good, it's the rider, after all, that makes the difference. We've always known that, of course. But in the swoon of the latest model introductions, in the excitement engendered by the latest technological advances, we sometimes forget.

A few years ago I was coming up the Blue Ridge Parkway after having spent several days riding down in the Smoky Mountains. It was late evening and I was running on fumes and caught in the minor urgency of trying to find gas and get the 60 miles further north to my campsite before darkness fell. I turned off the Parkway down what turned out to be one of the most crooked roads I've ever been on—riding the sharp, abrupt, incessant turns reminded me of nothing so much as a dog trying to bite its own tail. Halfway down the mountain I came upon two Harley riders, one a middle-aged fellow on one of Milwaukee's newer models—for some reason this guy struck me as being an MSF instructor—the other an older, white-haired gentleman on a much older model. They laughingly waved me past after a mile or so, but not before I was treated to one of the most hilarious fireworks shows I've ever seen. Stereotypes be damned—those two boys were every bit as much sport riders as those of us who revel in the latest Gixxer or R1 or Ducati.

Maybe there's a reason why the magazine is named what it is, after all.

October 2005, Sport Rider

The ATGATT Myth

*Sure, wear the gear. It's the
smart thing to do. Just know that it
won't keep you from dying.*

The shaded porch of the Mountainside Market is populated mostly by the locals of the little village during the week, just relaxing and catching up on things. But on weekends they cede it to the riders from near and far who've come to run the mountain.

As I pull into the parking lot and switch off the key to the Gixxer, my eyes scan the dozen-odd bikes already there, a mix of Harleys, race-replica sportbikes, and naked standards. I don't recognize any.

Shrugging out of my jacket, I hang that on the downside mirror, placing my helmet and gloves on the seat. The ear plugs go in my pocket.

The handful of cruiser riders, obvious by their attire, are sitting at the far-end table. I nod, bending to scratch the ears of the old dog who is always there, ever hopeful for a handout.

The air-conditioning inside feels good, a marked contrast to the warm, humid air outside. I take my time, wandering over to the cooler for a bottle of water and then down the aisle, where I finally select a small bag of peanuts. It's hardly been two hours since I stopped for lunch. I don't need much.

Back out on the porch, I settle myself on the bench against the wall, near the table in the middle where the four sportbike riders are engaged in animated conversation. Like the cruiser riders, there's no question which bikes they belong to.

After a long pull on the bottle of water, I open the bag of peanuts and begin to eat them one at a time. I'm in no hurry. As I slowly unwind, I catch snippets of conversation. One is a joke about the sparse gear the Harley riders are wearing. That brings a laugh and nods of approval. It's true, of course—the contrast between the race leathers the sportbike guys are wearing and the jeans, thin leather vests, half-helmets, and fingerless gloves of the cruiser fellows. But the condescension seems a bit much.

Twenty minutes later I'm ready to roll. The sportbike boys are planning on running the mountain again and I have something in mind. I need a little bit of a head start and that gives me something of an excuse to push the pace a little. The pavement is clean and dry and my ascent is the tiny slice of heaven that it always is.

On the western side, just past the summit, I steer the Gixxer into the pullout. Removing my jacket and helmet, I turn to the tailpack and withdraw my Nikon DSLR. Turning away from the bike, I switch the camera into focus-tracking mode, double-checking the frames remaining on the compact flash card. Walking over to the berm where I've done this before, I hunker down to wait.

It takes longer than I expect. A couple of single riders pass by, and I get shots of them. But the sportbike boys whom I left at the store a little while ago—and whom I had hoped to get some decent shots of as they carved through the corner—are nowhere to be seen.

Finally, I hear the low, unmistakable rumble of big-engine Harleys. A few minutes later they roll slowly through the corner. They're the same group that was down at the store and a couple of them, seeing me, wave.

Figuring the sportbike boys must have changed their mind, I put my camera away and head back myself. Halfway down, the reason for their delay becomes all too obvious—one of them is down. A sheriff's deputy is already there, blue lights flashing, so I don't stop.

But the irony doesn't escape me.

§

Riders who ascribe to the notion that wearing proper gear on every ride have an acronym that they use these days—ATGATT. As in *all the gear, all the time.* It's an important concept, one of the wisest that has ever gained traction in the motorcycling community. But while it represents a distilled bit of wisdom, one borne from decades of rider experience, it's unfortunately often presented as the perfect catch-all for rider safety. Hang out with riders for awhile and you'll undoubtedly hear it proselytized in all sorts of contexts. Most of those make sense. But a few don't. There's nothing like hearing it espoused, for example, in response to a horrific, fatal accident to make you realize that not everyone quite gets it.

What I am about to say may very easily be misconstrued, so I would ask that readers be discriminating in how they interpret it. I am most emphatically *not* suggesting that wearing a full complement of riding gear—helmet, leathers or riding suit, boots, and gloves—on every single ride is not the right and proper thing to do. It is, without question. But it is important to understand that wearing the right gear all the time—ATGATT—is not the rider safety panacea that it is often purported to be. It's one of the bigger parts of the puzzle, to be sure, but by no means is it the entire picture. Riders who focus undue emphasis on it risk being lulled into a false sense of security. And those who somehow feel that wearing the gear gives them a bye to take greater risks are asking for trouble.

First, an aside: helmets are so crucial to any meaningful dialogue about rider safety that I'm going to take them entirely off the table for purposes of this discussion. I know that the topic of helmet use is a very emotional one for many riders, but the medical evidence seems overwhelming—sufficiently incontrovertible to me—to beggar any further discussion. Others can debate that subject, if they like. I won't. I'm going to assume that everyone is wearing a fresh, high-quality, full-face helmet every time they thumb the starter.

With that assumption as the baseline, here's the deal: the grievous injuries that most of us truly worry about—death, dismemberment, or paralysis—are overwhelmingly caused by severe, blunt, impact trauma. Impact trauma which riding gear—save that helmet—*has limited ability to attenuate.*

Riders get hurt badly, in other words, when they hit hard, immovable objects. They get hurt when they miscalculate lean angle or traction and low-side into an oak tree; or when they blow a corner and end up caroming into an Armco barrier. They get hurt when they panic and lock up their brakes and go flying off a cliff. And they get hurt when that SUV makes the unexpected left-turn right in front of them.

In fact, it is the susceptibility to severe impact injury which makes car/motorcycle accidents so overrepresented in motorcycle fatalities. Other vehicles are the most ubiquitous hard objects on the road, of course. So it's no surprise that they represent the greatest threat to us.

The flip side is that most everyone knows that racetracks are the safest environments in which to ride aggressively. What many may not realize is that the singular reason that they *are* safer than the street is precisely because they minimize impact risks, they decrease the opportunities to come afoul of hard, immovable objects. And to the degree that one racetrack may be perceived by riders to be safer than another—it's invariably because the one has been more successful at eliminating impact risks than the other.

Future clothing technologies may change the equation, but for now the bottom line is this: to avoid that most serious class of injuries, riders must avoid severe impacts. And doing that falls far more to the twin umbrellas of rider judgment and rider skill than it does to the area of gear selection.

A cynic might conclude from all this that I don't believe in

ATGATT. Some might misappropriate what I'm saying to suggest that riding in shorts and sandals is, if not okay, at least not as bad as those in the serious motorcycling community have long asserted it to be.

Nothing could be further from the truth.

I think riding without a full complement of proper riding gear is inarguably stupid. Those who choose not to wear it are saying more about their experience, competency, and attitude than perhaps they realize. The serious riders amongst us, the cognoscenti who make up the backbone of this sport, know those riders for what they typically are—rookies, with an early exit already wired in.

But it does beg a reasonable question: if ATGATT can't mitigate the very worst kinds of accident scenarios, why is it important? Why do we continue to emphasize it?

It's a good question. And the answer is simply that good gear is remarkably effective at mitigating the whole range of less-than-grievous get-offs that are far and away the most common sort of crash. Good gear can prove supremely beneficial in keeping a minor crash… minor.

Want an example?

Go back and find your copy of the October 2006 issue of *Sport Rider*. If you don't have a copy, then order a back issue, or go find one in a library, or borrow a copy from one of your buddies. Whatever you have to do, find a copy.

Now turn to page 114. (That's the famous Parting Shot picture, for those of you who might remember).

There you'll find two of the most remarkable photos you'll ever see. There are stories inside of stories written inside them. I won't belabor them here. Suffice it to say, what should have been a relatively modest low-side, with a few scratched and bent bits on the bike and the need for a couple of Ibuprofen tablets by the rider and passenger, turned into something far worse. Something that neither will likely ever forget, both because of the emotional trauma they endured and because they'll probably carry the physical scars from that moment for the rest of their lives.

And all it would have taken was some decent gear.

So, no, I'm not at all suggesting that ATGATT is not the right and proper thing to do. I'm simply encouraging riders to understand that it's not the whole story. That it's only one part of the repertoire that a good rider must bring to bear in dealing with the risks that are inherent to our sport. And that—most importantly—wearing it shouldn't provide an excuse to do things we otherwise wouldn't.

So wear the gear, all of it, all the time. But also be sure and bring your skill and your judgment; your experience and your belief in yourself. Bring those, and the remembrance that there's not a situation out there that a good rider can't solve.

All those wielded together become your talisman, proof against the unexpected.

May 2007, Sport Rider

The Magic Line

The more-or-less straight sections are okay, the rider behind me staying reasonably close on my tail. But every time we enter a series of curves I glance in my mirrors and find the trailing headlight falling further and further behind. That, even though my pace is anything but fast. "Tepid" would be a better description.

Rolling out of the throttle a bit and mentally drumming my fingertips for half a minute is usually enough for him to catch back up. Then we'll hang together for another mile or so, until the next set of curves, at which point we'll do it all over again.

Our little ride actually had its genesis months before, when Steve, a colleague at work, heard that I ride. After the usual "what kind of bike do you have?" query, and my describing the three machines currently in my stable, his joking "when are you going to get a real bike?" rejoinder told me everything I needed to know.

Bad jokes aside, Steve is actually a great guy. And unlike the majority of Harley aficionados that I know, he's actually a quite serious rider, putting 20,000 miles or so on his two Milwaukee-built machines every year. And he himself complained to me that most of his riding buddies prefer the rather-shorter weekend breakfast or lunch rides to the longer jaunts that he favors. I took that as hope.

Getting our two schedules to line up was another thing. The couple times we tried to schedule something, one or the other of us was always busy. Eventually, though, we sorted out a Saturday morning which worked for both of us. It still being summer, I insisted on an early start. And Steve needed to be back by late morning so what we had in front of us was about four hours. Enough to hit some of the good roads I know, but not enough to do the somewhat longer loop I originally had planned.

Of my three bikes, the R1200GS was the obvious choice. Although BMW's big adventure bike actually possesses a surprising amount of sporting prowess—one of the motorcycling world's better-kept secrets—its greatest strength lies in its remarkable versatility. If ever there was a bike that can pretty much do it all, this bike is it. I don't own a cruiser—have never even ridden one, in fact—but I reckoned that the straight-up seating position of the GS and its flexible boxer-twin motor would at least allow me to do a kinda-sorta imitation of one.

Or, to say it a little differently: I've sent most of my life wondering how to be a smoother, faster, and better rider. On this day, for the first time, I'm wondering how you go slow.

Arriving at Starbucks, I'm about as casual as I ever get when out riding—Aerostich Darien jacket, jeans, BMW boots, short-gauntlet deerskin gloves, and my Arai full-face helmet. Steve's wearing chaps over his jeans, light jacket, work boots, fingerless gloves, and a helmet which is something between a beanie and a regular open-face helmet. There's the merest hint of awkwardness as the two of us sit at a table outside next to his big-engine Harley and enjoy a quick cup of coffee before we head out. It's clear we approach the motorcycling world from very different viewpoints.

When we first starting talking about hooking up for a ride, I mentioned that I knew a lot of good roads. Even though we both live in the same community it was clear Steve wasn't familiar with most of the routes I described—lesser-known secondary roads, the more gnarly and technical the better. Turns out he and his pals mostly stay on the bigger, straighter thoroughfares.

But Steve's enthusiasm is genuine. And he wields that big Harley with a comfortable precision. The problem is simply that when we get into the twisties, at a point where my GS has hardly begun to dip into its cornering capacity, his machine has already exhausted all of his. It occurs to me that if one is into 4th of July light shows, a bike like Steve's isn't a bad choice.

The other thing that strikes me—I've got lots of time to think about all of this—is that this ride is distinctly *different*. Our pace is so modest—"cruising" being very much an apt metaphor—that the sensation remains one of being disconnected, of simply sitting atop the bike while it motors along. We never get to that that threshold, that moment in time, when the tires and the frame and the suspension all begin working in concert. That point is a crucial, transforming moment for many of us. It's the instant when a bike comes alive. It's when our senses become melded to what the machine is doing and saying. It's the moment of intimacy when, with our head in the right place, we and the bike might become one.

It's the magic line.

If a motorcycle ridden at pace on a curvy road has any distinction from the same bike when it's being used in a more hum drum, utilitarian fashion—say, for instance, when it's seeing commuting duty—it's in the confluence of its multiple dynamics. At slow speeds the various elements of the bike work perfectly fine, but there's no real sense that they're ever really working together. The engine does its thing. The tires and frame do theirs. And unless it's very softly sprung, the suspension sits there in the background, hardly working at all. It's only when the pace picks up sufficiently to reach that certain threshold that all those pieces begin to work in unison.

Engineers probably have a term with which they describe that point of harmony. I simply think of it as the point where the magic begins.

When I get home later I'll tell my wife Ginny "that was the slowest ride I've ever been on." Which is okay, even for someone like me who spends an inordinate amount of time thinking about such things. I've often said that speed shouldn't be the end-all of riding a motorcycle.

Except. Except that I deeply missed that very close you-talk-to-me-and-I'll-talk-to-you interaction with my motorcycle that I normally have. This ride was kind of like being on a date where the talk is sparse and there's no sex afterwards. You're left vaguely wondering what exactly the point was.

Which is not at all meant as a criticism towards the cruiser riders out there. I've no doubt that there is an enormous visceral pleasure to be derived from a throbbing, large-displacement V-twin motor. Such an enjoyment is not at all dependent upon how fast you're going and, in fact, probably starts to diminish beyond a certain speed. But for those of us who mostly live in the sport and sport-touring world, it does matter. For us, the engine is only one part of a larger package. How that package responds to the road is everything. And for that to work there has to be at least enough speed to awaken it from its slumber. You have to cross that line.

Back at the Starbucks, Steve and I shake hands. "Thanks for the great time," he says. "I don't have a clue of where we were, but I loved those roads!" I smile knowingly. "Glad you enjoyed it."

As he mounts back up, Steve turns back to me one last time. "Next time I'll bring the Sportster."

December 2006, Sport Rider

The Third Layer

There are a small handful of things about this sport that are very important. This is one of them.

The breakfast back in Victorville had been filled with anticipation. After eleven days on the road, enjoying some of the best twisty-road riding that North America has to offer, I was finally in Southern California. If the previous week and a half had been the appetizer, I figured all those storied roads around here that I'd read about in the magazines for all these years would surely be the desert.

From Victorville it's just a few miles down I15 to Cajon Junction, where I pick up 138 westward into the San Gabriel mountains. And just a few miles from there California route 2— better known as the *Angeles Crest Highway*—begins its tortured, twisting 66-mile-long dance into the Los Angeles basin.

Past Wrightwood, things immediately get serious. As I spool up the aggression meter on the K1100RS and begin pushing harder and harder into the turns, it's obvious why this road has the reputation it does. The curves come in a delightful, flowing cascade. And as the miles roll under my wheels on this weekday morning, I find that I have the road almost entirely to myself. Only thing... I have this odd feeling of disquiet. There's something subdued and mildly depressing about the landscape. The sky is blanketed in a somber overcast. The road is littered with chunks of rock, large pine cones, and enough shale dust that I figure it's got to compromise traction. And there are numerous patches of black, burnt forest, with the odor of those apparently-recent fires still pungent in the air. All that, along with maybe a touch of suddenly feeling alone, so far from home, add up to something less than the most inviting of tableaus.

But garbage on the road is certainly nothing new to me. Nor is being far from home. There's something else here, too. Something edging with an increasingly incessant urging into my consciousness.

After whistling through pursed lips for the nth time, it finally comes to me what it is: this is a deadly road. Not just dangerous—lots of roads are that. No, this one holds a hard-edged, distilled lethalness that is rarely seen. Countless numbers of those beautiful, seductive curves lie naked in the sky. There's no earthen bank. No Armco. Not even a swatch of trees to stop you should you blow a corner. There's nothing but an abrupt leap into nothingness, hundreds of feet above the valley floor.

The realization of what that could mean imparts a decidedly surreal feeling. It gives me pause. And it will prompt me to write in my journal later that night "this is not a road I particularly like."

§

When we ride a motorcycle at speed there are three things that affect us. Three things that encapsulate the skills, knowledge, and wisdom that our sport demands. How we deal with those things—the three layers—will determine our fate as riders.

The first is the *technical* layer. This is what most riders think about when they consider their riding. It includes all those details, all the many nuances, involved in the actual mechanics of riding a motorcycle. Everything from what the road presents to how we manage ourselves and our motorcycle as we ride down it. When we assess the qualities of a particular road, for instance—its width, the quality of its pavement, its camber, the radius of its curves, that sort of thing—we're in the technical layer. Likewise, when we decide upon a certain spot to be our entrance point, this spot here to begin throttling up, and that spot over there as our exit, we're talking about the technical layer. When we're heading towards a corner and we make the decision whether to brake or not, and, if so, which brake and for how long and how hard—that's the technical layer. Our sight lines through a corner are part of the technical layer. And when we decide whether we'll sit straight up on the bike or pull our ass off the seat and put a knee slider on the ground that, again, is the technical layer.

The technical layer has everything to do with all the particulars of the road, the rider, and the motorcycle. It's the distilled essence of what we do. In a perfect world those things would be the sum total of what we would need to worry about.

Alas, the world is not perfect. And because it's not, we have a second layer: the *environment*. The environmental layer involves all those things which are changeable over time and which can influence how successful we are in executing the first layer. An obvious one is weather. If it's raining it's pretty clear that surface traction will be reduced. Time of day is another. We'll certainly ride a curvy road differently at midnight than we would at noon.

Other vehicles on the road are another pretty obvious environmental element. And that can range from an in-your-face SUV with a talking-on-her-cell-phone soccer mom shading into your lane; to there not being a vehicle at all but nevertheless adjusting your line around that blind corner because of the very *threat* that a vehicle might appear. Ever dial it down on a sportbike-popular road because of the concern that a rider coming the other way might overcook that corner in front of you? You were thinking about the environmental layer.

Oil, gravel, and other compromised-surface contaminants are other environmental factors. They're not quite as obvious as a rain shower pouring down on you or that vehicle coming your way, but they're important. There's not a rider alive who hasn't been caught out by them at some point. And most of us spend a fair bit of effort in trying to watch out for them.

But there are other less obvious environmental factors, too.

The harsh shadows that are thrown into a corner on a bright, sunny day often impede our ability to detect those same patches of oil or gravel. There's a subtlety to light and novice riders might not at first understand why many seasoned sport riding veterans actually prefer riding on a softly overcast day.

The environmental layer—it's all those dynamic elements which can affect the quality and the safety of our ride.

Which brings us, finally, to the third layer: *consequences*. The consequences layer speaks to us of all those things which are likely to conspire against us should we fail to properly manage the first two layers. It answers for us the question of the repercussions of failure. Of what might happen if, perchance, we *don't* make that turn.

A motorcycle racer visiting a new racetrack for the first time will be evaluating a lot of things during his initial sighting laps. He'll be looking for his entrance and exit points. He'll be calculating how deeply into the braking markers he can go before hitting the binders. He'll be assessing where the best places to pass are. He'll be thinking about the particular strengths and weaknesses of his engine/suspension package and where those match up well with the track and where they don't. He'll be figuring where he can make the most time. There's an awful lot that needs sorting in a short amount of time, in other words. But even with all that, he's looking at one other thing—runoff.

Whether on the track or on the street, having clear runoff is the single biggest factor affecting motorcyclist safety. When we turn on the TV to watch the latest MotoGP race and see the inevitable crashes that are part of the sport, it's notable that serious injuries are very rare, notwithstanding the extraordinary speeds at which these riders are often traveling. Having sufficient runoff so that they can slide unimpeded to a stop is the singular reason why.

American racetracks—almost all of which were designed for cars—fall well short of most of their European and Asian counterparts in that regard. Which is why AMA races must rely so frequently on air fences to provide a modicum of rider safety.

But the point is that a racer must assess the danger in each corner, the consequences of a mishap there, along with all those other things. When he does that, he's thinking about the third layer.

Public roads are far more complex than any racetrack, of course, and there are far more elements that a rider must confront when examining what lies past his apex. Everything from guard rails and trees and rocks, to mailboxes set atop 4x4 slabs of timber. In their worst incarnations, the third layer presents a rider with the certainty of death—like my encounter with the over-the-cliff-and-you're-gone corners of the eastern portion of the *Angeles Crest*.

Whatever it presents, the third layer is an easy thing to figure out. All you have to do is ask yourself the simple question: "if I blew it right now, what would happen?"

It's been my experience that most riders spend a lot of time thinking about the first layer. That's the fun stuff. It's what we all talk about with our buddies. It's what we read about in the magazines. It's what makes us all want to go out on that next ride.

Riders pay a modicum of attention to the second layer.

But, unfortunately, most riders pay scant attention to the third layer. We'll blithely ride past threats as if they weren't there. As if that corner with the fat oak tree six feet past our apex is no different from the one which opens up into a pleasant little meadow. Then, of course, we're caught out if something goes wrong.

Running a road hard needs to be more than simply line and camber and radius. We need to make that third layer part of our routine, corner-by-corner, how-hard-will-I-run-it calculus.

Back on the *Angeles Crest*, I clearly recognized those things. The sheer, breathtaking, danger presented by those cliffs made me dial it back several notches. It's what made me write in my journal, that first night, that I didn't much care for the road. But there's one last thing to know about all this: familiarity blinds us.

It softens the level of risk that we perceive and blunts our consideration of what might happen. It inures us to danger.

I spent five more days in Southern California on that trip and I rode the *Angeles Crest* every day. And every day, urged on by my growing familiarity with the road and the cornering delights it provides, I rode it harder and harder. By the time I finally turned back towards my home in Virginia, it felt like an old friend. The danger I had perceived when I first arrived had receded to some place of dim remembrance. And even today, a decade later, the joys of the road far outweigh my recollection of its dangers.

The third layer. It's such a simple thing. But it's the last piece of the puzzle. The final thing that holds the promise of keeping our ass out of trouble.

If we let it.

April 2007, Sport Rider

Who We Are

*It's more than just a bunch of
guys waving at each other.*

L orton road is easy, just a couple miles of gentle turns. Not having given much thought to what route I should take, I turn south when I get to the stop sign at rt. 1. Going north isn't an option, as that would mean having to cross four lanes of busy traffic. I don't know that I can do that.

Last night I spent a few minutes trying to ride on the grass out in my parent's field in front of the house. But it was mostly dark by the time we got home from the dealership and I kept stalling on the hill. Fear of dropping the pristine new motorcycle soon prompted me to abort those efforts. It seems that riding—on grass, at least—isn't quite as simple as I imagined it would be. It was an inauspicious beginning, to be sure.

This morning, though, the sun is shining brightly and I awaken with that catching-remembrance that something very special awaits. One of those red letter days you know you'll not soon forget.

Now, tentatively easing out the clutch and feeding in throttle, the orange RD350 bucks, hesitating at the less-than-expert control inputs it's receiving, but then settles as it picks up momentum.

Rt. 1 is straight and the biggest thing I have to deal with is the overwhelming sense of vulnerability that comes with being on the road with so much traffic. I'm amazed at how exposed I feel. But within a few minutes, as those first, maiden miles roll under my wheels, the sense of abject exposure begins to diminish. I slowly begin to relax and notice other things—the raspy sound of the 2-stroke engine, the rush of the landscape, and the coolness of the wind filtering through my denim jacket. A grin breaks across my face. Finally, I'm riding a motorcycle!

Cresting one of the small hills south of Woodbridge, I see the distinct form of another motorcycle heading towards me. I'm sufficiently wrapped up in my own piloting duties that I don't pay him much attention. But suddenly, as we close on one another, he raises his left hand in a casual, offhand wave. The gesture comes as something of a surprise—I don't know him from Adam, after all. But his acknowledgement strikes an instant, welcoming chord in me. I'm all too aware that I'm a rank newbie at this, but that doesn't seem to matter—simply being out here seems to be enough. It suddenly occurs to me that perfect strangers see me in a particular, different way, simply because I'm on a motorcycle.

"Wow, that is so cool," I think to myself, as I wave in response.

§

One of the first things that becomes apparent to a new rider is that... we're different; that this activity they've chosen is not exactly mainstream. That may come as a bit of a surprise to many—to the undiscerning eye the roads seem full of motorcycles, after all. But it is ineluctably true. Society presents us with a constant stream of reminders.

Much of it is warm and welcoming and inclusive. Like we've joined some sort of club. However long we stay in this sport, there will always be a community of like-minded souls ready to provide support, encouragement, and camaraderie.

But society as a whole still views us with a whole range of stereotypes. To them, we seem a little strange. They can't imagine why anyone would voluntarily embrace a risk-laden sport like motorcycling, all in the name of recreation. And they find the streak of independence which prompts such a choice to be vaguely disquieting.

In days past that unease was expressed a bit more overtly

than it is today. I still remember the high school acquaintance of mine whose mother refused to let me park my bike in front of her house. She was okay with *me* visiting, she just didn't want that bike parked out there. I guess she was afraid the neighbors would think that her family was consorting with hoodlums.

Today it's a bit more muted. Now we're more likely to simply get the occasional long, subtly disapproving look and pursed lips from the wait staff when we walk into a restaurant with our helmet.

Or the quizzical look at work when we're discussing plans for the weekend with our coworkers. Instead of a round of golf or an afternoon in front of the TV watching football, we happily announce that... we're going riding. Of course. What else would we do?

Worst of all, of course, is the extra attention we often receive from the law enforcement community. Police officers are already wired, by training and inclination, to focus on people who live outside of societal norms, so it's probably no surprise that many of them instinctively see us as scofflaws, already guilty. (I'll apologize in advance to the many fine police officers—many of them riders themselves—who don't look at us that way. It's just that a whole lot of them do).

Notwithstanding the negatives that occasionally attach to this sport, though, being a motorcyclist has been a grand, positive differentiator for most of us. In a world which is more and more homogenized, a world which is increasingly devoid of personal risk, choosing to ride is a clear and emphatic statement about who we are, what we value, and how we look at the world.

I know that for me, personally, riding has colored my life more than anything else I have ever done. My entire adult life has been defined by it. The people in my life are without question the most important thing in the world to me—being a husband, father, brother, son, or friend defines *what* I am. And my colleagues at work all know what I do, of course, how I relate to the work that they do—there's a tag that comes with that, too. But being a motorcyclist defines *who* I am. Everyone I know looks at me through that prism.

No one understands that better than my wife, Ginny. Notwithstanding that she definitely got the short end of the stick—having a husband, like most of her friends', who likes to putter around the house instead of continually heading off towards some distant horizon surely would have been easier for her—she knows that motorcycles and riding are an indelible part of who I am. They are etched into my soul.

A half-dozen years ago I pulled up to my house in my pickup truck after a not-so-great track day down at VIR. Hearing me drive up, Ginny walked out onto the deck. Seeing my sad, rueful face, she glanced back at the totaled carcass of my SV650 in the back of the pickup. Looking back at me, after assuring herself that I was okay, she slowly shook her head and offered "you need to find a cheaper hobby."

We both laughed. But we both also knew it was a joke—because it's always been much more than a hobby to me. Indeed, she has long assumed that I'll be out riding most weekends. On those odd occasions when I'm not, she'll be the one to ask if something's wrong. And if I'm in a grouchy mood she'll be the first to suggest "why don't you go for a ride?"

She knows me well.

I suspect that's the way it is for most of us. Riding a motorcycle doesn't call to everyone. It carries a level of risk which is anathema to most. And it demands a level of competence, a degree of engagement, which is unusual in today's modern society. Like an old-time craft, the skills and the wisdom necessary to be successful at it don't come quickly, but emerge only slowly, over time. Most people today simply don't have the patience or the inclination to deal with that sort of thing.

But for those of us who do, to that tiny minority who are drawn to it, the rewards are immeasurable. For us, riding imbues life itself with color, tinges it with adventure. It connects us to a time when people weren't perhaps quite so shy about how they lived. A time when everything wasn't a careful, exacting calculus of risk and reward. A bolder time when a fear of getting hurt didn't stand as an impenetrable shield to the simple enjoyment of life.

So, yeah, those of us who ride are definitely different. But it's a good difference. We carry something that once was common, but now is rare. Something of the distilled essence of what got us all here.

We're the last wolves, in a land of sheep.

August 2007, Sport Rider

800 Miles

He rode north through the gathering darkness, knowing now he would make it home and put a finish on this 800-mile day. He was only partially glad of that.

He rode the interstate now, after 600 miles of the small, curving roads that he delighted in. Cruising easily at 80, his was very nearly the fastest vehicle on the road, a sleek, faired missile. Sitting atop the motorcycle he did not usually see that. But detaching his mind he could see himself as he must appear to those drivers around him and it pleased him. Whether he was pleased about going home he wasn't sure.

§

He had begun early in the morning, intending to stay out the night. He headed west, seeking the same thing he always sought. Just before the mountains he stopped to buy fuel, a liter of water, and a biscuit. While eating he noted the sun bore down sharply, but the humidity was low. That meant he would not sweat much in his leathers.

Finishing his breakfast, he went back into the store and bought a small bottle of baby powder. Sprinkling a little on the seat of the motorcycle, he spread it with his hand. The powder clung to everything. He wet a napkin with water from the bottle and swabbed the side panels clean.

Six more miles and the mountain pass lay before him. He attacked it hard, rolling back and forth through the curling switchbacks. The powder relieved the tackiness of his leathers, allowing him to move easily from side to side. The only sounds were the heavy thrumming of the engine, muted through the ear plugs he wore, the rush of wind past his helmet, and the gentle scurrring of the footpegs as they touched down. He loved this road. He rode it well this day.

He did not stop at the top of the mountain, as he usually did, but continued over the crest to begin the long downward spirals, maintaining his brisk pace. Halfway down the mountain he finally encountered a slower-moving car, which forced him to check his speed. He thought about it, but then decided not to double-yellow pass the car. Too soon. Too close to home. There would be plenty of time for that later.

The road straightened on the valley floor on the far side of the pass. Had he the power to conjure the thoughts in his mind, he would have thought only of the road and of riding today. But as soon as he made the flat of the valley floor the road straightened and thoughts of home intruded. He wished he could cast them away. But he had no control over the images that coursed through his head.

At the far end of the valley he turned south on the valley road. He made good time, maintaining his pace at an even 80. He ran now down the length of the valley, with mountains over both shoulders. The valley road went directly south, but it was a lazy road and it moved around rather than through the local topography. For a straight, fast road, it had much character, the man thought. He could feel himself flowing with the cut and contour of the land, and that made him feel a part of it.

§

Her eyes wet with new tears, she looked at him flatly.

"What is it?" he asked, his tone measured, but with a hint of kindness.

"I'm afraid."

"Afraid of what?" he asked.

"Afraid that you'll leave."

Her directness made him feel hollow, and he paused in his reply, finally returning "you know better than that."
He chose his words carefully so they would not be a lie.

§

Entering the parkway at Leeds was like a freshening. It was always like that—any vestiges of fatigue from the two fast hours getting there falling away to new delight in the wondrous road which ran through marvelous country. He quickly established a rhythm which carried him in a rocking cadence back and forth through the sweeping turns. He set his speed at 65, but had to work to keep it there. The smoothness of the road and the engineered consistency of the turns made it possible to go much faster. But twenty over was already pushing it. He didn't need any more points.

The low humidity made for a cool morning along the mountain crests over which the road ran. Over his shoulders lay beautiful vistas into the valleys beyond. The man knew he should stop before the morning light was gone. In the tank bag he carried his good camera, the F4, a small tripod, and several lenses. But he could not make himself stop. The road mesmerized him, as it usually did, and he continued on.

Hours later he turned off the parkway. The road leading down the mountain was crooked and technical in an unpredictable, chaotic fashion. Its rogue character lay in sharp contrast to the effortless smoothness, the harmonious consistency of the earlier road. It forced him to work harder, to pay more attention. A half-dozen miles later, by the time he pulled into the diner in the valley down below, he was wide awake, enervated by the combination of risk and the exultation that came from surmounting it.

Lunch was lazy. Long after he finished eating he continued to sit there, drawing distractedly from the glass of ice tea while gazing idly out the window at his bike. Having already come some

400 miles he could feel the first tendrils of fatigue creeping in upon him, the first knots of soreness spreading from his neck into his shoulders. Yet he was loath to think about an end to the day. The perfect day, he thought, would be one that went on and on. Riding a high alpine road that never ended.

Even as he held that thought he recognized it for what it was. Even without her to remind him, he understood it.

He popped two Ibuprofen tablets as he prepared to leave. As he climbed back on the bike he wondered what it was about these two-wheeled machines that held such a fascination to him. Why was it that they exerted such a hold on him?

Returning up the mountain he marveled at how a road can look so different when running in the opposite direction. The rising elevation and having now a hint of what to expect gave the man an advantage, but that was offset by the mild lethargy that came from also having a full stomach. Funny how things even out, he thought.

Back on the parkway, he continued south, quickly again being lulled by the sublime rhythm of the road. An hour later his bladder prompted him to pull into an overlook. After taking care of that he retrieved the map from his tankbag and spread it across his seat. He had been considering where to stop for the night and, now, gazing at the map, his eyes turned towards the college town an hour west. Pulling his eyes back towards the purple line that represented the parkway, the man visually connected several of the faint, smaller squiggles that would get him there.

The next hour and a half were the best of the day. A rocking, broken, roller coaster of a ride, tracking along a small, shaded trout stream that had him bending towards the task with an intense concentration. By the time he arrived at the town the man's face held a satisfied countenance, belying his growing tiredness.

Dropping down into cruise mode, the man motored slowly up the main drag, absorbing the youthful vibrancy that college towns always seem to exude. He nodded at a couple of flirtatious coeds who smiled at him.

At the gas station he pondered his options. Hot supper and a cold beer sure sounded good. But the glow from that run down out of the mountains still held him. He was reluctant to let it go. As he returned the handle of the fuel hose and reset his odometer he did a quick calculation. He had already come 550 miles. And there was only an hour of daylight left. But the road still called. There wasn't much south of here. But there was a terrific road that tracked northwards, back towards the interstate. Back towards home. He paused, considering. He would not get back until late in the night. And most of it would be on interstate. But at least he would be riding.

Slowly pulling on his helmet he paused one more time, stepping back to gaze at his bike, the machine that had carried him so far, in so many ways.

Nodding quietly, he climbed back aboard and thumbed the starter. Then he pulled back onto the road.

July 2010, Sport Rider

A Matter of Focus

We frequently caution ourselves to slow down, believing that in so doing we'll be safer. Sometimes we're not.

The county road out of Oak Flat runs north through the Sweedlin Valley, following the crinkled wrinkles of the landscape. It's a pretty little road, narrow, with the modest traffic common to rural communities. Just the odd car or pickup now and again, on its way to town.

On this weekday John is running it alone, his R1100RT an agreeable companion to what is turning out to be a beautiful day. The road is heavily shaded along much of its length and the sun flashing through the trees makes it harder to see into many of the corners. But John is in cruise mode on this late morning and his relaxed pace means that the road demands little from him. The miles roll by in a mellow cadence.

Part of that is choice. John spends plenty of his motorcycling time running an aggressive pace—including some of his earlier routes this morning. But he recognizes that the narrow contours of this particular road best lend themselves to a more measured pace. A place to recharge the batteries while he moves towards the mountain pass he has in mind.

Part of it is simply the character of the place. The Sweedlin Valley is nothing if not picturesque. It's hard to ride through it for any distance and not appreciate the gentle beauty which lifts from the landscape. And as the minutes tick slowly by that beauty engenders an aura of well being. A beatific sense of joy in simply being on a pretty road, with a beautiful day in hand, enjoying it all on a terrific motorcycle. All is well.

It's a surprise, then, when the soft right-hander before him suddenly hardens—the apex a deception and his line towards it a mistake. The big BMW swings wide, begins drifting across the imaginary center line. Startled out of his reverie, his heart hammering in a sudden explosion of adrenalin, John pushes hard on the bars, quickly adding lean angle. The bike dips, hewing to the urgent new control input, but there's not enough time to catch up with the disappearing tarmac. In an instant John is entirely across the road, bouncing across the narrow ditch and into the grass field on the far side. The bike shudders in the suddenly-tenuous traction, but remains upright as John wrestles it to a stop.

Shaking his head in reproach, John silently chides himself for not recognizing the decreasing radius corner, even as he whistles a sigh of relief that nothing more had come of it. He pauses for a few seconds, thinking through what just happened. He takes a couple of deep breaths to slow his heart, then pulls in the clutch and rocks the bike to get down into first gear. Peering carefully in both directions, he eases back out onto the road, glad to have tarmac under him once again.

"Okay, let's pay attention now," he murmurs to himself.

§

What happened to John that day—being caught unawares at an idle moment—has happened to all of us at one time or another. It is an inevitable part of the riding experience. It brings to mind how our mental state affects our ability to respond to unforeseen events. To deal with the unexpected. And it points to the irony that a soft, easy pace has an aspect about it which, counter-intuitively, actually introduces risk.

John, long the chieftain of our little sport-touring group, is one of the most talented riders I know. Over the years I have followed along behind him on thousands of miles of crooked pavement and admired his consistently clean lines, his outstanding judgment of pace, and his ability to get down the road with a swift, spartan efficiency. He is one of those rare riders who are deceptive in their quickness. It's no exaggeration to say that he probably could have ridden that road that day at twice the speed he was.

Alas, John was in "cruise" mode, simply enjoying the day. He was running at a speed far less than the crisp sporting pace he usually runs. And that is what got him in trouble.

When we're railing, running a spirited pace, it demands exceptional vigilance and attention to detail. We're wired, noticing everything. We're active on the controls, almost anticipating what the road might throw at us and responding instantly. We're present in the moment, fully and completely engaged, 100% of our attention devoted to what's happening in front of us. We are at the height of our powers. It's what I call "working" the road.

Conversely, when we back down into "cruise" mode any number of irrelevancies begin to intrude into our thoughts. We daydream. We fantasize. We wonder and worry. Frankly, our mind is consumed with a countless parade of things about everything *except* riding through that next corner. A corner which we take for granted. We take it for granted because it's easy and because it requires little of our attention—our mellow pace has convinced us of that.

Until the surprise. The inevitable, unexpected wrinkle somewhere down the road. It's there, waiting, guaranteed. And when we come upon it there is the sudden mad dash within ourselves to marshal our talents, to find the solution, to craft a response. To put together something that works. Usually we do, and it does. Sometimes we don't, and it all goes awry.

Things happen quickly on a curvy road. There are flashes of insight. Judgments are made in an instant. And the time in which decisions are made and then executed is measured in milliseconds.

When we are riding at pace, with our minds fully focused on the task at hand, all that works well. When we relax, however—

something that a modest pace often prompts—we can easily find ourselves unprepared to deal with any surprises that might arise. And sooner or later there's always a surprise.

None of which is to suggest that we ought to ride WFO all the time. But being mindful of that natural tendency to relax when things become too easy, we can at least remind ourselves of the need to try and remain focused; that we need to actively work to minimize those mental distractions which frequently come calling; and that we may in fact be at greater risk during a very mellow ride than one which has a bit of an edge to it.

It does suggest an interesting thought: that the sweet spot for minimizing risk is not slow and easy; nor is it hard and fast. It's riding at a pace which is just fast enough to require constant attention. One where the road imposes upon us a sufficient stream of inputs and enough decision points that there is little time for our minds to wander.

The somewhat self-righteous response to that is that we should always be paying full and complete attention. Well, duh, of course—no one disputes that. But the reality is that we often don't. Take our car-driving brethren, for instance. Think of all the distractions which exist in that world: everything from listening to the radio to fumbling to find the next CD to talking on a cell phone to carrying on a conversation with other passengers in the car—not to mention the chronic day dreaming about everything under the sun. Frankly, driving is largely an unconscious activity for most people. They direct a relatively small portion of their conscious attention to the specifics of the road, the traffic, and the control inputs of their vehicle.

Motorcycling is a far more demanding activity, of course. And the consequences of an error are far more serious. But an experienced rider has similarly long since stopped devoting significant attention to the basics of piloting his bike. Much of what he does is subconscious.

The two things that will focus his attention are dangerous

traffic—long-term riders generally have a very nuanced instinct for traffic situations which might quickly deteriorate; or a road run at sufficient pace, one that has sufficiently compressed the evaluation and decision-making process, that it allows no time for idle thought.

A sporting pace, in other words.

Here's the challenge: none of us can remain on, fully-focused, 100% engaged, all the time. It's simply too exhausting. Our minds and our psyches require a break now and again.

So by all means enjoy those mellow, smell-the-flowers interludes, both for the rest they provide and the pleasure they evoke in their own right. But just be aware that they introduce their own brand of risk.

It's all a matter of focus.

August 2008, Sport Rider

Checkmate in Two

Dawn breaks slowly, emerging with a fitful reluctance. A light overcast hazes the sky, reflecting my mood, which is anything but ebullient. The thrumming in my head, the cottony numbness of my tongue, and the sandpaper which passes for my eyelids bear silent witness to too many beers and too little sleep.

Coffee doesn't help.

But we are here to ride, so come eight o'clock we've shrugged into our riding gear and are rolling down the mountain. When we get to the bottom I drop in behind Dave and immediately switch to autopilot, steering dumbly onto his wheel tracks.

I'm kicking myself for the late night and the surfeit of "okay, one mores," smiled to the pretty barmaid, like we were singers doing a bunch of encores or something. But at least the cooling breeze coming through the chin bar of my Arai gives faint promise that maybe I'll feel human again. Someday.

If there's a saving grace, it's that our group is larger on this run than most. Kevin has brought along a bunch of friends from North Carolina. Because of the new guys and the general unwieldiness of the group, Dave is keeping the pace down.

I'm glad when we pull into Watoga for breakfast an hour later. Eggs and toast and sausage and a couple glasses of ice water bring the first tendrils of relief. And when we walk outside the sky is likewise brightening, with occasional patches of blue appearing through the broken cloud cover. Maybe the day won't be such a bust after all.

Dave's plan for the day is ambitious. He has us heading south and west towards some squiggles on the Delorme Atlas we've never been on before. New roads and new mountains to try.

But first we have to get past the traffic through this section of West Virginia. Dave has us on remote, secondary roads wherever he can, but at some point you have to deal with rt. 219, the only major north-south artery through Pocahontas County. We're stuck behind a line of slow-moving cars when we get to the really nice stretch south of Droop Mountain. That sucks. And it's a struggle to keep our dozen-odd bikes together when we begin the double-yellow-line dance.

So it's with a palpable sense of relief when we finally turn off onto an obscure county route.

We haven't gone more than a handful of miles when Jim rolls around me and slots in behind Dave. It was his "anyone want to walk up to the bar?" last night that had prompted my present misery. Watching him now, I wonder if he feels half as bad as I do. He's one of the new guys on this run but is anything but inexperienced. He and I had reminisced long into the night about bikes we had owned, roads we had run, and trips we had been on. And he had spent much of yesterday goosing the throttle, pulling wheelies, and otherwise making it plain that he was impatient to get it on. Now, apparently, having passed a sign alerting us to the mountain just ahead, is that time.

Dave waves him on around, offering him a clear road. Jim answers aggressively, spooling his CBR 600 into a long, loping wheelie as he powers around into the front. He immediately lays down the hammer, putting quick distance between himself and the rest of our group.

I watch all this unfold with surprise. Our years-long protocol has been to choose a lead rider—usually John or Dave—let them choose the day's route, then stick to the roads and the pace that they select. Jim has just broken that unwritten rule.

But even as I am processing this development, I'm charged with an enervating, predatory excitement. A moment passes. Then with a quick glance in my left mirror I likewise pull out, punching a downshift even as I roll the throttle of my BMW hard around to its stop.

It takes me a minute to catch up to him, by which time we've left the rest of the group far behind. As I pull onto his tail he acknowledges my presence by bumping the pace even further. The curling road hardens as it begins the ascent and we both bend to the task with an intense scrutiny. Faster and faster. In moments I'm at the absolute limit of my comfort zone. I run a quick calculus of how much is left, painfully aware of the disadvantages of my BMW compared to Jim's Honda. The answer comes in a flash—not much. Our spiraling run has become lit by a harsh edginess, held together by the most tenuous of threads. I shake my head, knowing how unwise all this is. But I don't stop.

Halfway up the mountain Jim makes his mistake. He glances at his mirror for just an instant, to see if I'm still there. Just the merest sliver of a second. But it's enough. When he looks back his line has already shifted the few inches that make the difference, has hardened into inevitability. It takes him off the road into the grass.

Watching it all unfold, I am aghast. In the blink of an eye Jim is a full two feet off the pavement, heading straight for a large strip of Armco. I am certain I am about to watch a man die.

Instead, he makes the greatest save I have ever witnessed. He stays on the throttle, kicking up an enormous roostertail of dirt. Struggling against the sloping, off-camber dirt bank he somehow manages to work the bucking Honda back onto the tarmac, making it just ahead of the razor-sharp Armco.

"Are you okay?" I yell as I come to a stop alongside him. Flipping up his face shield he turns toward me. Even through his helmet I can see the blanched look on his face. There's a long second while we both absorb what just happened. Then he squeezes his eyes into a smile and flips his face shield back down and drops the clutch.

§

Riding at speed is not for the faint of heart. It punishes the unwary—or simply the unlucky—with a swift harshness. We preach moderation—and believe it when we're saying it. But then we get out there where the roads are fine and the possibilities seem endless... and our restraint is left behind in a trail of spun rubber and intoxicating petrol fumes.

So it behooves us to understand this craft of ours.

One of the subtleties that sometimes is lost even on advanced riders is the need to perceive the road in a holistic fashion. To understand it as a single thread, a connected whole. Too many riders simply ride each corner as it comes to them, treating each turn as an individual entity. Alas, that's not the fastest or safest way to get down the road.

This is easily seen on a racetrack, where a rider will sometimes take a deliberately sub-optimal line through one corner in order to better set himself up for a subsequent turn. The racer is interested in optimizing his time across an entire lap and is more than happy to lose time in one corner if doing so means he'll more than make up for it somewhere else.

Such thinking is not nearly as obvious in the complicated arena of the street, but it also applies there—where we're not just trying to maximize speed, but also to find the optimal balance among all the risk factors that exist. We do this subconsciously on roads that we ride a lot. We've learned through simple repetition what the road holds. And we've adjusted our lines and pace very subtly based upon that knowledge.

I'm going to suggest two things. First, that we *think* about this inter-connectedness of corners, that it become a conscious affect of our riding style. And, second, that we practice it in the hardest realm of all—on roads that we've never been on before.

"How do you do that?" is the obvious question.

The answer is that even strange roads give off faint tell tales of what lies beyond the apex of the corner ahead. The rise and fall of the landscape, how the light touches the trees, and how the line of the horizon subtly moves in front of us all provide clues. And the road itself will impart a rhythm that, once perceived, provides a starting point for understanding what lies ahead.

The reason why all this is important, the reason why we seek to see what at first seems impossible, is so we can place our minds there, down the road. For, like a chess master, the good rider is always thinking a few moves ahead.

The benefit is that the time compression that occurs for all of us at speed is lessened. Our mental pace unwinds. The rider with his head down the road is better able to go fast on the one hand. And to deal with the unexpected on the other.

Just don't look in your mirror.

May 2010, Sport Rider

Commitment

"Turn, or die."

The beginning parts were straight, as we left the shop and headed westward. The early morning sun warmed our backs, the day soft with promise. With no rain anywhere in the forecast, surely it was a good day to finally lose my track virginity.

I had hooked up with Alan and the half-dozen others thirty minutes earlier and I'd be lying if I didn't admit that my stomach was full of butterflies. I'd been to Summit Point dozens of times over the years watching the races, of course. But now, for the first time, I'd get a chance to actually get out there myself and see what it was like. Just thinking about it brought shivers of both excitement and fear.

It was also the first time for a new concept that Cycle Sport, the Yamaha dealership where I hung my hat, was trying out. The idea was for a "track day," where riders could ride the track at speed, but without the formality or competitiveness of racing. The instructors and control riders for the day included guys like David Nees and Randy Renfrow, local WERA racers for whom the racetrack was like a second home. Randy would turn pro the following year, exposing his talents to a soon-to-be-appreciative national audience. And a couple years after that he would win the first of his AMA national championships. But to me, then, they were just the pals I hung out with at the shop.

Rolling westward, soon enough we passed Berryville and the topography began to sharpen. The formerly straight tarmac began to turn curvy. A few miles on, David turned down a route I had never been on before, one contorted by twists and turns. In my first surprise of the day—in a day full of them—he turned up the pace. Despite having the fastest and most powerful bike among our little group, I immediately began to struggle. I considered myself a pretty decent rider but these guys were clearly in a different league altogether. Using the extra acceleration at my disposal, I lit it up down every section that was even remotely straight. It didn't make any difference. I lost ground on every corner, the gap between me and the others quickly growing. Soon, the boys were gone. I had been dropped, as they say. Like a piece of rotting cheese.

§

How does one go fast around a corner? In many ways it's the existential question of our sport.

The answer, at once both simple and complex, begins in our head. In how we decide what is achievable. In what we define as reasonable. And how we frame a task which at first seems straightforward—but which in fact is actually bound to a multitude of factors.

It starts with crafting a balance between our desire—do we want to just hit that corner briskly, really hard, or do we want to absolutely rail through it?—and the risk that we perceive attendant to each of those efforts. The backdrop to it all, of course, is the worry—perhaps morphing into outright fear—of crashing. For at some unconscious level we recognize that there are limits to our ability, the capabilities of the bike, and what the road offers. Exceed any of those and you go down.

Or, as I wrote some years ago, "how much fun shall we have today?"

Once we've made that judgment of risk versus reward, we move into the realm of the corner itself. To all the factors that dictate how we will traverse it.

There are the aspects of the bike itself. How the frame performs. How the geometry of the bike affects its steering. How the tires and the suspension respond to the road. How the characteristics of the engine either expand the opportunities for or else impose limitations upon the rider. And how the ergonomics of the bike either support or detract from the whole effort.

It's interesting that riders focus so often on the bike. They twiddle with suspension settings, believing there is some magic combination which will suddenly make them fast. Or they spend money on a new pipe, expecting that the handful of horsepower they gain will somehow make a difference.

It never does, of course. Much as we love the gearhead part of the sport, the truth is that the bike is the very least of the go-fast equation. A good rider will be fast on virtually anything with two wheels. And a lesser rider will still struggle, regardless of how capable his machine is.

Which leads us to the harder aspects of getting through that corner. They exist in a tier.

First is the environment. There is the road itself—its size and composition, how it tracks, the other traffic upon it, and the traction it affords. There is our visibility through the corner—a huge factor which often dictates the line we choose. There is how the road "flows"—how the sections before and after our corner affect our entry and our exit. There is weather, which can affect our traction, our visibility, our tires, our suspension, and ourselves. And finally there are the threats that the environment presents— those objects and characteristics that might bring us to grief should our trip through the corner not happen exactly as planned.

A good rider quickly and intuitively pulls these different threads together in his mind. A glance is sufficient for him to make the judgments he needs. He connects the dots in a flash of cognition.

Notably, it's also the one area where long experience is extremely beneficial.

Remember Michael Jordan's failed attempt at becoming a major league baseball hitter, despite his unquestioned, extraordinary degree of athletic talent? Well, it wasn't a surprise to most baseball experts, who had long known that becoming a top-flight hitter requires two things: major league talent—which Jordan certainly had; and a vast mental database of pitches thrown—the visual memory of tens of thousands of baseballs coming at you while you stand at the plate. Jordan didn't have that.

Same thing on a motorcycle. The rider with the visual memory of a few hundred thousand corners will instantly see patterns and subtleties in the environment which are lost on less experienced riders. Their judgments will be faster and more accurate.

From there we move into the hardest parts of getting through that corner—ourselves. The mental and emotional aspects that we bring to bear.

There is our familiarity with the bike. Our familiarity with the road. Our tolerance for risk. Our judgment of how we're riding at the moment—are we in the zone, or is this one of our off days?

There is our management of fear—the ability to surmount our oftentimes counterproductive survival instincts that Keith Code so accurately identified many years ago. And the flip side to that—the confidence that we bring to this corner. Do we truly believe in our ability to get through it at speed?

And at some level our intuition comes into play, sampling the ephemera of possibility, the tiny bits of truth given off in an obscure fourth dimension, guiding us through it all.

There's one more thing we need.

As we arrive at the corner itself, as we move from preparing for and assessing the corner to actually riding through it we need… commitment.

Many riders make the mistake of continuing to deliberate all those aspects we've talked about even as they enter into the corner. They are afraid to commit to the turn, wishing for just a few more feet of pavement to pass beneath their wheels, a tiny bit more certainty of what the corner holds.

Such vacillation is the death of good riding.

The irony is that most corner crashes are, upon examination, entirely avoidable. They don't occur because the rider overrode the corner. They occur because the rider overrode his belief in himself. He failed to commit to the corner.

None of which is to suggest that we ought to go charging blindly into the next corner, believing that confidence alone will get us through. We've all seen those young riders who are high on testosterone and risk tolerance and low on everything else. The guys for whom it has yet to occur that the deal isn't just to get through this next corner—but through all the corners.

No, clearly we need to intelligently assess all those characteristics of the corner as it emerges in front of us. But it does mean that there is a time for making judgments and establishing a plan; and then there is a time to actually execute that plan.

So commit to the turn.

Or, as a friend of mine once solemnly intoned, "turn or die."

March 2010, Sport Rider

Hard Times

When a motorcycle is more than a motorcycle.

I'm up at 4:30am, the darkness amplifying the mystery of the day to come. I'm glad for the hours of riding that lie in front of me, for sure. But the tinge of excitement that normally accompanies an impending trip is missing. So is the mild sense of urgency that usually prompts a hurried packing of my gear. I put the pot of coffee on and take a slow, leisurely shower.

Turning on the computer, I spend a few minutes scanning emails and checking responses from the search agents I've got working. Nothing.

After my second cup of coffee I finally rise and head outside. It doesn't take long to pack the bike. And by 6am I'm finally rolling.

The weather gods are smiling. Sunshine, brightly clear, low humidity, highs near 80. It looks promising for the boys over at least the next couple of days. It's hard to take a 5-day motorcycle trip and not run into some rain, somewhere. But it's always nice when at least the first few days are sunny and nice.

It's a little chilly at the moment—43 degrees—and my hands are cold even with the Olympia 3-season gloves and the heated grips on the BMW working away. But I'm fine otherwise. The heated liner under my Aerostitch is providing its usual magic.

Heading out rt. 211, I try to think of the last time I left early on a morning, with the whole day in front of me. Seems like it's been awhile.

Dawn is already well up and as the road slowly rocks back and forth, my shadow dances along in front of me. What was it I had written years ago? "…chasing my shadow towards Thornton

Gap." That's a really cool way to start the day.

Even with everything else going on—maybe because of it—
I'm suddenly glad to be out on the road. Especially since I almost
decided not to. Something about that 4:30am wake-up call.

There's a temperature inversion as I roll up the mountain at
Thornton Gap, and again crossing the Alleghenies just east of New
Market. Rising on the ascent both times, the chill quickly
evaporates, replaced by a suffusing, warm glow. My hands
quickly warm.

An hour and a half later I'm in Staunton. After gassing up, I
roll up to the Comfort Inn to find Mark and Barton already suited
up and on the side of the road, waiting for the rest of the group.
Five minutes more and I'd have missed them. Seeds and some of
the others are getting breakfast. And Earle has already left, leading
another group on a circuitous, westward swing through West
Virginia. His ambitious route will encompass over 500 select
miles on the way towards Little Switzerland.

After quick greetings—Mark, Barton, Lew, Eric, Andy,
Mike, and a friend of Lew's are in this little contingent—we roll
quickly towards Afton mountain and the Blue Ridge Parkway.
The morning chill is gone and there is almost no traffic on the
Parkway. Absolutely perfect. Our pace is normal for our little
group—70-80mph—and few things have ever felt so right. I just
love this road. And one couldn't ask for more than this great group
of talented riders to enjoy it with. The pace is just enough to get
my blood up a bit, and the devil on my shoulder is nattering at me.
But I hang back in the middle of the pack, as I mostly do anymore,
and that helps.

A hundred and fifteen miles later we roll down out of the
mountains. After gassing up, I decide that this will be my
turnaround point. I say my reluctant farewells, and as the group
continues on south I turn back north to re-run the Parkway in the
other direction.

I'm still in that glow of riding. That golden place where

everything feels just right. The place where one's world, for a little while, has no worries. With the clear skies and low humidity, the scenery along both sides of the mountains is just breathtaking. I notice it with quick glances as I fly north at a steady 70mph and know that I should stop and take some pictures. But I don't. The place I'm in is a gift, a drug I'm loath to let go of, for even a few moments. So I keep riding.

§

That little ride was in the spring of 2002. I didn't know it at the time, but I was six months into what would eventually turn into a fifteen-month stretch of unemployment. You like to think that such an experience is an outlier, a statistical footnote you hear about on the news. Usually it is.

Alas, given the economic turmoil today buffeting the globe, it was an experience which now seems to be increasingly germane to other riders.

Being unemployed sucks. As the weeks, and then the months, pass by, it raises a whole range of threats to one's lifestyle, ranging from the starkly financial, to the quietly emotional, to the utterly pragmatic. It can be a devastating experience.

One of the obvious imperatives the situation forces is the need to reduce expenses; and the corollary need to raise money, however one can. And since motorcycling is a discretionary activity for most of us, it becomes an obvious target. A lot of guys faced with those circumstances immediately look to sell their bike.

I'm glad I didn't.

Not that I didn't think about it—I surely did. Especially as the months dragged on and my financial situation became more and more dire. But in the end, it was my bikes that saved me. They gave me a place to escape to, a place of comfort and sanity, in a world which otherwise seemed to have utterly lost its bearings.

There were changes in my motorcycling world, of course. I had to put track days on hold. And I had to cut back on the handful of overnight trips that I usually take every year, as in my little jaunt to meet up with my buddies above. There was no way I could afford the several-hundred-dollar motel and restaurant charges that such trips inevitably bring. And even on day-rides I would eschew the cafes or fast-food restaurants which normally are the venue for lunch, instead pulling out the peanut butter and jelly sandwich I had packed along. You save every dime you can.

It doesn't mean you can't take trips. You just have to do them a little differently. Pull out that old, unused-in-forever tent and sleeping bag and it's amazing how cheaply one can travel. Camping has its own unique allure in the best of times. As a bastion of opportunity for those in strained economic circumstances it holds few equals. I took several multi-day camping trips during that otherwise forgettable time and they provided some of my most memorable motorcycling moments, ever.

Tires were the hardest—I went through seven sets that year. And it was the tire budget that quickly became the arbiter of how much I could ride. I found myself carefully calculating tire mileage—how much tread was left on each of my two bikes and when the next set would be needed—and allotting myself so many miles on a given day. Even with a strict mileage allowance, I spent a lot of money on rubber over the course of that year—seven sets of motorcycle tires aren't cheap. It was the sole luxury I allowed myself.

Mostly, it was the few hours I got away on otherwise mundane, average days that made the difference. I quickly fell into a routine of spending several hours every morning doing the job-search thing—and then going for a ride. As the months dragged on with little in the way of prospects, those mornings became more and more discouraging. But as dark and depressing as they became, I always had that afternoon ride to bring me back.

Those back-road jaunts never failed to make me feel better. They let me finish the day with hope.

To those of you who find yourselves in similar circumstances, you have my utmost empathy and respect. I know how hard it can be, how desperate it can make you feel. Short of death, divorce, or debilitating illness, it's probably the hardest thing any of us ever have to deal with. And although at the end of the day we all have to make the hard choices we think are right for ourselves and our family, I'd encourage you to think long and hard before selling that bike out in the garage.

It might just be part of the answer that you need.

July 2009, Sport Rider

Journey to Glass Mountain

Of young men and old men and
paying it forward.

It was on the descent of Sherando Mountain that the old man came upon the group of five sportbikes. On seeing the extra headlight behind them the lead rider bumped the pace, and so the old man made no effort to pass. He simply hung at the rear, enjoying the road and the visual choreography of the bikes in front of him.

His quick observation was that these were good riders, excepting the fellow in the rear, the one right in front of him. This guy was obviously struggling to stay with his mates. He blew the line on many corners and nearly ran off the road more than once. After a bit the old man backed off a ways, fearing that his presence might be contributing to the struggling rider's anxiety.

He didn't intend to stay hooked up with these riders, but after forty minutes of watching the numerous miscues of the fellow in the rear he was convinced that this was a disaster in the making. When the group pulled into the gas station, the old man followed them in.

After fueling, the old man walked over to the bench outside the door where the riders were milling around. Nodding to the young men, he introduced himself. They were a friendly bunch, obviously impressed with his ability to match their pace, and quickly included him in their laughing discussion of the road just run. When they began to suit up a few minutes later it was Jeremy, the young fellow in the rear, who asked if the old man wanted to ride with them. He didn't really want to, but the plaintive look on the young man's face made him reconsider.

"Sure," he said, after a moment. Then turning so the others

couldn't hear, the old man added "You need to take it easy out there."

Jeremy looked at him with a slightly pained look and nodded. "I know."

The old man hung with them for the rest of the afternoon. Despite his admonition to Jeremy, the young man continued to struggle. It was obvious he was determined to stay with his faster friends, but had neither the skill nor the experience to do so. The old man, convinced throughout the afternoon that he soon was to be witness to tragedy, breathed a sigh of relief when they finally pulled into the motel parking lot.

Two to a room, the ride leader tossed the key card to the old man. "You and Jeremy, okay?"

After dinner and a couple of beers at the restaurant across the street, the riders wandered back to their rooms.

Inside, the old man finished stowing his gear. Turning to Jeremy, he looked at the earnest young man. "How long have you been riding, son?"

"About six months."

The old man nodded, the answer having affirmed what he expected.

"You know you're going to get hurt, don't you?"

Jeremy looked at him with a blank expression. "Look, I know I'm not the best rider in the world. But my friends tell me I'm doing okay. They're all pretty experienced and they say that all I have to do is keep riding with them and do what they do and pretty soon…" His voice trailed off.

The old man gave him a hard look. "You believe that?"

Jeremy shrugged. "I dunno." He looked down, and then back at the old man. "How else do you get to be fast?"

The old man let the question hang in the air for a moment while he studied the boy's face. He started, and stopped. Then started again, more slowly. "You need to take a track school. And then you need to do another one. And then another. Then you need to do a bunch of regular track days." The old man paused. "And you have to live through the early days. That's how you get to be fast."

Jeremy looked at him. "I don't know. The racetrack seems pretty extreme. And anyway, I can't afford it."

The old man sighed, shaking his head. He pondered for a moment, then sat down on the bed, nodding at Jeremy to sit on the other.

"Look, there aren't any short cuts." The old man paused. He started to say something else, but then stopped.

"Listen Jeremy, when you go out tomorrow you need to do a few things. First, you need to stop hauling ass deep into every corner and then grabbing a big handful of brakes just before you pitch your bike into the turn. The speed you think you're gaining by doing that is a mirage. You end up rolling through the corner with less than optimum corner speed. And because your exit speed is less than it might have been you end up paying for it long after the corner is behind you."

"Forget trail braking," the old man went on. "Forget going deep into the corner at a speed you know you can't sustain. That just blows up your anxiety level. Instead, way before the turn decide what your entrance speed needs to be. Then set it. Roll into the corner and run that speed all the way through to the apex. At that point you can begin to add throttle as you slowly power out. That does a couple things. It settles the suspension early, giving you a higher corner speed with a whole lot less drama. It eliminates the distraction of braking and allows you to pay attention to the corner itself, your line, and what your tires are telling you. And it calms you down. Since you're no longer hurling yourself deep into the corner at at a speed you know you can't hold, speed which you have to scrub, you'll automatically relax."

The old man paused. "Motorcycles are really great at doing one thing really well—be that accelerating, braking, shifting, or turning. They're a whole lot less happy about having to do a whole lot of different things at the same time. So set your entrance speed early. You think you can do that?"

Jeremy nodded.

"Okay. Next, you need to be in the right gear well before you tip your bike into the corner. Shifting late is a distraction at the very point you can least afford it, and it unsettles the suspension."

"How do I know what gear to be in?" Jeremy asked.

"That's a good question," the old man answered. "It's something that varies a little bit from bike to bike. But here's a tip that works for most: Put your bike in the gear corresponding to the first digit of those yellow caution signs you see. So if the sign shows a maximum speed of 20 or 25, put your bike in second gear. If the sign says 30 or 35, put it in third."

Jeremy brightened. "That's easy to remember. But that seems like a lot lower gear than I've been running. Why would you do that?"

"Because you want to control your bike with the throttle," the old man answered. "By being in a lower gear you'll be running higher revs. That puts your engine in the fat part of its torque curve. The bike becomes much more tractable. It'll respond immediately to even subtle changes in your throttle position. You'll have more of both acceleration and deceleration instantly available. And you want that. You want that because you want to use the throttle as your primary control, the one thing you use to manage your speed, your acceleration, your deceleration, and even your line through the corner. "

"I guess I never realized you could do all those things with just the throttle," Jeremy said.

"No, it's not obvious," the old man replied. "And it's something a lot of riders miss. As you roll your bike towards a corner, use tiny changes in your throttle position to first set your speed and then, if need be, to adjust it."

"Okay, I think I can do that," Jeremy said.

"Good. Now do you know what positive throttle means?"

"You mean like to have the throttle open or cracked?" Jeremy asked.

"Exactly," said the old man. "Well the suspension on your bike is really designed to work well under only one condition: When riding down the road under positive throttle. If you roll off the throttle you'll instantly notice the weight shift forward. The front suspension loads and there is some degree of chassis upset. If you add in any braking, it gets even worse. So make any speed adjustments you need to well before you begin to tip your bike into the corner. Once you reach that point, stay on the throttle, no matter what else happens."

"What if I end up going in too hot?" Jeremy asked.

The old man nodded. "Yeah, that'll happen sometimes. It doesn't matter. Stay on the throttle, no matter what."

The old man paused. "Okay, last few things. Stay off the brakes. They'll get you in far more trouble than they'll get you out of. So stay off 'em."

"Don't hang off the bike and don't be trying to touch your knee to the ground. Lean into the corner with your inside shoulder, like you're aiming the sights of a rifle, but keep your ass planted in the seat."

"And look—look hard—at wherever it is that you want to go. Because that's where you're going to end up."

"You think you can remember all that?"

Jeremy nodded. "I think so."

"Good. The thing is, Jeremy, there are lots of techniques for riding fast on a motorcycle. Many of them are appropriate for a very advanced rider or in a controlled environment like a racetrack. But many of them don't translate well to riding on the street. But you do these things I've told you and you'll be alright. Later on, after you've gotten a bunch more miles under your belt you can try some of that other stuff if you want, but forget them for the time being. Okay?"

"Okay," Jeremy replied.

"And remember," the old man softly intoned, "riding is as much about this"—he tapped the side of his head—"as it is about any kind of technique you apply to the bike."

Jeremy nodded thoughtfully. "I'll try and remember that."

§

The old man awakened early the next morning, long before Jeremy or his pals would rise. He packed his bike quietly in the dark, with just the faintest tinge of light smudging the horizon. By his calculation he would be at Glass Mountain in about an hour, just when dawn was fully realized. How long had it been? Nearly twenty years since the trip over that pass with John, his old riding partner.

As he thumbed the starter he looked toward the room where Jeremy still slept. The young man who reminded him so much of himself, a long, long time ago.

"Good luck my young friend."

December 2008, Sport Rider

Old Age and Treachery

We were tired of the rain. You expect some, of course, on a six-day road trip. But after a couple days of off and on wet stuff—compounded by the mud—we were hungry for some clean, dry pavement.

Day one had been nice, a good omen on which to start the trip. And day two started auspiciously, with good roads and skies that, if not brightly sunny, at least weren't loosing anything upon us.

But then, as the day advanced and we descended deeper into the heart of Appalachia, rolling through southwestern Virginia, southern West Virginia, and into southeastern Kentucky, a light, misting rain had begun. Passing through the tiny towns of Inman and Lynch and Stoney Fork, everything was set off by a dull, depressing grayness.

Severe thunderstorms had pounded the area in the days prior to our departure and had left a layer of sand and mud on many of the roads. Crossing Black Mountain, the highest peak in Kentucky, the bikes felt like we were running on flat tires the road was so squirrelly. That forced a modest pace—a disappointment on what we could tell would be a terrific road in better conditions.

Worst of all was the limestone and coal dust from the many mines in the area which mixed with the misting rain to coat everything in a layer of gray sludge. By the time we stopped in Pineville for a late lunch, our bikes were covered in the concrete-mix-like goo. Even those of us who don't normally worry too much about such things shook our heads in dismay. It was easily the dirtiest any motorcycle of mine had ever been.

Day three had seen more rain—enough to cause us to abbreviate our day's ride and head back to the lake resort where we were staying. An early dinner and cold brews seemed the better part of valor.

And so it's no surprise that we were a bit antsy for some decent weather. When day four finally broke with clear blue skies and pleasant temps, we suited up in anticipation.

And so it proved to be. Other than a minor interruption when we stopped to fix the clutch on Lew's Ducati, the morning passed in a blur of good roads and laughing camaraderie. Tennessee has a lot of great motorcycling byways and we did our best to see as many of them as we could.

After lunch, Earle led us on a long, looping route intended to get us back to our home base back at the resort. Middle Tennessee is blessed with a rolling countryside not unlike the Virginia Piedmont I'm familiar with. And we couldn't have asked for a more perfect afternoon in which to enjoy it—perfect temperatures and an azure blue sky contrasting sharply with the deep green of the verdant landscape. The narrow ribbons of black roadway snaking through it all were simply the desert. We lost no time in getting down to business.

As happens, we occasionally would come upon a slower vehicle. No worries. Most people were cool and would pull to the right to help make room for our double-yellow passes. The usual sport riding stuff.

But not the Harley rider. As Earle rolled up behind him the guy was doing the posted speed limit—if that. Earle hung there behind him, obvious in his mirrors. But as the rest of our six-bike freight train quickly stacked up behind the cruiser pilot, he remained planted in the middle of the lane, seemingly oblivious.

Earle gave him a mile. And then, with no sign that the guy was going to move to the side, when a smidgen of space opened in front he dialed up his K1200S and swung around in a quick double-yellow pass. Lew went with him, the bass notes from his Desmodromic twin booming back towards us, a reproachful counterpoint to the Harley's own sound.

One by one, the rest of us pulled up behind the Harley and,

as soon as there was a little space, sped around him. When it was my turn, an instant after I began my pass a car appeared around the corner ahead. A flashing calculation told me I'd be fine and so I stayed hard on the throttle as I rolled the R1200GS a bike length in front of our cruiser friend. I had the merest glimpse of a white mustache on an aged face as I pulled past him.

That left only Eric, bringing up our rear. I kept an eye peeled in my mirrors for the tell-tale of his Triumph's headlight. A half-mile of hard turns later, there it was. Okay, all good. I relaxed. So long, Pops. We cranked back up to a sporting pace.

It was nearly a mile after that, as we emerged onto a slightly straight section, that I suddenly realized that Eric was riding my ass, something he doesn't usually do. And that there were now two headlights behind me, not one. Looking again, I did a double-take. The guy behind me was the Harley rider! Eric was still behind him!

Few things have surprised me as much in all my years of riding. Our pace over the last mile, while not grossly excessive, was certainly well beyond that which any Harley this side of a VR 1000 should have been able to match. I was stunned.

Mixed in with my disquieting sense of the impossibility of it all, my first thought was that he was an off-duty police officer and was after us for the double-yellow passes. My second thought was that maybe he was just pissed at us for having passed him that way. In any case I was torn between wanting to light it up and get out of there and wanting to stop and talk to the guy. Regardless of what it was that motivated his sudden hot pursuit, here clearly was an incredibly skilled motorcycle pilot.

I began to watch him closely, glancing in my mirrors as soon as I rotated up through each of the curves. This was a seriously good road, the kind that any sport rider would instantly fall in love with. The kind that would force all the cruiser guys into a slow toddle.

Only, not our new friend. For ten miles he stayed with us,

curve for curve. It was true that he would fall back a bit in the more serious stuff, but not by much. Not nearly as much as you'd think. Watching him, I just kept shaking my head.

It was ten miles of the most impressive motorcycle riding I've ever witnessed.

That evening, back at the resort and with beers in hand, Eric and I regaled our compadres with the story of the mysterious Harley rider. They had been oblivious to it all, of course, having been ahead of what was happening; having assumed that that guy had long since been dropped just like all the other vehicles we had passed that day. They were incredulous when they heard that he had stayed with us for all those miles.

"You know," I ruminated, "beyond the obvious difference in handling capability that our bikes had over his, the biggest thing that separated us from him was how close to the edge he had to ride on *every* corner. While we had plenty of margin, plenty of spare ground clearance to draw upon to deal with anything unexpected, he had to take his bike to the absolute limit of its capabilities on every turn. Over and over, for miles. All while knowing that if he misjudged a single corner by so much as a hair's breadth it would put him on the ground."

Even ceding the likelihood that he was intimately familiar with the road, it was a lesson for the ages. And it was an object reminder that good riding is far more about the rider, and what he brings to the table, than it is about the equipment.

That's sometimes a hard thing to accept for those of us who too-often lust after the latest sporting machinery. We use the performance benefits we ascribe to that new machinery as our justification for wanting it. We yearn for the reduced lap times we imagine it will provide at our next track day. And we day dream about how it will make those rocking Sunday rides so much better.

When, really, it's always been about us.

Smiling, I raise a silent toast to the old guy—to all the old guys—who got that.

But I still want that 1098R.

September 2008, Sport Rider

Questions Without Answers

Probably the thing we most fail to do.

The last vestiges of comfort are gone shortly after dawn, with the sun still low in the sky. By the time the first session begins, the suffusing heat and humidity which would mark the day are already rapidly climbing. Georgia in July is hot. It's surely not a day to worry about getting heat into your tires.

Nor is it a day on which one expects to crash.

But something is amiss. As I pull into the pits 20 minutes later I'm still trying to figure out what it is. It's not the bike, which seems reasonably sorted. Nor is it the track—the circuit here at Road Atlanta is providing the sterling grip that it usually does. But still, something doesn't feel quite right. I don't have that dialed-in feeling that I usually expect.

I shrug it off, chalking it up to first-session jitters.

But then the second session is the same. I feel a general sense of lethargy, a torpor which is reflected in my riding.

Heading out for my third session, my mind shoves aside the frustration and abides a moment of gladness at being here, with two full days of track time in front of me. Up the hill out of turn one, I drag my attention back to the task at hand. I'm still building speed out of the pits, searching for that synced-up feeling for pace that frames a day at the track.

I know I should give my tires a couple of laps. But as I start down the long, storied, back-straight I can already feel the exuberance building. A half-minute later I steal a quick glance at the concrete wall as I sweep past the pits. A voice in the back of my mind whispers a caution as I head into my first flying lap. But that voice is already being drowned out by a sudden determination to push through my morning disquiet and get to the crisp, fast laps that I came here for.

Slicing through turn two, I hold to that moment of restraint necessary before heading into the decreasing-radius turn three. Perfect. It sets me up for a clean entrance into the downhill esses. I nod in satisfaction as I head into those.

Pressing now, hard into the right-hander, I add a couple clicks of throttle. Although my boots are as high and tight on the footpegs as I can get them, my toe slider is nevertheless down on the pavement and my mind, in a curious bit of worry, imagines the tiny strands of plastic trailing off behind me. I wonder how long the sliders will last. I didn't bring a spare pair.

And then, in the flash of an instant, I'm down.

I'm awed by the violence. There is a cacophony of formless shape and color exploding through my field of vision and I realize that I'm tumbling, not sliding. There's a surreal sense of disbelief, a voice saying this can't be happening. But the sudden headache from where my helmet smacked down and the sharp pain from my right ankle tell me otherwise. I wonder how bad this will end up being.

As I finally come to rest against the tire wall across the grass outfield there's a quick sense of relief—a lot of things hurt, but everything more or less seems to work. Slowly sitting upright, my thoughts begin to congeal around a single question.

"What the hell happened?"

§

Crashing a motorcycle sucks. It is as stark a reminder as our sport has that we screwed up. The only good that can ever come from it is… a lesson. A lesson in what not to do again.

Riders crash for all sorts of reasons. With newcomers to the sport it's often simple inexperience that brings them to grief. They already have a built-in tendency to concentrate too much on the machine—to stare at the instruments and to over think what they are doing. They use an inordinate amount of their attention focusing on the bike rather than the environment. Combine that with the peer pressure that often comes with riding with buddies who may have more experience, and it's no surprise that new riders often fall down—with reasons that are usually obvious.

But what about the rider who has gotten through that phase, the intermediate and advanced rider for whom those basics have long since been assimilated? What causes them to go down?

Unfortunately, there's often not a clear answer. An experienced rider is operating his motorcycle at a very different level—including perhaps much higher speeds. He is exerting far more nuanced influences on its controls at the same time that he is interpreting very subtle cues from the bike. And he's doing all that while interacting with the road itself in a far richer way. Combine all that and suddenly the things that can go wrong have dramatically increased in number at the same time that they have become far more difficult to discern.

There are some things that stand out, however—causes that seem overrepresented in crashes by the cognoscenti. Among them would be things like cold tires, inattention, over confidence, pressing too hard, fatigue, and lapses of judgment.

Judgment, in particular—that parent voice inside our head that should be watching over everything—is frequently an early casualty in the prelude to a crash. Judgment isn't often viewed as a riding skill, a competency to be developed. And yet, as the progenitor of all our decision making—where should I ride today, what should I wear, who should I go with, what shall my pace be, what should my line through that corner be, and on and on—it sets the stage for everything that comes after. Absolutely, judgment should be nurtured. Alas, it's a lot harder to learn judgment than something like trail braking or how to wheelie. And it's usually the first thing we toss aside when we start having fun and get all happy.

None of these causes are new, of course. We've heard them all before. The important thing to realize is that these are all "soft" factors. They defy a quick understanding of what happened, rarely raising their head as a single, obvious cause of a crash. How, then, do we figure it out?

In the aviation world every crash is examined in minute, exacting detail. No stone is left unturned in trying to determine what caused it. And that information is then disseminated widely. You can actually buy books that are only about airplane crashes. Treatises that lay out in grim detail case study after case study of how it all went wrong up there. Similarly, aviation magazines frequently showcase crash or near-crash incidents, detailing the particulars of what real world pilots faced.

And pilots embrace that stuff, because they know that understanding what their counterparts went through—how some of the stuff those other pilots did worked, and how some of it didn't—may someday save their own ass.

That kind of critical analysis contrasts sharply with the attitude too often seen in the motorcycling community—where oftentimes our crashes are embellished for dramatic effect and where a busted up bike or a pair of scarred leathers are somehow seen as badges of courage. And where there's usually little or no attempt to seriously decompose the crash and come up with an answer to the question.

And therein lies the message: We need to intellectualize this sport of ours. When we crash we need to sit down and think long and hard about everything that preceded it and everything that was a part of it. We need to study it. We need to write it down. We need to examine our bike for clues. We need to go back and visit the place it happened, if necessary. We need to bend our minds to the puzzle until the cause—or, more likely, causes—reveals itself. The answer is there.

And then, understanding it, we need to add it to our body of experience—that list of lessons we don't want to have to learn a second time.

That's especially important if we've experienced more than one crash over a relatively short span of time. A decade ago, after having enjoyed dozens of incident-free track days over many years, I suddenly found myself the not-so-proud author of three racetrack crashes over as many years. A crash rate I found utterly unacceptable. That prompted some long and reflective thinking about what I was doing and how I was doing it.

If you're crashing multiple times, there's almost always a common thread that runs through them. You need to figure out what it is.

Those scarred leathers? They're simply a reminder that, for a single moment in time, we sucked.

August 2009, Sport Rider

Redskin Sundays

As I turn down Piney Mountain, any pretense that the riding season has much left to it quickly goes away. The air has that cutting coolness that prompts in me a shiver. Partly from the temperature. Partly from the knowledge that winter will soon be upon us.

It's not a surprise, of course. Summer wanes. Those long, lazy days full of light and warmth slowly disappear, the golden rays and that comforting heat gradually receding, like the tide. It's not all bad. At first it's just a little cool, not really cold. And with the falling humidity the air turns sharp and clear and wonderfully pleasant, just in time to enhance the colorful spectacle that the turning of the leaves provides. There are pumpkins and Halloween and the first fires at night in the woodstove. There's a new football season and the World Series. But even amongst all those happy things you know it's coming. And that knowing imparts a bittersweet tang to it all. And, soon, sure enough, there it is—a day you can no longer pretend it's "just a little cool." You stand out there on the train platform in the darkness of an early workday morning, seriously shivering, grousing at yourself for not wearing a jacket. The next day you do. And so it begins.

And then instead of leaving early on those weekend rides in order to beat the heat, you let the early morning hours slide away while you sit in a chair with your coffee and a book, waiting for it.

But it's bright and sunny on this early afternoon and I push those thoughts away. As I sluice through the slalom down to the creek I can't help but smile. The pavement is a little bumpy down through there but I know the line to take. The corners have that gilded feel that let's you know you're dialed-in. It's going to be a good day.

Past the log cabin, onto the little hundred-yard straight under the canopy of trees, exuberance takes hold and the spooling engine on the Gixxer lofts the front end a few inches. My smile breaks into a laugh.

And then my boots are back on the pegs and my eyes narrow their focus to the road ahead and my hands are grasping the grips with that ever-so-light touch that means serious business. The sound of the wind spilling over the cockpit fairing is overwhelmed by the rising exhaust note emanating from beneath me. Something both primal and new.

And for a handful of miles it's just the dance. The one that never grows old. The one that's part chess, part ballet, and part sword fight. If you asked me later to describe the world I passed in those few minutes, I couldn't. All I'd be able to conjure would be an image of aliveness along a spiraling roadway, threaded to a feeling of euphoric certainty. The old magic.

The stop sign at Orlean drops me back into the here and now. The dog at the corner doesn't run out to greet me like he usually does, and I wonder for an idle moment where he is. Inside, I suppose, like it seems the rest of the world is. I click down into gear and wheel slowly down the hill. A few hundred feet along, the parking lot of the country store—usually host to a few bikes— is empty. I nod knowingly. I'll have the mountain to myself.

Glancing at my watch, I note that the game started twenty minutes ago. I abide a moment's wonder of what might be going on. If there is any score. But as much as I'd like to be watching the game, doing this—being out on the road—is far more important to me.

That puts me in a very distinct minority—Redskins fans are a notoriously passionate bunch. But even a love as deep as football pales in comparison to the special magic that two wheels brings. Something you can do and experience and feel, not just watch. And as much as I miss not seeing the games, my reward for forgoing them is roads which are, for a few hours, uncommonly free of traffic. It wasn't just because of the temperature that I shifted my ride into the early afternoon.

For a dozen winding miles I don't see another vehicle. As I approach the bottom of the mountain the lack of traffic prompts me to take a gamble. Two years ago they dropped the speed limit on the eastern flank of the mountain from 55 to 45; and then later to 35. That, along with an intense level of law enforcement attention and a mountain of reckless driving citations was successful in driving away the sport riders who once used to flock here. I'm betting that the dearth of traffic today means an equally light LEO presence.

It's not a bet to take lightly. But a quick calculation tells me that I'll only be hanging out on that limb for eight minutes or so.

Even though it seems like an eternity since I've ridden the mountain at speed, as soon as I click down into third at the entrance to the long left-hander all that time slides away, leaving a memory as fresh as if it were yesterday. Like going home after a long absence, only to find everything just exactly as you remembered it.

There's the right-hand hitch, the decreasing-radius corner that was the scene of so many crashes back in the day, and then I'm into the main ascent, the bike flowing through the turns with an effortlessness so sublime that I'm convinced it must be preternatural. Like Zeus rising.

At double the speed limit the character of the road is different. It has a beckoning, come-hither quality, like the sharp knowing glance from a girl you once gave no thought to. You know instantly there's something here both dangerous and divine.

The mistake the squids used to make, of course, was not holding an even pace; not understanding that the speed they added in the little straight sections couldn't be sustained through the corners. They turned a road of wonders, with curves to be picked like so many beautiful petals, into a minefield they had to tip-toe through.

At the back of my mind there's the nagging worry of

encountering an oncoming trooper. But as I near the top something tells me this ride is blessed, and so I hold my pace over the summit. The left-hander with the Armco lying in wait to punish any miscue passes in a blur. And then the rest is a flying lap, with only a few minor tweaks to my line to accommodate a couple of diesel smears. Other than that it's a classic run, one to add to the thousand or so before it.

As the road flattens out in the valley below I'm torn between the delicious remembrance of what a stellar section of road that is, what an incredible hit to the senses; yet the pained knowledge that it is now mostly lost to us.

That was a thousand-dollar bet I put on the table.

Two hours later, sitting on the bench outside in front of the tiny general store drinking my bottle of water, I glance at the Suzuki a few feet away. It sits framed by the creek and the small white church in the background a hundred yards away, with the Blue Ridge Mountains rising behind them. Though I can't actually see it, in my mind's eye I can see the snaking trail of the Blue Ridge Parkway, way up in the sky along those ridgelines. I've stopped at the overlook up there before, similarly peering down into this little foothills valley trying to see this store, this bench, and this little gem of a road. I've never been able to, but that doesn't stop me from trying.

The flat angle of the sun and the lengthening shadows remind me that we're only six weeks away from the winter solstice. Next Saturday I'll be loading my truck with my .270 single-shot and .30-06 bolt-action rifles, a pocketful of careful handloads, and the camping gear I'll need for a week away hunting. And I know that as I still hunt those steep ridges west of our camp, rising to the very peak of the Appalachians, I'll frequently turn my gaze down along the vertiginous slopes and the hollows below defined by them, imagining the wonderful, crooked roads that run through them, and think of riding.

Standing, I tip the last of the water into my mouth, tossing the empty plastic bottle into the trash can beside the bench. The game should be just about over. Time to go home.

January 2009, Sport Rider

Road Rage

It's coming. Sooner or later.

"It's as good as Deals Gap," Jim said.

That got my attention. I looked at him with sudden seriousness.

"Really?"

"Yeah, really," he nodded.

That was years ago. Jim and I had been discussing good roads in the Mid-Atlantic region, as we often did. He had discovered this little treasure in the Eastern Panhandle of West Virginia on one of his recent adventures. And his comment had instantly made me want to go find it.

It didn't take long. On one of our trips just a few months later, Dave—another friend who was familiar with the route—had led us up rt. 220 to where the secret road began.

Alas. It was a very nice road, to be sure. It wound for miles through an isolated, rustic canyon. It was a pretty road, one to enjoy for its mellow character. Most definitely a fun road.

But it was no Deals Gap.

Sure, it had plenty of curves. But the road was narrow and abrupt, with sketchy pavement in spots. And guard rails that frequently came to the very edge of the pavement, forcing a rider towards the center of the road and seriously limiting the line one could take. Most of the curves were blind.

It was a road you couldn't really get your suspension working on. You most certainly couldn't rail on it.

I marked it in my mind as one of those pleasant little roads I'd welcome visiting again, but probably wouldn't go out of my way to do so.

Fast forward a handful of years and that's what I'm thinking as Michael, David, and I cruise northward. We had left our homes in Northern Virginia early in the morning and were now long into a 400-mile loop through West Virginia. It had been a terrific day so far. We had enjoyed a mix of roads—everything from technical, out-of-the-way county routes to bigger roads with high-speed sweepers, to a single, gnarly, oh-so-cool mountain road that connected nowhere to nowhere and made me glad I had brought my GS rather than the Gixxer or KRS. Now we're heading back north on rt. 220 and I'm wondering if we're anywhere near Jim's secret, good-as-Deals-Gap road. I wouldn't mind riding it again.

A few miles later I get my answer as Michael turns left. "Smoke Hole Road" is written on the little green sign. I smile to myself.

Michael and David are both excellent riders. Brothers, they grew up riding bikes. Now, decades later, they bring that relaxed assurance that comes from many years of riding. Michael is riding a Buell Firebolt and David is on an RC51.

Michael has led all day, adjusting our pace to suit the road we're on. I've been impressed by his judgment, running a crisp, fast pace where conditions warranted; pulling back our tempo where it wasn't.

Now, on this pleasant, narrow little road, Michael sets a relaxed pace that has us gliding through the turns with smiles on our faces. The road is demanding enough that even at our reduced pace there is little time for sightseeing, but we're able to steal the odd glance here and there at the bucolic landscape. The forest the route tracks through, the odd house or cabin that sit hard along the roadway, and the creek running next to us all add to the atmosphere.

It's around twenty minutes later, after we've run most the length of the road, that we come upon the truck. Because of our reduced pace we've been running pretty close together, our three bikes within a handful of bike lengths of each other. Third in line, I'm maybe two seconds behind David, just in front of me; and four seconds behind Michael.

I come around the blind left-hander to see a large, red Ford F-250 King Cab pickup halfway off the road, partially in the ditch on the left-hand side of the road. It's a surprising sight. He's deep enough in the ditch that his front axle is almost on the ground. It's the vision of that that has my attention in the split-second before I'm past him. It seems an oddly-poor job of parking if he was just fishing or hiking and it makes me wonder if he ended up there from having jerked to the side of the road to avoid Michael.

There's no time to sort out that question before we're around the next corner and gone.

Five minutes, and a handful of miles later, we get to the end of the road. David pulls up alongside Michael at the stop sign and the two brothers start talking. Thirty seconds go by. Then a minute. I can't hear what they're saying, but the length of the conversation tells me they must be talking about the truck. That answers the question.

Finally, Michael turns right, followed by David. I'm just easing out the clutch when the sound of screeching tires on my left prompts me to freeze. It's the red truck, which has come lurching up alongside me. I'm taken aback, first by the unexpected sight, then by the shouted obscenities by the four people inside. After gesturing profanely at me for an instant, the truck launches down the road after Michael and David. My first thought is that it has been every bit of six or seven minutes since the clear-to-me-now incident where Michael and the truck driver must have surprised each other on that blind corner. Normally that would have been plenty of time for the anger of a traffic altercation to subside.

This is not good.

I fall in behind the truck, trailing at a reasonable distance.

This is a bigger road, straight, and it only takes a few seconds for the truck to catch the two riders. They're doing the 55mph speed limit and either they don't see the truck, or they don't realize its import. After pressing within inches of David's ass for a few seconds, the truck jerks around in a pass. Once in front, it slows, trying to force them to stop.

Now fully aware of the situation, Michael attempts to swing around in a pass. The truck lurches leftward to block the road. Reacting, Michael quickly moves to the right, looking for space on that side. Just as quickly the truck does likewise, keeping the road blocked.

David, following and seeing the gap that has now opened up on the left, accelerates hard up that side. The truck, seeing it is too late to block the road, swings hard in an attempt to hit him. He is a microsecond too late, missing the RC51 by inches.

Several baited seconds pass as the truck continues to weave from one side of the road to the other, keeping it blocked, even as it slows.

Timing his move, Michael waits until the truck has moved to the right and then launches a pass up the left, just as his brother had done moments before. And again, the truck shoots left in an effort to hit the bike. Michael avoids being struck only by diving off the pavement, tracking a foot into the soft debris of the shoulder. I breathe a sigh of relief as the fishtailing Buell finally makes it around the truck and accelerates into the distance.

The truck now drifts to the right and stops, waiting for me. I judge I can get around him easily enough. But I'm not familiar with this road or what obstructions might lie ahead and a quick calculus tells me that I do not want this truck behind me. I pull up alongside to have a chat.

§

It's unfortunate, but anger on the highway is an increasingly common aspect of modern America. And as motorcyclists, we are particularly vulnerable. The open-vehicle freedom which attracts us to two wheels in the first place automatically makes us more susceptible to those who would turn to violence.

Some might suggest a macho, in-your-face response when confronted with an angry driver. To that I'd simply offer that—Hollywood scripts notwithstanding—a motorcycle makes a very poor platform from which to wield a weapon or otherwise play the tough guy.

The best thing, if you can't defuse the situation, is to simply get out of there. Use the one advantage you have—your bike's speed and maneuverability—to put space between you and your attacker.

Our little tete-a-tete that day? It turned out okay. I discussed things with the occupants of the truck for a couple of minutes and by the time I pulled away a hint of perspective had begun to seep back into their thinking.

Michael and David were waiting for me a mile up the road. "Get going," I motioned emphatically. It had been a close-run thing. I wanted time and distance between us and that truck.

Be careful out there.

October 2009, Sport Rider

Solo

This.

After refueling, I'm quickly back on the Parkway, glad for its coolness. More stops. More pictures. But after awhile, as the afternoon progresses, I begin to have that pressed feeling. Like I'm late. I had planned on staying at Deals Gap tonight, in one of their cheap motel rooms since I need to dry out my gear before I can consider camping again. I'm not sure what time they close, but I figure it's at least another couple hours past Cherokee, the southern terminus of the Parkway. I'd rather not ride all that way only to find them closed.

My amped-up pace is ever so sweet. The Blue Ridge Parkway is a mesmerizingly wonderful ride at almost any speed. But ramped up, with the motorcycle pulling g's through the corners and the suspension working and the tires gliding with a smooth suppleness across the twisted landscape, it's the absolute best. It's the reason I come here.

I do have one more stop I'd like to make: the Cowee Mountains overlook. And as I pull in I'm reminded that it is, indeed, a piece of work. It has that classic postcard look of ridgeline-upon-ridgeline stretching far into the distance. It's where I got one of my favorite motorcycle pictures ever—the shot of Anton right at sunset, dressed in his Aerostich, looking off into the distance in the fading light.

There is no sunset today—it's only just 3:30pm. I pull out my camera and while I get ready to fire off a few frames, amongst the several other people there at the overlook, I notice the single other motorcyclist is a girl. Young and pretty, I look around for her companion, and then slowly realize that she's alone. Damn. You don't see that very often.

After taking a few shots I walk over and introduce myself. She's riding an old Harley Sportster and her tag says she's from Michigan. She's not loaded all that heavily—but heavy enough to realize that this is no little day trip. She's actually on the road. Really, damn.

It's always been curious to me that out of the millions of guys who ride motorcycles, the number who ever take a serious trip—go someplace overnight—is comparatively small. And of those that do, the number who ever do it alone, without the solace and security of one or more companions, is smaller still. I've never known a woman to.

Her name is Jennifer. She's from Kalamazoo, Michigan. And she's a schoolteacher. Which explains how she has the time to do what she's doing. But doesn't go anywhere near towards explaining where she got the courage to do such a thing. I'm impressed. She's got more balls—or whatever passes for such in a pretty young woman—than most men I've known.

While talking, I mention I'm staying at Deals Gap. She brightens and says that's where she's headed as well. She starts to get dressed as I do and I wonder if I should take that as a cue that she wants me to ride with her. Looking at her rig I know she'll be a lot slower than I am. And I'm already late—maybe too late. Mostly though, I don't wish to intrude or appear like I'm hitting on her. I'm figuring that any woman embarking on a trip such as hers might just prefer to be alone. So after wrestling with that decision for a few moments, I wish her well and head on my way.

If I was in make-up-time mode on my way to the overlook, I'm *really* in it now. There are 40-odd miles of the Parkway left—maybe my favorite section of all—and that devil that so often sits on my shoulder is nattering at me. We make up time, blitzing by every vehicle we encounter.

I get to the store at 6:02pm. They're still open—for another minute or two. And, yes, they have a room.

Graham County is dry. You have to go to Tennessee,

through the Gap, and then back again, to get any beer. What a shame.

After I unload my gear in my room, that's what I do. My first run through is pretty ragged, like it usually is. The pavement is excellent. The Tennessee Highway Department just finished re-paving the entire stretch through the Gap a few weeks ago. And while doing that they slightly extended the aprons on the insides of some of the corners. Except for the gravel—there's a fair amount of that in spots—the road is in the best shape I've ever seen it.

Twenty-odd miles on the other side of the Gap is the closest place for beer. I pick up a six-pack of Budweiser, and then head back. Not far down the road there's a little dive. I had breakfast there a year ago with the two guys rooming next to me—who had brought 21 spare tires and a tire-changing machine with them. Since I'm already pretty cooked, I decide to just go ahead and get something to eat there.

My run back through the Gap is better. I remember that I prefer the Tennessee-to-North Carolina direction. The road camber is better.

With my beer iced down in the sink, I spend an hour or so unpacking all my wet gear and hanging it to dry. I set up my tent and leave that out in the grass. My sleeping bag I hang from the top bunk of the two twin beds. Clothes and bags I spread all around the room, hanging them wherever I can find a spot.

I'm fading, but glad to be done. I help the guys next to me unload their bikes when they pull in. Then we sit around for a few hours, the half-dozen or so of us staying at the campground/motel, watching racing videos and drinking beer.

I turn in sometime after 11pm. There's no sign of Jennifer. I shouldn't have left her.

§

When we think of taking a motorcycle trip, most of us

automatically think of doing that with others. Having riding buddies along with whom we can share the joys of the road is a pretty cool experience, after all. The laughter and the camaraderie and the end-of-the-day recounting add immeasurably to the pleasure of a road trip. Not to mention the security that comes from knowing that you've got help at hand should some mishap occur.

And yet a solo trip—something that most motorcyclists never even consider—brings its own unique rewards. The most immediate difference is the freedom that comes from not having to consider anyone else. You can go where you want, when you want. You can stop when you choose, cut the riding day short—or make it longer—all at your own whim. You don't have to periodically check your mirrors to make sure your buddy is still there. You don't have to calculate anyone else's fuel range, because they've got a bigger or smaller tank than you. And you can ride at whatever pace suits you, modifying it as you see fit during the course of the day.

A solo trip is also inevitably a more introspective experience. When you talk to someone… it's mostly to yourself. It's amazing what you can come up with, the problems you can solve, and the issues you can sort through, when on a road trip by yourself. A few days alone on the road may just be the best salve there is for those thorny issues of life that touch us all.

A trip by yourself can also be interesting in ways that a group ride never is. There's something intriguing about a lone biker out on the road. People are drawn to it. It seems to speak to some distant, inner longing that most people have, but few ever actually act upon. Whereas our interactions with strangers tend to be brief and superficial when we're out with a bunch of buddies, it's been my experience that people find a lone motorcyclist far more approachable. The interactions are richer. You stand a much better chance of actually meeting people when you're by yourself.

Mostly, though, a road trip by yourself speaks to an

increasingly rare quality in this day and age: self-reliance. It's the flip side to having someone always there to lend a hand. Instead, you get to deal with whatever may come, all by yourself. That may sound a little frightening to some, but it also brings an intangible sense of adventure and accomplishment. It imbues the trip with a special feeling that is hard to describe. I'll never forget standing at an overlook looking out over the Pacific Ocean, 3000 miles from home, and glancing in quiet amazement at the 2-wheel machine which had brought me alone all that distance. There's magic in that.

Alas, most riders seem afraid to embark upon such a trip. Which is why I was so surprised and so impressed by Jennifer. And, yes, she ended up being perfectly fine—showing up at Deals Gap the next day. Like all good solo travelers, she had simply molded her itinerary to changing circumstances that first day, staying overnight near Cherokee.

Nothing will ever take the place of those multi-day trips with our buddies. But a solo trip is special in its own unique way.

You should try it.

May 2009, Sport Rider

Surfing Asphalt

L eaving is always bittersweet. After a few days on the road you always want to get home and see your family. But there's also that twinge of regret that the trip is over.

But I push those thoughts aside as we walk outside the diner. With a good breakfast under our belts, we have the better part of a day's ride still in front of us. There remains much to look forward to.

Glancing at the sky, I make note of the broken cloud cover. The soft overcast is welcome. That will temper the heat later in the day. More importantly, it will provide good visibility into the turns.

"How's your tire doing?" I ask Rasmus.

"Fine," he replies. "Still holding at thirty-nine pounds."

I nod in satisfaction. We had pulled the roofing nail yesterday morning and the plug had held all through the long day of riding. He'll get home just fine.

Suiting up, I glance around the small West Virginia town one last time. It'll be three months before we'll be back. Turning back to Kevin and Clyde and Rasmus, we shake hands.

"Have a safe ride back."

They'll be turning off a handful of miles down the road, heading south to their homes in North Carolina while I continue on east, alone, into Virginia.

Rolling, I fall in behind them. Our pace is relaxed and for ten minutes my mind wanders, as our southeast route tracks through this country that I love. Thinking about the few days of riding that we just enjoyed. Thinking about home. Thinking about work tomorrow. Mostly, thinking about the mountain that lies ahead.

At the turnoff Kevin looks back and salutes. I point at him.

The descent begins right after that. I accelerate into the first hard turn, only to have to slow as I come upon a slow moving pickup truck. I abide that inconvenience until halfway down the mountain, when the short straight exiting the 10-mph horseshoe gives me the opportunity for a double-yellow pass.

At the bottom I pass the tiny general store, the church, the firehouse, and the dozen-odd homes comprising the picturesque little village of Valley Grove. The two faded gas pumps at the store remind me of the late summer afternoon I drifted in there on fumes many years ago. It's funny how, over time, we lay little bits of memory here and there across the landscape, like Easter eggs.

Running along the creek, my mind begins to bear down, my focus narrowing. The mountain I've idly been considering since we finished breakfast is just ahead. It's one of the best mountain passes in Virginia. Thinking about it prompts that old anticipatory tickle in my gut. It's where things get serious.

With expectation hanging in the air, the throttle spools under my hand—an almost involuntary response—as my boots slide back on the pegs.

Passing the turnoff down into the draft—just a handful of miles from the camp where I hunt—I do a quick calculus of the likelihood of encountering deer. It's higher than I like. I toy with that thought for a brief second before putting it aside. I'm not going to not do this.

Over the bridge and across the creek and the ascent begins. The road tracks at a flat, upward angle for the first two hundred feet, then breaks hard left into the esses which climb the mountain. My blood up, I hold steady on the throttle.

Like a downhill-rolling snowball slowly gathering strength, I can sense the increasing flow of energy around me. The first corner is a moderate-speed turn—30mph is painted on the yellow caution sign. It comes like a softly lobbed toss from a lazy pitcher. The line is obvious and the bike hews to it with precision. I feel the same odd thrill I always get when first hitting a string of corners at speed.

The next handful of corners are similar. Easy, with steady radii that make for classic lines from entrance to exit. They act as a prologue, giving the bike and I a bit of time to get wired together, to be ready for the harder stuff just ahead.

I no sooner think that thought when the 15mph caution sign signals that I'm there. The hard right-hander tightens halfway through the turn. "Easy," I whisper to myself, tempering the urge to throttle up too soon. I let the tires drift out to the middle of the tarmac—the very edge of what passes for my half of the road. Then I'm throttling up into the left-hander which immediately follows.

The road is very different now. It moves in undulating, misshapen coils, as if the builders of the original wagon track here two centuries ago had begun, sober, at the bottom, only to take a pull on the bottle with every increment of elevation gained. And then, halfway up, suitably sauced, had abandoned any sense of engineering decorum.

However it came to be, it makes for a fine, highly technical motorcycle road. It forces one to think. To divine what is here.

Pressing hard, I search for every advantage I can find. My line is dictated as much by the subtle lifts and fall of camber as by the direction of the road itself. The bike feels alive, responsive. As I hold myself light in the seat, it molds itself to the road, as if it were a living part of the earth.

Camber is a wonderful thing. It introduces a third dimension to our riding. Usually subtle, it forces us to see nuances in the pavement if we are to make use of it. In that sense it is a gift to experienced riders—as neophytes usually don't even notice it's there.

Here, nearing the summit, with the bike alive beneath me, I can only smile. The descent is a several-mile downhill slalom—tight, harsh, and abrupt—but sufficiently open that I can carry just enough speed to smoothly connect the transitions. I'm covered with that afterglow of a good-road-run-well when I finally cross the river at the bottom.

Things mellow after that. I relax down into the seat as the road unkinks itself into the meandering, relaxed curves that define the valley landscape here.

A few miles further along my GPS surprises me, pointing left down a road I've never been on before. I debate for a couple of seconds whether to take its cue—my normal turnoff is a few miles ahead and leads to Cherokee Draft, one of my favorite little roads. I'm loathe to lose the opportunity to run it. But after an instant's pause, the mystery of an unknown road wins out.

It's a tiny, tortured little road hardly more than a single lane wide and I'm soon smiling to myself. One of those little jewels that is devoid of traffic and is unknown to anyone except the odd farmer or two who live along it. Once again I nod an appreciative thank-you to Mr. Zumo.

At McDowell things get serious once again. Rt. 250 climbs two mountains as it heads eastward into Virginia's Piedmont. As I approach the stop sign turning onto it I have the same urgency I always have here—the impulse to quickly jump ahead of any eastbound traffic. The road is tight enough that passing opportunities are few and far between.

I'm in luck today. A glance back shows the road to be clear.

As an hour before, there is a pregnant sense of expectation as I begin the first ascent. And like that one, it quickly amps into a barely contained rush of energy up the mountain.

This is a bigger road than that other, but every bit as serious. And whereas the road camber in that one was subtle, this one is anything but. The road engineers, trying to moderate the severe turns, made it obvious.

Like a pitcher in the seventh inning gazing out at the scoreboard and suddenly realizing there are no hits displayed there, I finish the descent of the first mountain with the realization that I have just enjoyed a perfectly clean run. How many years has it been since that happened?

Hoping to maintain that string, I press hard into the second mountain. This one is tighter, edgier. Glancing at the GPS shows the purple line curling back on itself, like two fingers held together. That hairpin leads into the very tight upper section, the one so coil-bound and where you lean the bike so far over that you swear it surely must fall over.

It doesn't, of course. Instead, the bike thrums beneath my feet, alive, like a surfboard upon the water.

As I leave the second mountain behind I have yet to come upon another vehicle. I shake my head in wonder.

Some days are a gift.

September 2009, Sport Rider

The Elephant in the Room

Pretending it's not there.
Until we can't.

Even knowing it was coming didn't really prepare me. When I walk outside the humid, balmy warmth of the air surprises me. The contrast between the sleet and the snow and the near-single-digit temperatures we were experiencing just a week ago is remarkable.

It prompts a sense of urgency. I had planned on getting out today anyway, ever since hearing the forecast a few days ago. But the liquid air sparks a sudden need to get moving. I hurriedly air up the tires and pack my gear.

It doesn't take long, and in just a few minutes I'm rolling. A little hitch north, and then westward, into the ridgelines I've hardly seen since last fall.

Alas. My pleasure in getting out is quickly tempered by conditions—the roads are heavily coated in salt and sand. I expected that, of course, but the grimy reality sets in like a quick rebuke. The compromised pavement will hold many surprises today, none of them good. It will not be a day to rail.

That's okay. After a winter of unusually sparse riding opportunities I'm just grateful to be out. Even at a somewhat reduced speed and with an extra dollop of attention directed towards what the tires are doing, the BMW feels wonderful.

At the stop sign I turn onto Blantyre. Up past the pond the road is busted up in places from winter frost heaves. In some sections they come so frequently and my line changes are so abrupt that it feels like I'm riding an old time trials course.

But Midway Road is in pretty decent shape. It has the salt and sand, but none of the broken pavement, thankfully. Easing out past the church, I glance to my left, my eyes sweeping quickly across the field to the edge of the woods beyond. A mild overcast shadows the sky, but I see no deer. I sharpen the throttle a hair, even as my mind drifts back.

This was the road that brought me back after my last street crash, fifteen years ago. Its patchwork of sharp edges and swiftly-breaking blind curves both raised the demons in my head, and allowed me to slay them. It had been a stern teacher, forcing me to look at the question.

The nice weather reminds me that a lot of riders will be out across the region today. And last night's Daytona 200—long my own personal demarcation between winter and spring, and the herald of a new riding season—means that weekends will soon once again be full of motorcyclists riding these roads. The glorious awakening we see every spring.

But I also know that even as the springtime extends its annual offer of renewal and hope, it also has a darker underside. A lot of those riders will crash. Some because of being rusty. Some because they're trying to match their buddies, trying to do things their experience is not yet ready to support. Some, just because.

I think back to July 2000. I was at Mid-Ohio with Reg Pridmore, attending one of his CLASS schools. When he came into the dining room at the hotel his face held a sorrowed countenance. He had just received a telephone call that his friend Joey Dunlop had been killed at a roadrace in Estonia. It was shocking news. That an icon of the sport like Joey could come to such a fate just seemed so… wrong.

But of course it happens. It had happened to Wayne Rainey seven years before that, in the Italian Grand Prix. His freak, paralyzing crash had likewise shocked the roadracing world.

Those are the times you think about it.

Stuck behind a car for the last mile doing exactly the 45mph speed limit, I grow impatient. After exiting the little hamlet from which the road derives its name, I pull around in a quick double-yellow pass. The first of the season.

It's dark for the next half-mile, the straight section up the hill, running through the canopied forest which grows right to the very edge of the blacktop. With the distraction of the car fading behind me, I settle into the seat, listening with satisfaction to the slightly coarse Boxer twin. Thinking about the section just moments ahead, over the crest, one rich with technicalities, I add a little more throttle.

It's always worse when it hits close to home, of course. Andrew's crash last November had been a sobering reminder that even the best of the best are not held apart, immune from the vicissitudes of chance.

And that finally begs the question. The one we all avoid. The elephant in the room. Would we ride if we *knew* that we were going to crash? Would we ride if we believed there was much chance that that crash might be catastrophic?

I don't know. What I do know is that we wrap the question in denial. We preach training and awareness and wearing good gear and saving it for the track—and there's no question that those are all good things and there is truth in them. But what is also true is that we hold to those mantras like they were talismans, holding the question at bay. They give us a rational basis for thinking we've managed the risk. They allow us to believe it will never happen to us.

But that's a myth. I know quite a number of multi-decade riders, men who have riding resumes spanning vast tracks of time and hundreds of thousands of miles. But I know only one who has never crashed. Forrest's sterling record is not an accident—he brings not only a strong competence to the table, but what also may be the most consistently steady judgment I have ever seen in a rider. But there's also no question he's a statistical anomaly.

You and me? We're going to fall down.

Which brings us back to the question.

Over the crest, having left the forest behind, the light

brightens. The road tracks crookedly through a mixed landscape of small fields interspersed by small patches of woods. There are occasional barns and houses and small groups of livestock, but I notice none of them. The road has become intense, demanding everything. Blind curves come like flash cards from a teacher, only seconds apart.

Gently adding throttle, the motor harkens to that sweet spot, the sublime edge where the torque it lays down has married with the tires to express their traction in a perfect kiss with the pavement. The motorcycle comes alive. And for the next two miles there is that quickening in my heart, drawn from somewhere eternal.

I think of my old friend Randy Renfrow. Of the countless evenings we spent shooting the breeze back at his old shop in Springfield. We talked about everything under the sun. We talked about bikes. We talked about the motorcycle business. We talked about WERA and roadracing and the bumpy surface at Summit Point. We even talked about crashing. But, no, we never talked about the question. We were young men, full of the immortality that all young men assume is theirs.

The road quiets, unkinking just enough that I can relax a bit, exultation trailing in its wake. And suddenly there, in that mix of elation and joy, I begin to see a glimmer of an answer. Not to the question. For the more I think about it the more I realize that it's a question that can never really be answered.

But to the reason we do what we do, in spite of the question. Why we do it in the face of the unknowable.

It occurs to me that despite the several grievous injuries that Randy received while riding, it wasn't any of them that killed him. It was a tragic accident at home that did that.

Turning left at the stop sign, I gently roll on the throttle. Even through my ear plugs I can hear the engine softly spooling. My mind stretches ahead, conjuring the next section of what will later become the map of my day's ride. Cromwell Road, a couple miles ahead, sounds good. Fifteen miles of undulating pavement, a slightly softer cousin to the road I've just finished. It'll make for a lovely, ziz-zag route westward to the Blue Ridge.

My eyes fall to the old, faded Vanson summer-weight gloves on my hands. It's such a pleasure to be wearing those instead of my bulky winter gloves. And the whole season stretches in front of me. I abide a moment of gladness.

I don't know the answer. But that's okay. I know enough.

June 2009, Sport Rider

The Motorcycle Camp

"**Y**ou're taking the flame thing, there?" she asked. "Flame thing? FLAME THING?! It's called a backpacking stove," I replied. "And, yeah, I'm taking it."

Ginny laughed. "That's no stove. And, anyway, I've seen you with a stove. What are you taking it for?"

This time it was my turn to laugh. "No need to make fun of me. All I'll be using it for is heating water."

"Why?" she asked.

"Well," I explained, "after riding all day in summer's heat and humidity you're usually pretty grungy. Now, imagine you're camped at a primitive campsite—no shower and no way to clean up. With my stove here I just heat up a bit of water, add it to the cold water I already have, and use my little fold-up basin to clean up in. Just like at hunt camp. Simple."

Ginny nodded slowly, obviously not convinced that that sounded anything like fun at all.

§

Camping has a romantic sort of aura to it. It conjures up images of far-away places. Of campfires and self-reliance and adventure. And like pulling a much-loved rifle from the gun cabinet before a deer hunt, the paraphernalia of camping is similarly evocative. Tents and camp stoves and sleeping bags trigger an emotional response, a stirring of the juices. Mix them with motorcycles and you have, for me at least, as powerful an anticipatory feeling as it gets.

I've spent the last week getting ready for this little trip. Five or six days away, with just a rough idea to head down the Blue

Ridge Parkway into western North Carolina. A working trip, since I need to get some photographs.

The challenge is putting together a kit which is not overly cumbersome or that adds too much weight. Especially given the great roads I expect to be on, it would be a shame to diminish the handling of my motorcycle. With that as my mantra, I work hard to pare things down to only the basic stuff I truly need.

I'm gone at 6:30am. It's just light. Even in the early morning one can tell that it will be hot. The air has a liquid feel to it, the haze and humidity a physical presence. But right now it's simply gorgeous. The world is just awakening, with tired drivers heading groggily north and east toward work. There is a feeling of great fortune to be heading the other way, on a motorcycle, to be gone for at least a little while. *Head out on the highway, looking for adventure...*

I arrive at Price eleven hours later. Plenty of time to set up camp and get some supper before needing to be up at Raven Rock, seven miles away, for the sunset. So that's what I do. While pitching my tent a fiftyish fellow on a bicycle rides by my campsite. "That's definitely the way to do it," he says, nodding towards my BMW. We talk for awhile. He seems genuinely interested in starting to ride, so I tell him about the Suzuki SV650 I used to have. He seems quite serious, asking good questions and obviously making a mental note of what I tell him.

He leaves after a few minutes and I quickly finish setting up camp. Then I climb back on the bike and relaxedly ride back out to the campground entrance, where I register my site, pay the fee, and talk to an older couple there doing the same thing. I've always found a motorcycle to be a good icebreaker and conversation starter. Most folks seem genuinely interested, especially if you're traveling alone. And it seems that most men have had some experience with motorcycles, of some sort, at one point or another in their life.

Supper will be a 4-piece wing dinner from the KFC in the

little town down off the mountain. Stowing that in one of my saddlebags, next to the bottle of beer and packet of peanuts, I head back up to the Parkway. In just a couple of minutes I'm back at Raven Rock. I probably have a good hour before the sun sets. A trio of teenage girls are parked across the way, sitting on a blanket, having their own picnic. Chatting away happily, as girls are wont to do.

As I'm finishing my dinner, a fellow on a VFR rides in. John is a local and rides up here a lot. We talk for awhile and I congratulate him on the terrific roads he has in his backyard. He knows it. And he knows how lucky he is.

A second fellow drives in while we're talking and comes over to join us. He's in his car today, but has an old beater GSX-R750 that he rides. He and John have never met but it turns out they know some of the same people. They both mention the bad crash a couple weeks ago on the right-hander just south of the overlook, where two guys overcooked the corner, went over the cliff, and had to be medivac'd out. Same thing everywhere—the really good roads exact a high price for not getting it right.

Back at camp, it's just turning dark. I light my candle lantern and fire up the "Flame Thing," heat some water, and wash up. Then I sit in the dark outside my tent and drink the now-only-slightly-cool bottle of beer and munch on my peanuts. It's been a good day.

Retiring, I find there's absolutely no breeze and it's sweltering inside the tent. I get back out and fuss with the fly a couple of times, first loosening it, then pulling it away altogether from the no-see-um netting on the tent. I'll remember that later.

I'm up at 5am, while darkness still blankets the ground. In just a few minutes I'm dressed and ready. The sky has but a tinge of light to it as I roll out of there. I consider doing something with camp—I've left everything rather scattered around in a mess—but figure since its dark and I'll just be a few miles up the road, there's little need.

Two hours later, the light outside the cafe is kind of grayish, the way early mornings often are. As I'm finishing up my coffee I notice the parking lot seems to have darkened just a bit. Is that rain? Damn, I sure hadn't expected that. Neither the sky last night nor this morning during my photo op at the overlook had given any indication of precipitation. But as I walk outside I see it surely is. A light drizzle is coming down. I dress hurriedly, glad I already refueled last night. The rain picks up steam even as I'm dressing.

By the time I get back to the Parkway it's raining hard. And by the time I ride the few miles down to Price it's coming down in buckets. I already know what I'm going to find.

My camp, which I've left entirely open—bags, stove, lantern, and other miscellaneous stuff just lying about—is saturated. My tent, from which I had pulled the fly last night for ventilation, lies entirely exposed and now has a couple inches of standing water inside. My down sleeping bag is sopping wet. *Everything* is wet. And the rain is still coming down hard.

Talk about miserable. I'm buttoned up in my Aerostich Roadcrafter riding suit. Leaving that on, along with my helmet, I remove my gloves and begin breaking camp. Of course I'm sweating like a pig in no time. I feel like a frigging astronaut trying to work with all this gear on.

The campsite is deliberately set up with these tiny little pebbles spread everywhere. The force of the rain has kicked those onto everything, so in addition to everything being really wet, it's now all covered with these little pebbles. They stick to my wet hands, which helps with the spreading. It's a holy mess.

Soon enough, all things considered, I've got everything packed up. As I pick up my duffel bag and lash it to the rear of the seat I ruefully note how much heavier it is. When originally packing for the trip I had been happy that I had kept the weight of that duffel down pretty well, to that of half a woman, more or less. Now, surely, it weighs as much as a whole woman. I shake my head sadly. I always figured that if you're going to be hauling around the weight of a whole woman, you ought to at least be getting sex out of the deal.

§

And so unfolded one of my more unflattering episodes in motorcycle camping. Lest you think I offer it to dissuade you from giving it a go, nothing could be further from the truth. That little morning was, in fact, more humorous than anything. It remains one of the more memorable moments I've spent on two wheels.

And that's the real point—motorcycles and camping were made for each other. Individually, they each bring one closer to the real world, one unfiltered by glass windows, air conditioning, high-def TV, and all the other conveniences of modern life. Together, they provide a remarkably unvarnished view of the world.

Just make sure you secure your tent fly before leaving camp.

January 2010, Sport Rider

The Old Warhorse

Never forget.

I'm late, the lame result of having stayed up too late last night watching that movie. The sun is already high in the sky by the time I head out to the shed. Opening the door, I start towards the R1200GS, as I usually do when heading out for a ride of long miles or indeterminate direction. Its amenities and comfort and jack-of-all-trades expertise is a wonderful thing.

But then my eyes fall on my old K1200RS, sitting there in the shadows in the back corner of the shed. A tinge of guilt washes over me. How long has it been? A couple months, on that little ride up past Antietam? And before that… I can't remember.

I debate mentally for a moment. I'd honestly rather take the GS, a bike whose lazy comfort I've grown quite fond of in recent years. But that feeling of guilt just won't go away.

I wonder if the battery even has enough juice.

It takes a few moments to push the three other motorcycles and the two bicycles out of the way. With the narrow path thus created, I slowly wheel the KRS out of the shed into the sunlight. My guilt gets a boost when I see the dust on the tank and the cobwebs between the windscreen and mirror. But it starts instantly and out of that surprise I suddenly know I've made the right choice. Fifteen minutes later I've got the tires aired up and the bike wiped down, looking somewhat presentable. Tossing my small duffel in one of the saddlebags, I shrug into the Aerostich, pull on my Arai, and finally head down the driveway.

After spending so much time in recent months either bent to the severe crouch of my GSX-R1000, or else sitting upright on the GS, the midway position of the KRS seems oddly strange. But looking down at the cockpit and the bars and the windscreen—a view I once knew well—prompts a sudden flood of memories, reminders that quickly gain strength as I turn out onto the road. They should. I certainly put enough miles on this motorcycle back in the day.

Past the duck pond, up the hill and around the bend, the hard pull of the turbine-like engine reminds me of one of the reasons I always loved this bike. On-throttle, it flows through the corner with an uncanny grace. Under my helmet, I break into a smile.

It's funny. Bikes are so individual—with sounds and smells and looks that are unique. As my speed builds those sensory inputs draw up around me, breaking through the haze of forgetfulness brought on by bikes of newer vintage and reminding me of how it used to be. Like meeting up with an old girlfriend.

Slowing at the stop sign, I pause, debating for a moment, then turn left.

The old route.

It's three miles to town, and then two minutes to get past the two traffic signals. Wending down past the high school, the landscape quickly turns rural again. Past the left-hander where I always worry about deer, and then the pace picks up. Within moments I'm already having to back out of the throttle, rediscovering the deceptive smoothness of the bike—70 in a 45 doesn't work just yet. *Patience*, I tell myself. I hug the white line near the shoulder through the long sweeping right-hander—the one where cars are always drifting across the centerline. And then a few quick miles and suddenly there's Panorama appearing on the left, a small, obscure ribbon of black emerging out of the woods. One of the secrets I discovered many years ago. Now I can relax a bit.

Coming from the much lighter Gixxer or the taller, more spacious GS, the KRS seems dense and heavy. As if it was forged from a solid piece of billet. But as I head into the first set of downhill esses it flows into them with an effortlessness that reminds me of how well it comports itself at speed. Kind of like that date with a beautiful but slightly heavy girl who shocks you with what she knows when she stays over.

It might be a little long in the tooth, but it was that broad-ranging competence that first drew me to this bike lo those many years ago. And re-remembering that, I'm struck by the oddity of how easily we forget such things when something newer and shinier comes along.

Turning onto Crest View, a still-curvy but slightly more open road, I bump my speed a bit. My guilt has given way to a simple gladness that I'm once again back with my old friend. I'm not sure why I ignored it for so long.

This route I'm on, this collection of good roads stitched together to fashion a motorcyclist's delight, is one I've ridden a thousand times. Most of those miles were on this bike. There are many shared memories along here.

It's an hour and a half before we stop. Not until we've crossed the Blue Ridge Mountains and tracked deep into the forest beyond, to a remote valley fastness known to only a few. I pull into the small park and pull up hard next to the gate. With the engine shut down it's suddenly very quiet. That's one of the things I like about this place—you almost always have it to yourself.

Walking the couple hundred feet to the small wooden structure housing the primitive men's facility, my eyes sweep the path in front of me, mindful that I'm without a weapon. I've seen bears up here a couple times. But I've not seen sign of them in recent weeks, and I don't see any today.

Back at the bike I break out my sandwich and crackers and bottle of water, walking the twenty feet to the picnic table. Munching slowly on lunch, my eyes periodically pause over the old BMW. I do that with all my bikes, of course—gaze at them with a combination of happiness and awe and appreciation. But it seems especially evocative with this red K-bike. My old warhorse.

Many of us have a bike that we're especially connected with.

A bike that, through countless hours and long miles we've become intimately acquainted with. Maybe because it's our only bike. Or maybe we simply like it best, and by virtue of that it gets the nod over others when it comes time to ride. However it is, you end up on that machine through the slow wear of time. What comes out on the other end is a burnished thing that is not nearly as shiny or bright as the day it was wheeled off the showroom floor. But what you get in return is an understanding between you and the machine that is almost preternatural.

It's then that the road tests in the magazines no longer apply. You've gone into a different place.

Looking at the BMW, I'm reminded of all that. I think of all the places we've been. I remember how for years I would tell myself that when the chips were down, this is the bike I'd want to be on. I remember all the times of mild angst when swapping bikes with someone, and how, no matter how terrific or new their machine might have been, there was always that sense of relief when getting back on mine.

The memories are as varied as the miles themselves. Everything from mundane one-day weekend rides like this one to multi-week adventures that traversed half the continent. Everything from the bliss of some of the curviest and best motorcycling roads in the world to the very worst interstate slogs—and everything in between. There was the hurricane we rode through. The rides at night. There were the times of being frozen. And then being baked. Mostly, though, through it all, it was simply being struck by a sublime magic. And, then, how many countless times, sitting and staring in wonder at the machine that might do that?

Nodding to myself, I stow my trash and mount back up. Thumbing the starter, I hear it yet again, the old music. Glancing at the sky, out of old habit, I judge what the afternoon will bring. Not that it much matters. A slow rolling U-turn returns me to the road.

Throttling up, there's that old lift as the machine comes alive. A smile tugs at my lips. We've hardly started yet. Looking down at the tank, I nod in thanks at that realization. "We still have many miles to make, old friend."

December 2009, Sport Rider

The Perfect Pillion

We missed the chicken. Our arrival in Brandywine was just a few minutes later than usual, but that was enough. Pulling up to the firehouse, the doors were shut.

Wheeling the bikes around, we disappointedly motored the half-block down to the little park. We'd have to find something else for lunch.

Pulling up next to the strange, green sidecar rig, we dismounted and began shrugging out of our gear. Dropping the Aerostich Roadcrafter on the seat of my BMW, I gave the unusual 3-wheel hack a sidelong glance as I walked towards the picnic table, next to which our two young guests stood smiling.

Joachim and Annette were a German couple in the midst of a 9-month, round-the-world journey. My buddy Dave had met Joachim—traveling alone at the time—the year before at an overlook up on the Highland Scenic Highway. A quick friendship had developed and a few months later when Joachim offered that he and his girlfriend were embarking upon their big trans-global trip, Dave had suggested that they spend a few weeks at his house in Arlington.

And so it was now, after having spent several months traveling northward through South America, as the couple rolled towards the east coast they were meeting us for our annual 3-day Labor Day run. They'd be following Dave home at the end.

After the usual introductions and greetings, and a few minutes hearing about their trip so far, we discussed where to get lunch. The little town of Franklin, a dozen miles down the road, seemed to make the most sense.

Mounting back up, John and Dave took the lead, followed by *Hannibal*, the heavily-loaded sidecar rig of our new friends. Kevin on his Ducati and Jay and I on our BMW's fell in behind them. As our loosely strung gaggle rolled westward I couldn't help but stare at the strange contraption in front of me. The sidecar itself was homemade, based on a frame that Joachim had had welded to his own specs. It was attached to an old BMW Airhead.

It also didn't hurt that Annette was quite fetching. The combination of a pretty young woman, the unusual sidecar outfit, and the adventure obvious in their round-the-world trip all combined to create a fascinating and alluring package.

What it didn't prepare me for was what came next, a mile and a half on as we approached the ascent of the mountain between us and Franklin. As the sidecar turned into the first sharp bend, Annette lifted herself from her seat in the car and swung her ass far to the outside of the rig, hanging on but by the slender handle obviously placed there for that purpose.

After absorbing the sight in a moment of stunned amazement, I broke out laughing. It was exactly what you'd expect to see during the sidecar races at the Isle of Man. But seeing it demonstrated by a pretty girl, deep in the mountains of West Virginia, was the very last thing I expected.

Kevin and I glanced at each other. He too was laughing. We just shook our heads.

What we would learn over the next couple of days was that Joachim and Annette both were quite accomplished motorcyclists, with extensive experience riding in Europe. Annette fell in love with Kevin's 900SS and would end up buying her own 916 within a couple of years. In the meantime, it quickly became clear that these young Germans were anything but your run-of-the-mill motorcycle tourists.

Fast forward three weeks and we're back on the road again—this time on a week-long trip to Deals Gap and the mountains of western North Carolina. Joachim and Annette have been joined by Andreas and Karin, another German couple who have flown over to experience the storied roads of Appalachia.

With the sport-riding potential of the area in mind, *Hannibal* has been left at Dave's home in northern Virginia. The two visiting couples are riding two-up on spare bikes lent by Dave and Jay. Our pace rises accordingly.

The days pass quickly in a blur of terrific roads, good company, fine food, and fascinating scenery. Our German friends are duly impressed.

As the week winds down the tires on the Yamaha Joachim is piloting begin losing what remaining tread they have. We decide to put Annette on the back of my BMW for the return trip home.

Early the next morning we begin the 574-mile ride north up the Blue Ridge Parkway and Skyline Drive. Andreas, with Karin on the back of his bike, and me, with Annette on the back of mine, quickly drop the others. The two of us, having adopted an extremely aggressive pace, quickly tag-team our way up the spine of the Blue Ridge. Swapping the lead at periodic intervals, we take turns finding the one line that might work at our elevated pace.

In retrospect, it was easily one of the most reckless, imprudent pieces of riding I have ever done. Riding hours on end at 80-90 mph, two-up, when the speed limit was half that, was clearly irresponsible. I certainly won't try and defend what we did, only offering the sad excuse that exuberance and youth and hooking up with another very fast rider can be a combination fraught with peril.

But I did learn a few things. For I had found the perfect pillion.

§

Nearly all of us have carried a passenger on our bike at one time or another. Some of us are quite experienced at it, having ridden with our wives or girlfriends for many miles.

And most of us have said pretty much the same thing before having that newbie passenger climb onboard for the first time:

"Just relax. Keep your feet on the pegs. Don't do anything unexpected. Lean with me. Wait for my signal before getting on or off." Depending upon how well we know her we might or might not have told her to hang on tight.

And that basic level of instruction works, after a fashion. For most people, backseat riding on a bike never gets much more sophisticated or any more complicated than that.

What I learned from Annette, though, is that an active, engaged passenger can make an enormous difference in minimizing the inevitable handling disadvantage that comes with riding two-up. Far from simply hoping for a modest, somewhat neutral level of disharmony from the back seat, an active passenger can actually contribute to the proceedings, counteracting much of the disadvantage that their extra weight brings.

Annette sat very close, first of all, so there was essentially one body mass on top of the bike, not two. And rather than simply sitting back there casually enjoying the ride, she watched the upcoming road with the very same intensity that I did, shifting her gaze over one shoulder or the other as the road unfolded. Because she was a sport rider herself, she knew exactly what I was thinking and what I was trying to achieve as I lined up each turn. She didn't just "lean with me." She pulled herself hard to the inside with the same significant effort that I did. Had we been wearing race leathers with knee pucks instead of Aerostich suits, her knee would have kissed the tarmac at the same time as mine. She was anything but the pleasant backseat passenger most of us are used to, in other words. She was every bit as actively engaged there on the back of my bike as she had been weeks earlier when swinging her ass out of the seat of *Hannibal*.

And that's probably the best example there is. Think of those sidecar racers. Those crazy guys you see every spring at the Isle of Man. Sure, one of them is nominally the pilot, the guy doing the steering. But, really, both of them are doing equal work in getting the car around the course.

What I learned from Annette is that you can have very much the same thing with that passenger on the back of your bike. Someone who is actually as much a copilot as they are a passenger. And that it can enable you to do things two-up that aren't easy to do when hauling around your more relaxed, I-think-I'll-just-sit-back-here-and-enjoy-the-view passengers.

All it requires is that you first find that girl who likes sportbikes as much as you do. One whose favorite sport isn't football or baseball or soccer—it's MotoGP and Superbike racing. She'll have her own bike. And she'll love those good roads every bit as much as you do.

And then you just have to convince her to get on the back of your bike, instead of riding her own.

Good luck with that.

April 2010, Sport Rider

Learning to Listen

*Motorcycles speak to us in so
many ways. Yet, so often, we don't
hear.*

The man awakens to the sound of rain. He is
disappointed, but not surprised after the darkening
clouds he rode through yesterday afternoon. He
turned in last night hoping against hope.

It prompts in him now a lassitude, a less pressing desire to
get going. After showering, he dresses slowly, considering his
options. By the time he has retrieved a cup of coffee from the
store a hundred feet away he concludes that it is here to stay. The
sky is a solid mass of gray and the rain, though not heavy, falls
with a steady patter that suggests it is not going away any time
soon. The handful of other bikes in the parking lot sit there
quietly, with no indication that their owners are yet astir.

Shrugging into his Aerostich, the man inserts his earplugs
and dons his helmet and cinches up his gloves before stepping
outside the room. Pulling the door closed behind him, he steps off
the porch into the wetness. The sense of immersion, of being
thrust into an unwelcome environment, is immediate. Years from
now he'll see rain in a very different way. But on this morning he
hates it.

Brushing aside the puddle of water that has pooled on the
seat with the back of his glove, the man swings his leg across and
thumbs the starter. Pushing through the enveloping thrum of the
rain, the sound of the engine adds a sudden richness. Even through
his irritation at the weather, the man can't help but smile.

Motoring slowly down the parking lot of the motel, the man
turns up the slight incline to the road. Under the sign that says

"Crossroads of Time," he pauses for a moment, then turns west.

From the store, the road into Deals Gap lifts for the first two hundred feet. On weekends it's the canvass upon which riders frequently launch wheelies and other demonstrations of prowess for the benefit of those hanging out at the store.

But the man is not inclined towards such shenanigans—and anyway there is no one outside on this wet weekday morning. He accelerates slowly up the hill, mindful that wet roads and cold tires are a combination rich with unhappy endings.

At the top, the trees close in, providing a canopy over the road. Even on a socked-in day like today, the diminishment in light is noticeable. In the last of his idle thoughts, the man makes note of this. Then the first curve breaks in front of him and suddenly he has time for nothing else.

Yesterday evening's run to The Punkin Center had been dry. Even with that benefit he had struggled to find its rhythm. Following the long day on the Blue Ridge Parkway, with its smooth, even gradients, Deals Gap was a challenge. His first run through had been ragged. The return trip back to the motel was better, but still not great.

Now, the wet road impels a tortured caution. Even as the first couple of miles pass and the man knows his tires have built some heat, he is aware that the swiftly arriving transitions and the abrupt nature of the turns hold a special danger. He rides with great care.

It's with a sense of mild relief when he finally drops down out of the gap and the road straightens. Ten miles on, when the sign for The Home Place emerges out of the gloom, he's glad to get off the bike.

He takes his time with breakfast. After eating, he sits there with a cup of coffee, warming his still-cold hands and thinking about the contrast between yesterday's lovely 600-mile ride and today's less-than-promising start. He thinks especially of that fellow he met.

It was mid-afternoon, as the sun began giving away to broken cloud cover, that he had passed the overlook. The flash of red as he rolled by and then the unmistakable look of the front-end in his mirrors as the bike pulled in behind him made his heart skip a beat. A Ducati 916.

Suddenly nervous in the presence of such august company, the man at first had a hard time concentrating on the curves ahead. But after a bit he settled down and for thirty minutes he and the Ducati rolled in lockstep down the Parkway. Every step he made, including the frequent double-yellow passes as he came upon slower traffic, was matched instantly by the rider behind him.

After awhile the Ducati passed him. A slow, rolling pass on a straightaway, with the black-leather-clad rider nodding and lifting his hand as he came around. After settling in front, the Ducati slowly began bumping the pace. Already running 25mph over the limit—well into reckless driving territory—the man wasn't entirely comfortable with that. But he moved to stay with him anyway.

For another thirty minutes they continued, a flying rush across the mountains. The man marveled at the smooth grace of the rider in front of him. There was an almost uncanny fluidity to his movements. And although he himself was riding at the very edge of his comfort zone, the Ducati rider gave no indication of being the least bit discomfited. When the Ducati finally slowed and pulled into an overlook, the man followed.

Dismounting and pulling off their helmets, the man was shocked by the sudden appearance of white hair and a grizzled countenance in his erstwhile riding partner. Far from the young hotshoe he had expected—this guy had to be every bit of seventy. But the fellow's face quickly crinkled into an easy smile.

"Nice day, huh?"

"Indeed it is," the man nodded, recovering from his surprise. "And that sure is a beautiful bike you've got there."

"Yeah, it does pretty well," the old guy offered.

They ended up standing there, chatting amiably for awhile. Until the old fellow began getting ready to leave.

Just before he pulled his helmet on, the old rider looked back at the man, as if intuiting the question that had hung there since they pulled in.

Tipping his head to where the two bikes sat side by side, the tiniest hint of a smile touched his face. "You have to listen to them. If you can do that, they'll tell you everything you need to know."

And then he was gone, the bass sound of the Desmodromic twin receding in the distance.

Suddenly eager to get going, the man swallows the rest of his coffee and pays his tab. Outside, the rain has lightened into a broken sprinkle. Maybe it won't be such a bad day, after all.

The ride to Tellico Plains is easy. Traffic is light and the man is happy for the cocoon-like dryness inside his Aerostich. In spite of himself, he finds himself grudgingly beginning to enjoy the ride.

He makes a brief stop for gas in town, but otherwise doesn't tarry. The road ahead hangs in his thoughts.

The Cherohala Skyway is only 40-odd miles long, but is one of the man's favorite routes. More open than Deals Gap, it allows for greater speeds and gentler transitions. He reasons that the latter, especially, will be a welcome quality on a day like today.

It starts soft and easy, gentle swirls at the bottom. But as the road climbs in elevation the topography hardens. The man holds his speed, concentrating on being smooth through the turns. He quickly finds a cadence that works.

There are patches of fog as he approaches Stratton Gap, where the road peaks. But past that, into the descent, the air clears.

It's harder now—the turns are serious and going downhill it's more difficult to stay off the brakes. The man struggles to hold the pace.

Pondering, he thinks back to what the old guy had said.

Through his earplugs he can hear the engine and the rush of wind past his helmet. And beyond those, softer, more subtle, he can hear the rain and the whine of his tires against the wet road.

But instinctively he knows these are not what the old fellow had meant.

Another handful of miles passes as he toys with the question. And then it comes to him.

Down deep there is a murmur. Not of a sound reaching his ears. But rather a stream of soft stories coming to him through his seat and his hands and his feet and his thighs and his fingertips. Every place he touches the motorcycle is speaking to him. He is amazed he never quite got that before.

And so he begins to listen.

March 2011, Sport Rider

Packing Light

After fueling, I replace my tank bag, then wheel the BMW around the corner to the McDonalds next door. John's R1100RT and Forrest's VFR are already there. Seeing the bikes sparks that wash of excitement that I always get at the beginning of these multi-day motorcycle trips of ours.

Inside, I nod greetings to my riding pals as I head to the counter. The pretty girl takes my order and smiles back at my obvious happiness.

Carrying my tray back to the table, I join my friends. "Heard from Neil?" I inquire as I sit down. John shakes his head with a small smile. Neil is legendary for his lateness. His crazy hours at the Pentagon mean he's usually up wrenching and packing until two in the morning, just hours before we depart, on these trips of ours.

We wait an extra fifteen minutes, but when he still doesn't show we head outside. We know he'll catch up.

As we get to the bikes we hear the familiar sound of an approaching V4 and another red VFR, a twin to Forrest's, pulls into the lot. I'm struck by the sight. It takes me a moment to realize it's Neil.

He's wearing his usual red Honda leathers and, Candace, his girlfriend, is attired in a conventional synthetic riding suit. That part's all normal.

What has us staring in amazement are the twin, vertical pillars that pass for their luggage. Neil has fashioned what looks like a three-foot-high pack on the rear of his back rest. And in front, he has mounted what has to be the tallest tank bag I have ever seen. It cants a bit to one side, like the Leaning Tower of Pisa. He can just barely see over the top.

I break out laughing. Neil is an exceptional rider—he'll shortly become an MSF instructor for the Air Force—but his bike is the most unwieldy combination of weight and mass I have ever seen.

I walk back to my bike, shaking my head, glad that Neil will be with us for the ride down but wondering how in the world he'll manage that ungainly setup.

The things we do to go three out of three.

§

Having enjoyed many dozens of multi-day motorcycle trips over the years, I sometimes forget that the "what to bring" question—something I sorted out long ago—remains a challenge that so many riders new to these long distance trips still wrestle with. So often we'll have a newbie along and he'll bring everything but the kitchen sink. He thinks of all the things he *might* need, however remote the circumstance, tosses each of those into the pile, and then wonders why his formerly lithe motorcycle looks and handles like a porcine mess.

My first piece of advice, then, is to embrace the old Boy Scout motto of "be prepared" when it comes to mind, body, and spirit—but to be wary of it when it comes to *stuff*.

The key is to carry the things you'll need to be dry and reasonably comfortable—but no more. If it helps, here's my basic kit:

For outerwear, I'll usually have a long-sleeved cotton shirt; a reversible, fleece-on-one-side, nylon-on-the-other electric jacket liner; an electric vest; several pairs of gloves; and, sometimes, if the trip includes camping or some other venue where I can't relax barefooted at the end of the day—a pair of sneakers or sandals. If there's any chance of seriously cool weather, a pair of fleece pants gets added.

For innerwear, I'll usually have two pair of boxers, two pair of t-shirts, and two pair of socks—in addition to those I'm wearing. Having three sets of those means you're square for a 3-day trip. For longer rides your options will be do some quick laundry during the trip—not as hard as it might at first sound—carry more, or begin to smell rather the worse for wear as the days unwind. Take your pick.

I also carry a pair of lightweight khaki outdoor trousers—the kind where the legs can be zipped off to convert into shorts—and a synthetic long-sleeve camp shirt. These together serve both as my "dress" clothes and as backups to my normally-worn jeans, should those get wet. Very versatile, and they pack down small.

A small kit of toiletries and a cotton laundry bag round out the innerwear stuff. Toss in the book or two I almost always carry, a couple of bike magazines, and, sometimes, a small laptop, and that's it for all the stuff on the back of the bike. It all goes in the saddlebags if I'm on one of my sport-tourers; or in a large seat pack if I'm on the Gixxer.

Some people don't like tank bags. I love them. They provide simple, quick access to all those things we readily need to get to. And most of them have lots of pockets for all those many small miscellaneous things we tend to bring along—everything from spare batteries to hi-lighters for marking up maps to extra ear plugs to face shield cleaner. Speaking of maps—don't forget those.

In the main compartment I'll always have a high-quality digital camera and several lenses, sunglasses, and, depending upon the trip—sometimes a gun.

I won't belabor the question of whether or not to take a firearm, other than to point out that it's a serious question that deserves a lot of serious thought. If you do decide to take one, think it through very carefully. Don't make the mistake I once made years ago and inadvertently end up in Mexico with a suddenly-very-illegal Glock 9mm.

Also don't forget that you need to carry all this in addition to the normal tools and maintenance gear that you always carry. You do have a tire repair kit and a way to inflate it afterwards, right?

§

I've carried this basic kit, with remarkably little variation, for years now. I arrived at it, after much thought and experimentation, mostly because of a few basic considerations:

Being cold sucks. Being wet sucks. Being cold *and* wet really, really sucks. So you need to have enough clothing to be able to layer properly under any conditions you're reasonably likely to encounter. The electrics are a considerable help with the warmth part, largely obviating the need for even-more bulky clothing.

The Aerostich riding suit I usually wear is sufficiently weather resistant that I don't feel the need to carry separate rain gear. Having that weather protection always there, in your primary riding garment, is a convenience that's hard to describe to someone who hasn't experienced it. No more hurriedly struggling into a rain suit on the side of the road while rain pelts down upon you. No more sweating so much *under* your rain suit that you wonder why you bothered in the first place. With the 'stich on, riding into inclement weather means only having to put the rain cover over the tank bag and swap gloves for the waterproof pair you've brought along. Having done that—something easy enough to do if the skies even begin to look threatening—you simply ride in and out of the weather as it presents itself. You're once again focused on the road, and riding, instead of the sky.

The Aerostich, as good as it is, is not entirely waterproof. Riding through an extended, heavy rain, you will get a little wet. And hanging around later at the motel or condo or campground with a wet crotch is, well, kind of miserable. You're going to want that extra pair of trousers.

Next to electrics, fleece jackets and pants are the hot tip for staying warm and comfortable once it gets cool. Unfortunately, they're *really* bulky.

There is a subtle—but nonetheless certain—satisfaction that comes from packing light. I don't know why that is, beyond that retrieving and putting away stuff in a loosely-packed pack is a lot easier than one which is stuffed to the gills. But whatever it is, it tends to color not just those moments when packing or unpacking, but the entire ride. Conversely, there is some kind of negative-energy frustration which always seems to accompany heavy and tightly-packed loads.

So pack as lightly as you can. On one of my recent 3-day trips I was planning to bail due to a family medical situation. I was just going to meet up with my pals and ride with them for a half-day, then return home. It was Ginny who urged me to "take your stuff, just in case." I took just a hint of her advice, tossing a spare pair of skivvies and a toothbrush into my otherwise empty saddlebags.

Turns out she was right. I wasn't needed at home after all and ended up staying for the entire trip.

It was the freest I have ever felt.

December 2010, Sport Rider

Priorities

It's something of an impromptu decision. I originally had planned on working around the house this morning. The fence still needs to be cleared of the root from the oak tree which has wrapped around it. And the late-winter pile of wood still sits in a heap, waiting to be stacked.

But *weather.com* is forecasting an oppressive day in the mid-nineties, with humidity to match. It doesn't take me long to come to a different decision.

Closing the laptop, I'm imbued with a sudden urgency. It's already after eight. I take a final, quick swallow from my cup of coffee, then head to the kitchen to rinse the cup and give Ginny the news of my change in plans. She's not surprised.

Swiftly pulling my gear together, I hurry through the packing of the bike and the airing of my tires. Even at this early hour, the air has a viscous, heavy feel. By the time I put the compressor away tiny beads of sweat have broken out on the back of my hands.

Still enveloped in that sense of urgency, my continuing impulse is to just get going. I start to pull on the Aerostich, only then to pause. "It'll only take five minutes," I tell myself.

Back inside, I spend those five minutes making a peanut butter and jelly sandwich and then a half-dozen peanut butter crackers. Wrapping those in plastic wrap and dropping them into a brown paper bag, I add a couple of Twinkies. Done. That'll be my lunch in a few hours.

Twenty-five minutes after making the decision to go, I'm finally moving.

Tracking south, traffic is light. I work consciously to detach emotionally from the feeling that I should have planned this better, should have left a couple hours earlier, should already be in the mountains. I've got what I've got, I tell myself. It'll have to do. But the hint of irritation hangs there, a gentle reproach.

Ninety minutes later I pull into the gas station at the foot of the mountain. As soon as I roll to a stop the sweat breaks out under my Aerostitch. Like flipping a light switch. I shrug out of the suit and drop it on the seat before reaching for the fuel hose.

Inside, the air conditioning is shocking in its coolness. I take my time before heading back outside with my liter of water and packet of donuts. Standing there in the shade next to the door I enjoy my simple breakfast, the white confectioners' sugar sticking to my fingers. Gazing at the sky, I note the opaque haze hanging there like a far-flung blanket, reflecting the heat. There will be thunderstorms in a few hours. But it doesn't matter.

Gazing at a knot of sport riders riding past the gas station, heading up the mountain, I'm struck by a desire to hurry, to jump on my bike and catch up with them. But I fight the urge, forcing myself to remain standing there for another couple of minutes. When I do finally begin to suit up, I do so with a purposeful deliberateness.

The ascent of the mountain is a joy. Long, winding, shaded sweepers track up its western flank. I roll into them hard, eager to get to it. In five minutes I'm at the top, where I pull off onto the short service road. At the stop sign I turn right.

The difference is remarkable. It's ten degrees cooler up here. Added to the winding road that now stretches in front of me for miles and miles, it's clear that this was exactly the right decision. I allow a self-congratulatory smile.

The next two hours are golden, dropping me into that place where everything falls away, leaving only a singular focus on the road. The scenery, beautiful as it is, arises in my consciousness only as brief snippets of quick wonder, before merging once again into the ephemera, a hazy backdrop to the black ribbon held in front of me.

Traffic is lighter than I expected. Every ten minutes or so I come upon another vehicle, and within a mile or two do a quick double-yellow pass. But mostly I have the road to myself.

The only detraction from my morning is the mild worry of coming upon a cop. My pace is clean and crisp, the natural tempo where the bike and I and the road have synced into an effortless partnership. But regardless of how right the pace feels, it's still 25mph over the limit—an honest 25mph, according to my Zumo—well into reckless driving territory. After running the self-debate I always seem to have on these rides of mine—the math of probability and consequence—I decide not to worry about it.

After awhile I come upon two riders pulling out from an overlook in front of me. Accelerating quickly, their pace first comes up to match mine. Then, after a couple of miles they begin to slowly add to it. First a single mph. Then another couple. And then shortly a couple more.

It's a tease, like following a rider on the racetrack who is running a tenth or two second faster laps. There's that invisible pull as you sense the ground between the two of you slowly increasing, and the unconscious response where you amp your own effort to keep it from happening.

But it's only a few more mph, and it's instantly clear that these are very good riders—and that prompts its own curiosity—and so I accept the gambit.

As I edge towards the boundary of my comfort zone, and the ever-so-slight beginning ripples of disturbance in my riding rhythm that that represents, I see no evidence that the riders in front of me are undergoing any kind of similar transformation. They continue to move down the road with an unperturbed, swift certainty. It is a pleasure to run behind them, watching their ballet.

Shortly after noon I reach my turnoff. After the pace of the last couple hours, the slow, meandering 20mph speed imposed by the narrow, paved trail leading up the mountain feels strange. But this is one of my favorite places and I take an odd satisfaction from the snaking crawl up the mountain.

At the top I shut the engine off. The sudden quiet, leavened only by the soft stirring of the breeze and the lilting music of nearby songbirds, is a palpable pleasure.

Breaking out my bag lunch and what's left of my now-only-slightly-cool bottle of water, I settle down beside my bike. I'm now very glad I took those extra five minutes.

I eat slowly, enjoying the break and the solitude and the still-yet anticipation. I'm thinking of something.

When I'm done I withdraw the Delorme atlas from my saddlebag. I already know the page number. Sitting back down, I study the pattern of squiggles which represent the roads and the topographic etchings which depict the landscape. I can almost see them in my mind's eye. Tracing my forefinger along one road in particular, one I've long wondered about, I come to a decision.

It takes me another hour and a half. Down out of the mountains and west across the valley. At a featureless crossroads, I'm torn. If I turn left, the sign indicates it's eleven miles to Jerome – and I need gas. But the sky to the west is quickly turning darkly gray, and I'm suddenly reluctant to let this go, to maybe miss it. So I continue on.

As the mountain rises in front of me, I appraise it the way a man does on first meeting a beautiful woman—with a combination of desire and restraint and wonder.

Then I'm there and the road has hardened, curling into whatever mystery lies ahead. For a moment I consider a softer approach, simply holding speed through the corners, to conserve my fuel. But, no, this strange, beautiful road deserves better. I downshift a gear and then, quickly, another, and the engine spools into the serious part of its powerband.

The next four miles are a delight, with the road twisting into a dance for the ages.

I'm laughing as I crest the summit and begin the descent. Right into the heart of the dark storm clouds which I've ridden so earnestly to get to, and which are now starting to spit drops of rain.

But it doesn't matter. I'm glad for this glorious day. I'm glad for this glorious motorcycle. And I'm smitten with what the road below may yet hold.

I'm sure I'll find gas somewhere.

October 2010, Sport Rider

Raising the Game

The man awoke early on the second day, the tease of anticipation stirring in his stomach. The motel room was dark, save for the red glow from the LED of the bedside alarm clock. Twisting, the man glanced over at it. 5:10am.

Padding to the window, he pulled the drapes aside and peered out at his bike, lit by the soft glow of the overhead light under which he had parked it. In all the years, across all his trips, he had never had a problem with anyone messing with his bike, his gear, or his campsites. But he still felt a moment of relief every time he confirmed that everything was okay.

Forty minutes later he was showered and dressed and the bike was packed. Walking the hundred feet to the small motel office, he nodded a smiling "good morning" to the woman behind the desk and walked over to the corner, where he selected a Styrofoam cup from the stack and filled it with coffee. He loitered for the two minutes it took to consume a lemon Danish, studying the several paintings hung on the wall, then turned and headed back outside. "Have a great day," he offered as he left.

He would have enjoyed a slow, measured getaway, slowly sipping his coffee while the anticipation quietly built. But the brightening sky was a solid mass of gray and the man knew rain was on the way. It impelled an urgency in him to get moving.

Suiting up, he injected the subtlest bit of deliberation into the getting-started routine: climbing aboard the bike, settling into the coolness of the seat, listening with satisfaction as the engine turned over, caught, and then settled into a purring idle. He allowed the pleasure of all this to wash over him for a moment, the prelude to the day. Then he eased into gear and turned slowly onto the road that ran in front of the motel.

The early miles were special, as they always were. The road was smooth and the air held a liquid presence, wafting through the crack in his face shield and curling around his neck. He knew he would be hot and tired later. And probably wet, as well. But for now it was as perfect as anything ever gets.

The road tracked northward into a range of low mountains, the two-lane route breaking into a series of smaller roads which then spread across the broken topography. The man called them "ridge roads" because of the way they held mostly to the upper elevations of the landscape. He loved them both because of their picturesque beauty and because they were so technical.

At the tiny village of Harperstown he paused at the stop sign. It had been a few years and as his eyes swept slowly down the two blocks worth of loosely placed buildings that served as the center of the villa, he searched for any signs of change. Satisfied, he turned west.

Almost immediately the cobweb of little roads narrowed and began the twisting, broken dance that gave them their character. Their abrupt, staccato cadence made riding them a study in concentration and quickly executed transitions between throttle and brake.

The man knew instantly it wasn't working. The soft overcast made for perfect visibility into the corners. He was well rested. His bike had fresh tires and suspension. And traffic was nonexistent. But none of that mattered. The road held a curious aloofness. Try as he might, the man could not find the thread that would bind it to him.

He tried different things. He adjusted his seating position, pushing his ass back another inch and pulling his boots in tight on the pegs. He clicked down a gear to move higher into the engine's powerband. And he studied his corner entrances with an even greater intentness, seeking to discern what they held.

But his riding continued with its touch of raggedness, its hint of unease.

It didn't bother him overly. Being out of sync wasn't unusual. It happened to everyone on occasion. But it was mildly frustrating to be in the midst of such great roads and not be able to ride them with the aplomb he normally took for granted.

After awhile the rain began. As soon as the first drops began spattering against the pavement the man began looking for a safe spot to pull over. There was no shoulder on this remote little road, and few other hints of civilization. He ended up pulling off in the dirt in front of a cattle gate. Moving with practiced ease, he quickly swapped to his rain gloves and put the plastic cover over his tank bag and double-checked the zippers on his Aerostich.

By the time he climbed back aboard the rain was coming down in a light, steady shower. The road he was on—gnarly and technical in the best of conditions, what with its quick, blind curves and sharply radiused corners—was suddenly quite treacherous with the added dimension of the rain.

Unable to use his brakes to full effect, and because the abruptness of the road did not lend itself to a single, smooth arc across its length, the man had no choice but to slow down. He dropped 20mph off his pace and strove to strike a balance in his gearing—low enough to give him some engine braking but high enough so as not to over-torque his wet tires.

As if that weren't enough, within a few miles the wind kicked up as well. Inconsistent, it swirled around him in quick little bursts, strong enough that he could feel the on-again, off-again, kite-like effect it had on his bike.

Despite the horrid conditions, the man continued to search for what was amiss in his riding. Every bit of attention that he could spare when not consumed with judging what was left in his tires went to reflecting upon that.

Forty minutes into the rain he came upon an old country store. Pulling in front of the two gas pumps, he slowly dismounted. The pumps had no cover overhead and so he left his helmet on while he refueled. Then he walked his bike over to the bench under the overhang next to the door, where he finally shrugged out of his Aerostich.

Inside, he took his time, wandering slowly down the several aisles. When he took his box of Fig Newtons and bottle of water to the register, the old fellow there looked at him with a hint of a grin. "Nice day for a ride, ain't it?"

The man smiled back. "Couldn't ask for much better."

Back outside, he sat on the bench and slowly opened the box of cookies. Gazing at his bike, he studied its lines, its mystery. Even just sitting there, he could feel its strength.

Out beyond, the rain continued. The man lifted his eyes towards the horizon obscured by trees. He knew what was there.

Suiting back up, the man took particular care to make sure everything was buttoned up properly, that the zipper at his throat was cinched up tight, that the collar of his Aerostich was up, that the short gauntlets of his gloves were flat inside his jacket sleeves. Then he mounted up and pulled back onto the road.

The light dimmed slightly as the road tracked away from the clearing where the store sat and moved back into the trees. The man made note of the subtlety, but otherwise did not worry about it. What he did think about were his tires—which were now both cold and wet. But they'd have a bit of heat in them shortly.

After a couple of miles the man made the slightest change in his corner entrances—adjusting his line the width of a hand and going in just a hair deeper before spooling his engine for the exit. In a few more miles, in the tiniest hint of aggression, he added back 10 of the 20mph he had earlier dropped off his pace. And after a bit he added most of the other 10mph as well.

He now rode at the nubbins edge, and he knew it. The thread was as thin as a razor. But it was a thread he held in his head with a sudden clarity.

The road was peculiar in that the apices of the turns often lay at the very crest of the hills—and both were often blind. A road pregnant with threat. But it didn't matter. The music playing in the background no longer held any sour notes.   And the man moved across the landscape with a confident certainty.

August 2010, Sport Rider

Road or Track

The sweat drips into my eyes, the salt stinging. Once again I pull my upper arm across my brow, the already-damp t-shirt sponging away the moisture. Then I dip the paint brush back into the bucket and return to applying the back-and-forth strokes against the side of the barn. It's not hard.

The new paint is a deep, rich blood red, contrasting sharply with the faded, yet-to-be-painted section. Even knowing it will lose a hint of its sheen once it dries, it pleases me. It's just a little darker than the Ducati 1198SP that sits in the shade inside this very same barn, just a few feet away. Parked in a row on the concrete slab along with the other three bikes. The thought makes me smile.

An hour later the side of the barn is finished. There is still one more to be done, but I judge that one side is sufficient for today. I can finish the rest of it next weekend.

It takes only a few minutes to stow the ladder and put away the gear. After cleaning the brushes I turn the hose on myself, reveling in the shock of its coldness.

Walking back to the house, the kitchen is filled with the smells of a slow-cooking Sunday dinner. Ginny is at the stove. I pull a glass of ice water.

"How long before we eat?"

Ginny pauses. "Probably an hour. Maybe a little longer."

I gaze out the window, contemplating.

"Okay," I finally say, finishing the glass, "I think I'm going to go run a few quick laps."

"Don't be too long," Ginny says. "And be careful."

Back at the barn, it takes me only a moment to strap on the back protector and shrug into the Dainese leather suit. Pulling on my helmet, I turn to the bikes. I'd really like to take the SP, but the fresh tires I put on last weekend are supposed to be for the upcoming track day at Mid-Ohio. After debating for a moment, I swing a leg over the S1000RR. It still has plenty of gas from last Sunday's ride up on the Parkway with John and Kevin.

Motoring slowly down the hundred yards of gravel road, I glance up and see Mark, the farmer who owns the land adjacent to me, on his tractor a quarter mile away. He waves and I lift my hand in return. A little further and the gravel turns onto the hard-paved macadam. Just past the small, hand-painted sign that says "Hughes International Raceway." I do a quick figure-eight on the small, rectangular section of pavement that serves as the "pit" and then head out onto the track proper.

Just over a mile long, the course is simply a fifteen-foot wide swath of pavement laid down in my lower pasture. At eight turns and some modest elevation change it's far from the most technical track I've ever been on. But it's mine and only two hundred yards from my front door. I can run it whenever I want.

The BMW spools quickly. I hold to little more than a brisk street pace for the first half-dozen laps. Even that is enough to drop me instantly into that place where it's all smooth and automatic. One of the benefits that comes with utter intimacy.

With heat in the tires I lift my consciousness for a moment, surveying everything. Then I squeeze the throttle, bringing the edge. Making everything harden.

But not too much. I'm terribly aware that there are no corner workers here. No ambulance. No quick response should something go awry. The line is drawn thin, but not too thin.

Still, it's enough. The BMW flows through the turns with a studied grace. And as I exit the last turn onto the short section past the pit, I think of how incredibly lucky I am.

And then I wake up…

§

And so there's my fantasy. Not fame. Not fortune. Not a mansion of a house. And not a staff of servants to be there at my beck and call. No, were my ship to come in, the one thing I'd want would be my own personal racetrack.

Alas.

I was reminded of it when some riding buddies and I were recently talking about track days. One pal has so embraced his time on the track that he has completely forsworn riding on the street. He's not the first rider I've known that came to that conclusion.

It's really not all that surprising when you think about it. To the neophyte, or to the rider who has never experienced it, the racetrack can seem like an utterly intimidating place. Its elevated speeds, its intensity, its storied history of danger, and its seemingly much-higher-crash-per-mile ratio all conspire to present an environment that seems altogether frightening.

Guys will tell you they can't afford it. More often than not the real reason—even if they don't admit it to themselves—is that they are afraid.

But those who somehow manage to surmount that trepidation, who are able to experience the purity and the euphoria of the racetrack, often come back transformed. I've known a couple riders who did a track day or two and called it a day. But not many. More often guys end up spellbound by the experience.

Ironically, among those who become zealots of the racetrack—the ones who forevermore give up riding on the street—the reason most often given is safety.

The cognoscenti have clearly learned a higher truth. But isn't it strange that both the virgins and the veterans fly the same flag?

For me, choosing between the street and the track would be like choosing between two children. I can't do it. I love them both far too much.

Against the purity of experience that the track offers—the mind-expanding and skill-enhancing crucible that beckons like an otherworldly light—the street brings a vast richness. The street may be more dangerous. But it also is far more varied.

A few weeks ago I took a Friday off work and—with three days in hand—packed a few things, kissed Ginny goodbye, and headed down the road. I had but a vague idea of where I was going—just a name on a map that had long intrigued me.

A day and half later I sat a few feet from my bike, hundreds of miles from home, wrapped in that good tiredness that comes after hours of riding hard-curving mountain roads, watching a golden sunset slowly descend around me. It was one of those magic moments that come unbidden to the street rider, unanticipated, and yet offering a transcendent look into something bigger and more important than we'd have guessed was there. Call it a quiet euphoria. Those moments alone are worth it all.

And then you add the other enduring advantage that the street holds—its simple accessibility. Riding a racetrack requires at least a modicum of forethought and planning. You have to decide days or weeks or even months in advance that you're going to ride on a particular day—and then commit to the logistics and expense to make it happen. If circumstances change, or your wife is in a sudden bad mood that day, too bad.

Riding on the street can be done just about any time you want. My pal Kevin was working from home earlier this week. With a forecast of snow for the following day, he knew he might get stuck not being able to ride for a few days. So on his lunch hour he jumped on one of his bikes and took it out for a little spin. Then he brought it home and took his other bike out for a similar quick twenty miles. Just a spur of the moment kind of thing.

In a similar vein, I can't count the times I've washed away the detritus of a bad day by going for an impromptu after-work ride. Heck, just knowing that my bike is sitting out there in the shed, waiting for me whenever I'm ready, brings a powerful bit of mental ease. What's the old saw? You never saw a bike parked outside a psychiatrist's office.

And so no, I can't imagine not having that immediacy, that ability to ride at the slightest whim. It's an advantage the street will always hold.

Unless you own your own racetrack.

April 2011, Sport Rider

Time Warp

The greatest gift of all.

We're gone just after dawn, while the cool morning air still lingers over the landscape. We've got a long way to go and need to make as much time as we can before the inevitable summer thunderstorms emerge later in the day.

The ride up the day before yesterday already seems like a lifetime ago.

George, having already done this ride countless times, takes the lead. Matt, Parks, and I fall in behind him. Pointing our bikes south and west, we begin the 500-mile trek back to the Virginia's.

For the first hour the roads lay straight across the flat land. Good roads for making time. Fine roads for gazing in idle wonder at the agricultural heartland here in central Ohio. But boring otherwise.

I'm still lit by yesterday's experience. Enervated by my return to the racetrack, after fourteen long years. It was the most extraordinary ten hours I can ever remember.

And so in a way the flat landscape with its minimal demands on my attention is welcome. It allows me to replay in my mind the circuit there at Mid-Ohio. To remember the rush that rolled over me as I swept through its storied turns. To consider the unleavened joy of commanding The Keyhole; or the disbelief that came with flying unscathed again and again through the off-camber, decreasing-radius turn eight; or the exhilaration that accompanied each flying lap through turn one. And to remember, too, the difficult turn seven at the end of the long back straight. I never really did get that sorted.

I'm already thinking of when I can return.

By mid-morning the topography begins to harden. The flat farmland gives way to rolling hills. Trees grow closer to the road. The distance from one turn to the next begins to shorten.

As if by unspoken assent, the lilt in the air—that unconscious rhythm grasped by us four riders—rises by a note. A tinge of aggression emerges, evidence of it held aloft by the subtly changed note of our exhausts. It hangs there, as if asking a question.

At our fuel stop everything is paused. We go through the simple mechanics of pumping gas and relieving ourselves and quaffing a cold bottle of fresh water. Nothing is said. Nothing need be. We all feel it.

Back on the road, crossing the river, the mountains loom. Even as the road narrows, turns crooked and abrupt, our pace rises. The air turns cooler from the shadows and from the rising elevation. But I hardly notice. I am captured, floating in the moment, marveling at the utter delight of flying up this road.

With its airy elevation, its shadowed, blind corners, and its rocky escarpments, our route here has little in common with the 2.4 mile circuit we spent all day yesterday riding. And yet there is something akin here. Some connection.

When I rolled into the pits after my last session yesterday I was saddened to see the end of a glorious day. But I was also charged with an incredible high, the endorphins coursing through my bloodstream like small bolts of lightning. They had hardly dissipated overnight.

Now, I fly on their wings. Upward, the serpentine road throws feints and jabs, illusions and puzzles. Obstacles to the unwary. But they matter not. My wheels seem to hardly touch the pavement, my bike to have shed half its weight. There is an otherworldly certainty to all this.

Past the crest and now carving swiftly into the descent, George has set a blazing fast pace. A glance at my speedo confirms what I already know—we are running far faster than on our trip up this same road two days prior. And, yet, even as somewhere in the distant reaches of my mind I recognize that this ride is at the very outer limits of what is possible on the street—and ought to be extraordinarily hard—it's not. It is, instead, effortless.

Something quite amazing has happened.

§

Waiting to step into the on-deck circle, you pick up a plastic-covered iron donut and slide it over the knob at the handle end of the bat. With a light tap of the fat end on the ground, you lift the now-much-heavier bat and cleave it through the air a few times. The laden bat aggravates you. But you persist through a half-dozen swings. The muscle memory comes quickly.

Now, dropping the weight and stepping to the plate, the bat seems child-like in its lightness. You've gained a little bit of extra bat speed and you know it. If the pitcher chooses, through accident or will, to serve one up across the fat part of plate, there might just be something worth seeing.

Something like that is what I experienced—what all of us experienced—on that ride home from Mid-Ohio many years ago. I have relived it enough times since, returning from a track day at some distant racetrack, to know it isn't a fluke; or some sort of once-in-a-lifetime metaphysical gift.

Its reality is based upon our perception of life around us. As we move through the world we absorb the pace of things. We become habituated to the speed at which events occur. They establish our internal clock, the rhythm via which we interact with everything.

That clock speed, that rhythm, isn't the same for everybody. I remember being startled the first time I watched a self-made video of Reg Pridmore circulating a racetrack at speed, commenting on each corner as he traversed it. Even deep into triple-digit speeds, even while piloting his sportbike through incredible lean angles, his voice coming through the speaker was as subdued and relaxed as if he were sitting in an office chair.

Then I realized why: the seat of a sportbike, circulating a racetrack, *was* Reg Pridmore's office. A closed-circuit road course—what to me, what to most of us, was a special, unusual environment—was to him anything but. After thousands of hours and uncounted miles upon them he was as used to that environment as I was to that office of mine back at work.

Here's what happens: our first time on a racetrack is filled with trepidation, our first laps at speed overwhelming in their sensory inputs. There's a reason we end up floating in a sea of endorphins and adrenalin.

But as the laps add up we very quickly begin to become accustomed to the much higher raw speeds on the straights and the faster pace through the corners. That initial trepidation is soon replaced by crooked grins and a swiftly growing confidence. After awhile a buck fifty no longer seems like the fearsome, extraordinary thing we once imagined it to be.

That's the conscious effect. Subconsciously, our brains are busy rewiring our neural pathways. They are recalibrating that internal clock of ours—the speed at which we mentally process all those motorcycling-specific inputs that we have to deal with.

And at the end of the day, what we end up with—in addition to a desire to come back and do this again as soon as possible—is a very different clock speed.

Back out on the street, everything suddenly seems different. Our new-found ability to process road inputs faster has the effect of slowing things down. Whereas before a 75mph freeway clip might have seemed fast, all of a sudden it feels remarkably sedate. And that set of esses near home that we previously felt challenged by… now seems like child's play.

Alas, this amped up mental clock speed is not permanent. As the days and weeks and months pass, a rider's mental clock will slowly revert back to his previous street-based rhythm. He'll still retain the cornering, braking, and general bike-handling skills he earned from his time on the racetrack. But his mental perception of events will no longer hold that magical edge.

Which is why an occasional track day is a benefit for nearly all street riders, regardless of how many years of experience they might have, or how advanced their skills. Beyond being simply fun, and a great tune-up for those bike handling skills we all depend on, a track day is an opportunity to re-juice that mental clock speed.

The racetrack has long been recognized for its ability to teach. It is an environment of such purity, a place capable of such dramatically accelerated learning, that it is no surprise that it comes so highly recommended by those who have experienced it. There is no better or faster place to learn advanced riding skills.

But its hidden secret is in what it does to our minds. The strange time warp that it fashions, and then places at our feet. That may be its greatest gift of all.

September 2010, Sport Rider

The Golden Hour

The tie that binds.

There's still an hour of daylight left, but the veil of fatigue that descended over me across the afternoon sits there like a golem, unrepentant. And so when the road breaks out of the trees into a clearing, with the three white buildings set hard into the woods across the field, I flash to a quick decision.

Rolling out of the throttle, I let the hundred yards to the exit wind down in a slowing cadence. Turning the BMW onto the small exit road, it's only a quarter mile to the white buildings. Pulling up to the single island in front of the restaurant, I dismount with a sense of relief. My exhaustion is palpable.

Pulling off my helmet, I eye the two pumps, one regular, one mid-grade. I don't see a slot for my credit card. "Pre-pay Only," the sticker on the pump reads.

Walking inside, the air conditioning is a sudden, sharp contrast to the warmth outside. I hand a twenty to the pretty young woman behind the counter. "How much?" she asks. I shrug. "Put it all on there."

Back outside, I lift the nozzle on the 89-octane pump and flip the lever around. It's one of those old pumps. No LCD screen. No Start button. Just the old black numbers behind the glass window that spin around in sequence, like those of a slot machine. Like the odometers on old bikes, where you could walk up and glance down and see how many miles were on them. As my tank slowly fills I listen to the loud hum from the pump and watch the rolling digits and think about how things change.

Inside, the girl gives me eight dollars and change. "Do you have a room?" I ask. I'm thinking the question is mostly rhetorical, given the dearth of cars at the small, 50's-era motel next door. But she dutifully pulls the book out and runs her finger down the page.

"Yep, we do," she nods. "It's fifty-five dollars."

"That's fine," I reply. I'll take it."

"You know there's no TV or phone?" she asks.

I give her a small smile. "That's alright."

The metal key with the plastic hang tag has a large number '3' written on it. I walk the fifty feet to the room and unlock the door, having to jiggle the key to make it work. Light spills into the small, dark room. Two tired double beds are separated by a small table with a lamp upon it. At the foot of the beds, right next to the door, is a small bureau, chipped and marked by time. The tiny bathroom has room only for a toilet, a sink stained with rust, and a 3-foot square shower stall.

I take everything in with a glance. Despite its obvious struggle against the pull of time, the room is clean and neat. Fresh towels are hung on the rack. The beds are made up well, with starched sheets and the bed covers pulled up snug. And the faded carpet, though worn, is clean.

Just like it was nine years ago.

Leaving the door open, I walk back to the gas pumps and wheel my bike across the gravel parking lot, dropping its side stand in front of the room. In five minutes I have unpacked my sparse belongings and set them upon the bureau. And in another five minutes I am back at the small restaurant adjoining the office.

There are only six tables. I settle in at the one pushed back in the corner. Another pretty girl takes my order. And while I wait for my dinner of country-fried steak, mashed potatoes and gravy, green beans, and ice tea, a late-middle-aged gentleman sitting on a stool in the other corner entertains me and the three other customers with his banjo. There's a pickle jar on the table beside him for tips.

When I'm done I leave a five on the table, walk over and

drop another into the pickle jar, and make the few steps to the office. Extracting a single beer from the cooler, I step to the register and hand the first girl, the one who had checked me in, my check.

"I had apple pie and ice cream, too," I offer, pointing out the missing item on the check.

Back at my room, I pull off my boots, retrieve my book, and sit down in the metal chair just outside my door. The sun has fallen below the trees and there is perhaps thirty minutes of daylight left. I study my bike, five feet in front of me. Enjoying the way the soft light edges its shape.

I think back to the last time I was here. Instead of a book, I brought a bunch of motorcycle magazines on that trip. Road tests. Suzuki's new GSX-R1000 had just been released and I had a thought in mind.

I smile at the memory of that long-ago evening. Then I pick up my book.

§

I awake in the darkness. Holding my wrist up to catch the faint light from the porch outside, I squint at the watch face. Five-forty. I lay there half awake for another ten minutes, then climb out of bed. After showering I carry my small duffel back to the bike, stowing it in the saddlebag. It's still dark as I wipe down the tank with a damp towel.

I had asked the girl last night what time they opened for breakfast. "Eight o'clock," she answered. I don't want to wait that long and so will have to find my coffee somewhere down the road.

With one last look around, I leave the key and a five on the bedside table, then pull the door closed behind me.

A handful of cars are now in the parking lot, late night travelers who got in after I went to bed. I'm conscious of that as I thumb the starter, the sound of the engine embarrassingly loud in the early morning stillness. I motor slowly across the gravel lot to the road.

It takes only a few seconds to get back to the Parkway. At the stop sign I pause for just a moment, enjoying the darkness and the quiet and the whole day that lies in front of me. And then I turn south, throttling up.

The bike spins up beneath me. "Fourth gear. Forty-five mph," I tell myself. I'm almost preternaturally aware of the deer out there. "Just take it easy."

But even as I tell myself that, the first curves are falling beneath my wheels. Curling, languid scrolls of the pavement that pull me first left, and then right. They offer me that mesmerizing gift that has brought me here, that is the reason I do this, but is somehow always better than I remembered. It always seems so new. As if last night's sleep had made me forget the magic that lay here in this moment. The pull of the bike and the road and the land slides over me in an exhilarating glow, washing everything else away.

The faint tinge of light that smudged the eastern horizon when I left is now leaking into the air around me. Up ahead, the edges of my headlight beam, the boundary between what I can see and what must be imagined, begins to soften.

The air has the tiniest hint of chill to it, snaking around my neck and through the chin bar on my helmet. It prompts a shiver, just enough to heighten my senses. As if to emphasize the newness of the day and the perfection of this moment.

Looking down, I realize my speed has crept up, drawn there by something beyond me. I smile to myself, remind myself of the deer, and bring it back down.

But I know it's an argument that in the end I can't win. The thing that has me here, the thing with its own pull, its own gravity, long ago pulled me into its orbit.

As the quickly brightening landscape unfolds around me, I can see tendrils of mist floating from the ground. They impart a magical, otherworldly sense to things. It is a world I have entirely to myself—in twenty miles I have yet to see another soul.

As the orange disk of the sun begins breaking above the horizon the thought crosses my mind to stop and take some pictures. To pull out my tripod and camera and try and capture some of the extraordinary beauty that surrounds me.

But even as I think that, I know it is for naught. For to do so would mean setting down, for just a few moments, the sublime, gilded feeling of this motorcycle at speed, on this good road, upon this good land.

And I cannot stop.

January 2011, Sport Rider

About the Author

Jeff Hughes has been riding fast motorcycles for over four decades. Deeply passionate about the sport, he has ridden hundreds of thousands of street miles, thousands of racetrack miles, and has collected the many varieties of experience one might imagine along that journey. Through sunshine and darkness, heat and cold, dry and wet, rubber-side-down and rubber-side-not-so-down... he has experienced it all. He continues to make his home in the foothills of the Blue Ridge Mountains of Virginia, and still rides every chance he gets.

Made in the USA
San Bernardino, CA
22 December 2019